D0394367

RED AND BLUE AND BROKE ALL OVER

ALSO BY CHARLES GOYETTE

The Dollar Meltdown: Surviving the Impending Currency Crisis with Gold, Oil, and Other Unconventional Investments

RED AND **BLUE**
AND
BROKE ALL OVER

RESTORING AMERICA'S FREE ECONOMY

Charles Goyette

SENTINEL

SENTINEL
Published by the Penguin Group
Penguin Group (USA) Inc., 375 Hudson Street, New York, New York 10014, U.S.A. • Penguin Group (Canada), 90 Eglinton Avenue East, Suite 700, Toronto, Ontario, Canada M4P 2Y3 (a division of Pearson Penguin Canada Inc.) • Penguin Books Ltd, 80 Strand, London WC2R 0RL, England • Penguin Ireland, 25 St. Stephen's Green, Dublin 2, Ireland (a division of Penguin Books Ltd) • Penguin Books Australia Ltd, 250 Camberwell Road, Camberwell, Victoria 3124, Australia (a division of Pearson Australia Group Pty Ltd) • Penguin Books India Pvt Ltd, 11 Community Centre, Panchsheel Park, New Delhi—110 017, India • Penguin Group (NZ), 67 Apollo Drive, Rosedale, Auckland 0632, New Zealand (a division of Pearson New Zealand Ltd) • Penguin Books (South Africa) (Pty) Ltd, 24 Sturdee Avenue, Rosebank, Johannesburg 2196, South Africa

Penguin Books Ltd, Registered Offices: 80 Strand, London WC2R 0RL, England

First published in 2012 by Sentinel, a member of Penguin Group (USA) Inc.

10 9 8 7 6 5 4 3 2 1

LIBRARY OF CONGRESS CATALOGING IN PUBLICATION DATA

Goyette, Charles.
Red and blue and broke all over : restoring America's free economy / Charles Goyette.
p. cm.
Includes bibliographical references and index.
ISBN 978-1-59523-082-9
1. Free enterprise—United States. 2. Liberty—Economic aspects. 3. United States—Economic policy—2009– 4. United States—Economic conditions—2009– I. Title.
HB95.G69 2012
330.973—dc23
2011041763

Printed in the United States of America
Set in Minion Pro with Frutiger LT Std
Designed by Daniel Lagin

In memory of my father,
Dr. Ed Goyette, Jr.,
a philosopher

CONTENTS

Is the prosperity of the American people in terminal decline?

Yes.

Unless . . .

RED AND BLUE AND BROKE ALL OVER

America Crosses the Line

Today is already the tomorrow which the bad economists yesterday urged us to ignore.

—**Henry Hazlitt**

The Line Between Prosperity and Poverty

Shortly after he graduated from the Air Force Academy in 1967, Roy Miller, now a retired colonel, was assigned to Williams Air Force Base in Arizona. Flying missions between Williams and bases in Southern California over the next five years frequently took him along the border with Mexico. He thought the differences between what he saw on the Mexican and American side of the border odd. Most obvious along the populated areas that straddled the border were the streets and roads: generally paved on the American side but tending to be dirt or gravel on the Mexican side. It was apparent that the houses and commercial properties were poorer on the Mexican side of the border.

What was it about that imaginary line that divided prosperity from poverty? he wondered. The terrain was no different; the natural resources were the same; the people, for the most part, were no different. Why was there a clear economic division between the United States and Mexico?

The line that divides prosperity from poverty is even visible in popular satellite imagery of the earth at night. The stark contrast of dark and light across the Korean peninsula apparent in images from space is actually the border that separates North Korea, plunged into darkness when the sun goes down, from the more dynamic and illuminated South Korea. There are the same people, language, cultural heritage, and natural resources on both sides of that line. What accounts for the difference?

Miller answered the question he pondered flying along the Mexican border this way: freedom works. Although things have begun improving there, Mexico has a long history of statism to overcome. In just the last hundred years this includes a socialist constitution that preceded even the Soviet constitution, restrictions on religious liberty, the nationalization and collectivization of agriculture, the commandeering of other private property, and the exiling of opposition political leaders. In 1937 Mexican president Lázaro Cárdenas enthusiastically welcomed Leon Trotsky, exiled from Russia by a power-consolidating Stalin, to a new home in Mexico. Perhaps there was a rush of statist exhilaration with the arrival of the celebrated Marxist, because the next year, 1938, Cárdenas nationalized Mexico's petroleum industry. Since then Mexico has suffered default, devaluation, and hyperinflation. As recently as 1982 Mexico's banks were nationalized. The United States, freer for having been spared the severity of a good deal of Mexico's statism through much of its history, is more prosperous.

North of the line on the Korean peninsula is the perfect police state: Stalinist, secretive, xenophobic. North Korea is probably the most thoroughly militarized nation on earth. Lacking free speech and characterized by fear from widespread internal spying and religious persecution, it has one of the world's worst human rights records. The state controls everything from the press and education to literature, the arts, and sports. It is a centrally planned command economy in which property rights are nonexistent. In Pyongyang, the capital, the city lights are turned on in a pretense of prosperity for special occasions, such as a visit from the New York Philharmonic; afterward it is plunged back into general darkness. Things are dramatically freer south of the border. South Korea has a per capita gross domestic product more than fifteen times higher than the North's. Freedom works. It's the difference between night and day.

Can the conditions that are responsible for the lights going dark on the other side of a line and paved roads turning to dirt at a border prevail here? Given America's current economic distress, this is a question that must be asked. The story Miller told me years ago of his thoughts as a young pilot flying along the border came to mind as America's economy began to slide, because

Colorado Springs, home of the Air Force Academy that Miller had attended, and representative of nearly every other city, county, and state in America, has been forced to make cuts. In the face of collapsing tax revenue, Colorado Springs let a third of its streetlights go dark and let its roads go unpaved.

Colorado Springs is not entering the new dark age alone; it is making a budget move that is being implemented in cities and along highways all across the land. Declaring a fiscal emergency, the mayor of Fresno, California, proposed turning off a quarter of its streetlights. Rockford, Illinois, has turned off thousands of its city streetlights as well. Elsewhere across the country, the cost of repairing and repaving asphalt roads has become prohibitive. Some are being ground up and returned to gravel. Paved roads have been reduced to gravel in North and South Dakota, as well as in thirty-eight of eighty-three Michigan counties. A 2010 *Wall Street Journal* story reports that roads have been left to erode in Ohio, Alabama, and Pennsylvania.

Perhaps our current financial limitations are only those of a passing moment. Perhaps the Washington minds that failed to see the economic crisis as it loomed before us—those who helped the debt grow to monstrous proportions—have now been gifted with new vision and we will soon be restored to our former state. Perhaps we will be made whole by a continuing faith in the Republican and Democratic consensus, a state religion based on deficit spending and other Keynesian economic claptrap that has America buried deep in debt and dangerously dependent on the kindness of foreign creditors. Perhaps the tax-subsidized governing classes that led us into this economic slough of despond can now provide a map to guide us out.

Or perhaps not. Perhaps this is only the beginning of the new normal—a future of fewer streetlights and paved roads, as well as fewer jobs and opportunities.

If the "heroics" of government spending—trillions in bailouts, rescue plans, stimulus spending, subsidies, and debt monetization—had resulted in real production, the economy would be robust, unemployment would be low, and Americans would be wealthier. Instead the money has been used destructively. Good money has been taken from people who made sound economic decisions and given to investment bankers who made reckless decisions. Productive people have been taxed to buy worthless paper from billionaires who should have known better than to buy it for themselves. In the spirit of the destruction of wealth that passed for economic genius in the Great Depression, back when the Roosevelt administration had crops plowed under and farm animals destroyed, billions of dollars of debt have now been cavalierly loaded onto the backs of little children so that sodium silicate could be poured into the engines of perfectly good automobiles to ensure that they never run again. It's been cash for clunkers, cash for caulkers, cash for appliances, cash for unions, cash for government buildings, and cash for politically connected green projects. And there's even been cash for the wives of fabulously wealthy Wall Street tycoons. That's the one that takes the "let them eat cake" award. Christy Mack is the wife of Morgan Stanley chairman John Mack, and Susan Karches is the widow of Morgan Stanley investment banking group president Peter Karches. With no discernable background or experience in finance, the two women set up an offshore company that got $220 million in Federal Reserve funds to buy commercial mortgages and other securities. The 2009 deal came with the enviable provision that if the investments proved profitable, the investors got to keep the profits. If things went sour, the taxpayers would eat ninety percent of the losses. A lot of loose money has been sloshing around in the Treasury and the Federal Reserve in programs like these, and this is especially glaring in a critically indebted government and an economy in which the people are told that the best they can hope for is a "jobless recovery." A what? "Jobless recovery" falls into the same class as a lifeless resuscitation: the operation was a success, but the patient died. It's the new normal.

It has been generations since Americans' faith in the economy has been this badly rattled. The American dream, composed of home ownership, the certainty that things will continually improve, the assurance of a comfortable retirement, and the assumption that our children will have a better life than we had, is being shaken by deep-seated concerns that our prosperity may be taking a giant step backward.

We can easily identify the dynamic growth of prosperity throughout history. The story of mankind has been one of ever more freedom (freedom from rule by tribal chiefs, kings, churches, and totalitarian states) accompanied by growing—indeed, by an explosion of—human prosperity. This correlation of freedom and prosperity is self-evident in both the long sweep of history and in the lines that divide poverty from prosperity along national borders today. Freedom works.

To assess the prospects for the prosperity of the people, one need only assess the state of freedom in America. Just how vital is freedom today as measured against its vitality in our own short national history? What is the relative strength of our freedom today as measured against that of competitors beyond our borders? If Americans are uncertain about their economic future they will find answers by making this assessment of the condition of their liberty. They will find that freedom has been double-teamed by Republicans and Democrats alike; it has been sucker punched by the red gloves of one and has taken a hit on the blind side by the blue gloves of the other. American freedom is on the ropes.

And while freedom may not be down for the count yet, there is no political quick-fix recovery for the pounding it has been taking. No matter what you have been told, as it stumbles to its feet the next election will not make it resilient. Nor will another round of electoral reform. No change in campaign laws, term limits, balanced budget amendments, or any other mechanical fix that can be put in place and run on automatic can restore us to our prior state of freedom, abundance, and opportunity. Our problem requires something other than process tinkering.

Politics as Usual

The inescapable conclusion is that both parties are to blame for the fading of the American dream. Einstein's oft-cited observation that no problem can be fixed from the same consciousness that created it applies to the deflating promise of America. The restoration of the American dream will not occur as long as the political discussion remains constrained by the old voices of the Republicans and Democrats who marched us into our present economic morass. The Tea Party movement has been on sound footing only to the extent that it has proclaimed itself independent of the political parties.

The narrow range in which those established voices spoke was on display in the national debate on the Obama health-care legislation. The Republicans were reduced to accepting the presuppositions of government interventionism, arguing in the main that they represented more effective management of the enterprise. Republican National Committee advertising called for a "responsible plan" and a "bipartisan plan." Finally the talking point, endlessly repeated, was to "start over on health care." Except for the constitutional stalwart congressman Ron Paul, Republicans were unable (or unwilling) to articulate an argument against a state-directed health-care system.

As the debate reached an end and it was time to vote on the 2,400-page bill, House Speaker Nancy Pelosi crossed the street to the U.S. Capitol carrying the same large gavel that had been used in the House when the original Medicaid bill was passed into law in 1965. With their own hands stained by years of red ink, Republicans weren't in any position to point out that the Medicaid plan Pelosi was so pleased to mimic faces a $38 trillion shortfall over the next seventy-five years. That's more than two and a half times the nation's gross domestic product.

With choices about the philosophy of governance limited to the tired nostrums of Democrats and Republicans, no wonder a feeling of disenfranchisement is growing. More Americans identify themselves as independents than Republicans or Democrats, while Gallup reports that a majority of Americans are so dissatisfied with the performance of Republicans and Democrats that they say a third party is needed. A March 2011 *ABC News/Washington Post* poll found a mere twenty-six percent of Americans are optimistic about "our system of government and how well it works." That's a record low. But it is not just a question of satisfaction. At issue is the legitimacy of the state itself. In August 2011 Rasmussen Reports released a poll of likely voters that found that a mere seventeen percent—a new low—believe the federal government has "the consent of the governed," from which, the Declaration of Independence insists, government's "just powers" must flow. Among the disenfranchised are people who have seen their jobs disappear, their savings exhausted, and their homes foreclosed. They are people whose old, fine hopes for retirement have gone dry; their trust in their childrens' future has withered. Some are angry that their own responsibility is being rewarded with the bill for bailing out the irresponsible. Others are distraught that their faith in the empty assurances of government plans like Social Security now threatens to prove their undoing. Some feel remorse for the past; for others, it's fear of the future. What has happened to our prosperity? What has become of the American dream?

The Dollar Meltdown examined the generational destruction of the dollar and extrapolated the debt crisis for investment purposes. There can be no doubt that the scale of government debt means a lower standard of living for the American people. But that is only part of the story. As foreboding as the debt is, the obstacles to renewed opportunity and well-being go beyond what the numbers reveal. Under the cloak of the Republican and Democrat orthodoxy that approved the debt as it compounded, other ideas were smuggled into

America's economic life. Just because some politicians damn the debt they created now that it is a crisis of unmanageable dimensions does not mean that the other statist ideals and dispositions that entered our national ethos with the debt are gone. These collectivist ideals, inimical to our freedom and destructive of our prosperity, are those that seek to subordinate the individual, generally by economic and authoritarian measures, to the will of the nation-state (hereafter referred to as the "state"; where the individual states of the United States are intended will be clear in context). These statist ideals and practices, so prominent in the mortgage meltdown and its ongoing aftermath, when Republican and Democratic majorities alike insisted on socializing the losses of private banks and corporations (whose profits of course remained private), and so visible in the war-making prerogatives and police-state authority recently assumed by the state, must be reversed. But first they need to be identified.

But there is more to the task at hand than identifying today's destructive policies of the state and reversing them, for they can incarnate tomorrow in new and equally destructive forms. Instead, the case for freedom itself must be explicitly made. Celebrating freedom in the words of songs and mindless slogans is simply inadequate to the challenge of our age. Perfunctory acts of reverence for aged documents and classroom rituals are poor substitutes for the clarity of vision modern Americans must have in an age of crisis. If freedom is to prevail, its case must be stated anew, as Friedrich Hayek suggested, in each generation and in the language of the times. This book was written to help make that case in the context of today's waning prosperity and, if it is successful, to enlist and arm new champions of liberty. Now. Before it is too late.

The title of this book, *Red and Blue and Broke All Over*, is intentionally ambiguous. It describes both a financial and a philosophical condition. Red and blue are convenient and graphically useful ways of referring to the two parties: red representing Republicans, just as red states, red districts, and red voters are Republican ones; and blue describing Democrats, with blue states, blue districts, and blue voters being Democratic. While the title describes America's national government as broke, and the people made poorer, it also describes the politics of the Republicans and Democrats as broken. The country is financially insolvent because the Washington parties, red and blue alike, are philosophically bankrupt. Their shared statist philosophy needs to be exposed—and abandoned—before it does us any more harm. On the other hand, the subtitle is not ambiguous about the book's objective: *Restoring America's Free Economy*. Only by understanding the bankrupt philosophy of statism and replacing it with the philosophy of freedom will a return to prosperity be possible.

This book consists of three sections. Section I, *Liberty*, is about the state of freedom in America. Like anything else in life, from brushing your teeth to performing maintenance on your car, there are serious consequences for negligence. Americans have been neglecting freedom and have been free riding on the achievements of people from generations gone by. This neglect is showing up now, and is reflected in our economic prospects. If Americans are serious about restoring their prosperity, they will have to take a realistic look at the Republicans and Democrats who have been managing (or mismanaging!) our political and economic affairs for generations now. Economic orthodoxies have been held in common by both parties. These doctrines have advanced in Republican and Democratic administrations and prevailed despite the control of Congress being handed back and forth. As science-fiction writer Philip K. Dick ironically noted, "In a one-party system there is always a landslide." Mesmerized by state authority, and blinded by their own partisanship, few authors, analysts, and commentators active in the public debate realize that both parties worship in the same statist church and share obedience to the same economic priesthood.

In Section I you'll also learn about the nature of wealth and prosperity and get a taste of the disdain statists have for your freedom. You'll find out about the price system and property in a free economy and why they are indispensable, as well as discover what happens in their absence. You'll also learn about spontaneous, self-organizing systems, dynamic and essential components of our prosperity. They perform wonders, but can only do so in an environment of freedom. And if you'd like to know who lost the Constitution, you've come to the right place. Hint: as tempting as it is, you can't blame it all on politicians or the media.

Section II, *The State*, is about the nature of government and its primary activities. You'll find out why freedom works and why the state doesn't. Few people ever think about state central economic planning. Republicans and Democrats both love it, but it is one of the most destructive activities of the state, right up there with warfare. In fact, you'll learn why centralized economic planning requires the state to wage war on its own people.

It will become clear in this section why the most dynamic things going on in our economy are those furthest away from the state's bureaucrats, bodies, and boards. Think about the astonishing improvements in just a few years in things like TVs, computers, and phones. Here is where you find the most consumer satisfaction. Not to mention the way prices have come down! Things move so fast in these areas that the state can't keep up with—and interfere—the way it would like. Then compare these wonders to activities in which the hand of the state is most visible. Things like the Transportation Security Administration (TSA) and airport security, health care, and public education—activities with some of the least consumer satisfaction and sources of endless public friction.

We'll also take a look at fascism, a deadly outcome spawned by the pairing of state and corporate DNA, and follow it quite logically with a close-up look at crony capitalism. Author Michael Lewis, who chronicles Wall Street, quipped that America stands at a crossroads, and Goldman Sachs now owns both of them. How do they get away with it? You'll know after you've read about the Wormhole Express. You'll also find out how the state and the Federal Reserve transfer wealth to favored recipients and how their activities are hidden from view, or at least from the view of the state's lapdog press. Not all crony capitalism is on a national scale, either. There are probably cronies right in your neighborhood. Crony capitalism leaves you poorer. What you'll learn about it will leave you outraged!

Freedom is not well loved by everyone. It has its enemies, especially those whose control is threatened by *your* freedom. Among the tools they employ to secure control are dependency, conditioning, and fear. Such enemies of human freedom have been around for a very long time; history is filled with notorious examples. But a few visionary writers have thought about how freedom's enemies may operate in our future. Present trends suggest that they are on to something. Careful attention paid to their description of the enemies of freedom will reward you with special insight into future challenges developing today. It's also important to take a closer look because when our freedom goes, our prosperity goes.

Section III is called *Dead Ahead*. The dollar is a currency in decline. Government debt will bring it down. Not in some far-distant future, but dead ahead. The international standing of the dollar will change dramatically. The process is already under way. The state's debts mean massive money printing, too. And that means we will experience a ruinous inflation. But there is something we can do to begin to insulate ourselves from the widespread monetary and fiscal calamity—that is, if the Republicans and Democrats get out of our way. It's important because it can help to cushion the dollar endgame and help rebuild our prosperity, too.

One more thing is dead ahead. Just as the Roman republic came to an end and Rome became an empire when Caesar crossed the Rubicon, America has crossed that line, too. The American republic has given way to empire. But the change has cost us dearly and we are now entering the twilight of the American military empire. It's the end of America as policeman of the world and trying to make the world safe for democracy. It was foolish when Wilson tried it and it remains foolish today. Although the transformation of America from a republic to an empire has meant power for some and fabulous riches for others, it has made enemies around the world for the rest of us, robbed us of a good deal of our freedom, and bled dry our wealth. We won't be able to restore our prosperity until the empire ends.

I'll also share some warnings about the future we choose and the larger things we sacrifice in further subordinating our liberties to the state. This part is important because freedom creates more than prosperity. It is also a way to improved human relations, it smooths the road to the brotherhood of man, and it clears the pathway to peace. *Red and Blue and Broke All Over* does cover a lot of ground and it does so from what, for some, may be a fresh yet unfamiliar libertarian perspective. But it's a message whose time has come. Because it's time to face facts: we can't continue down this red and blue primrose path if we're serious about restoring America's prosperity.

A free economy works wonders. The American people's prosperity can be restored. It's actually not complicated, but that doesn't mean it's easy.

SECTION I
LIBERTY

CHAPTER ONE

Wealth and Prosperity

Prosperity is not simply a matter of capital investment. It is an ideological issue.

—**Ludwig von Mises**

Prosperity

Prosperity is something much greater than wealth. Prosperity refers to the wellsprings of human ingenuity and enterprise from which long-term wealth and human improvement bubble forth. The ancient Romans made important contributions to the implementation and refinement of property rights. They established trading colonies as far away as the east coast of the Indian subcontinent before the time of Christ. And they developed civil engineering skills that enabled them to build roads, aqueducts, and other marvels that supported populations that could barely have been conceived elsewhere in antiquity. In this way they created long-term prosperity for themselves. The later plunderers of Rome got wealth, emptying the treasury of the empire, but they did not get prosperity.

Similarly, despite billions in cash that have flowed into the Persian Gulf oil states for generations, that money has not been turned into long-term prosperity for the people, as the seething discontent that spawned 2011's Arab Spring revolutions in the Middle East has shown. The Saudi royal family, the Al Sabahs of Kuwait, and Libya's Kaddafis have had their palaces with gold bathroom fixtures, but the capital is spent abroad in places where opportunities abound. When the wells of the desert kingdoms run dry, so, too, will the wealth.

On the other hand, where the right conditions exist, prosperity will follow, even on barren ground. Hong Kong is a rocky land of steep slopes set against mountains of volcanic material, only about a thousand square kilometers altogether. It has no oil or natural gas. Russia, the largest country in the world, is rich in natural resources. It is the world's largest exporter of natural gas and second-largest exporter of oil. Yet Hong Kong's superior prosperity is evident at both birth and death—and throughout life in between. While Hong Kong has one of the lowest infant mortality rates in the world, Russia's infant mortality is the highest among the developed nations of the world. People brag about their fine automobiles from other developed nations: Italian, German, Japanese, American, and even British cars. But nobody brags about Russian cars or anything else made there. Because in fact, other than its natural resource commodities, Russia produces almost nothing the rest of the world wants: not cars or computers or clothing; not cell phones or flat-screen TVs or electronics or software; not industrial equipment or medical devices or motion pictures. Tiny Hong Kong, with one-twentieth Russia's population and without its raw materials, still manages to export more to the rest of the world each year than all of Russia. Per capita income in Hong Kong is more than three times higher than in Russia, and the World Bank reports life expectancy in Russia is sixty-eight years; in Hong Kong it is eighty-two, fourteen years longer.

The oil sheiks may be rich as Croesus. Gas, oil, and gold may provide the autocrats of Russia wealth. But in Hong Kong wealth is *created*. That is the key to prosperity.

There are preconditions for the creation of prosperity. Chief among them is freedom. We'll come back to prosperity, but first a closer look at the nature of freedom.

Freedom

It is important to be clear about the meaning of freedom because the question will come up again. Among those who have thought deeply about the issue are economists including Nobel laureate Friedrich Hayek, Murray Rothbard, and Ludwig von Mises, who was a mentor to both. All three are representatives of the Austrian school of economics. It is called Austrian economics not because it is practiced there—it isn't—but because many of its leading figures, including Hayek and Mises, were Austrian. The contributions of the Austrian economists are many, and include a clear explanation of the painful business cycle of booms and busts, the result of needless policies by central banks like the Federal Reserve, and the false signals and "malinvestments" that result from their interventions. Their observations about freedom are not mere intellectual abstractions, but are grounded in the common human experience of the matter. According to Hayek, freedom is the condition "in which man is not subject to coercion by another or others." Man is free when he retains the possibility of "acting according to his own decisions and plans" rather than being "subject to the will of another" who "could coerce him to act or not act in specific ways." Rothbard is clear as well that freedom is an interpersonal issue, which he refers to as the "absence of molestation by other people." And Mises: "Freedom and liberty always refer to interhuman relationships." Rights guaranteeing liberty are negative, says Mises, observing that "in the realm of state and government, liberty means restraint upon the exercise of the police power." Clearly, freedom has to do with the way in which men live together and depends upon freedom from coercion by other men. It does not have to do with freedom to transcend the laws of nature. I cannot complain as I fall off a cliff that someone has taken away my freedom to fly. Freedom is also not the same thing as democracy or the right to vote. A slave can remain a slave, Hayek reminds us, even if given a ballot. Indeed, an entire nation can vote away its freedom.

The axiom at the heart of this book—that freedom creates prosperity—is put to the test in the living laboratories of nations today just as it has been throughout history. The *Economic Freedom of the World* index published by the Fraser Institute assesses the correlation of freedom and prosperity in countries around the world. Not surprisingly it concludes that countries with more economic freedom have substantially higher per capita incomes and tend to grow more rapidly. Economic freedom is good for everybody, even the most poor. The poorest ten percent of the population in the freer countries have earnings many times higher than the poorest in less free countries. Not only is life richer, it is also about twenty years longer in countries with the most economic freedom. The annual *Index of Economic Freedom* conducted by the Heritage Foundation together with the *Wall Street Journal* reports a similar correlation between freedom and economic well-being. The 2011 survey reports that economies it rates as "free" or "mostly free" have incomes more than three times the average levels in all other countries and more than ten times the incomes in "repressed" economies.

What is the state of freedom in America today? Is it waxing or waning? The shape of our economic future can be discerned in the lengthening shadows cast by the growing intrusions of the state.

To see how those shadows have grown in America's short history, Jacob Hornberger, president of the Future of Freedom Foundation, describes some of the conditions that prevailed from the nation's founding to the late nineteenth century:

- There was no income taxation (except during the Civil War), Social Security, Medicare, Medicaid, welfare, economic regulations, licensure laws, drug laws, immigration controls, or coercive transfer programs such as farm subsidies and education grants.
- There was no federal department of labor, agriculture, commerce, education, energy, health and human services, or homeland security. There was no SEC, DEA, FEMA, OSHA, or EPA.
- There was no Federal Reserve System, no paper money, and no legal-tender laws (except during the Civil War). People used gold and silver coins as money.
- There were no foreign military bases and there was no involvement in foreign wars. The size of the military was small.

Now take a closer look at the intrusion and outrages of government in our lives today:

- The U.S. Supreme Court has decided that police may kick down the door of your home or apartment without a warrant based on what they or their dogs smell inside the home. At the same time, the U.S. Ninth Circuit Court of Appeals says you do not have a reasonable expectation of privacy in your own driveway, nor does it think you have a reasonable expectation that the government isn't tracking you. It has ruled that U.S. government agents can legally sneak onto your property in the middle of the night, place a secret GPS device on the bottom of your car, and track your every move—without a warrant. And the FBI has been allowed to employ "roving wiretaps," which need not specify the place being bugged or require determination of the actual presence of the person being targeted.

- The Department of Health and Human Services used $650 million in stimulus money of the desperately indebted nation to fund antiobesity campaigns.
- A presidential commission issued a report recommending mandatory mental health screening for schoolchildren, including pre-school-aged children, with or without parental consent.
- The FDA is raiding and strong-arming Amish farmers in the state of Pennsylvania for fear somebody may be drinking raw milk without its permission.
- From December 2007 to July 2010 the Federal Reserve secretly provided $16 trillion in loans to bail out politically connected U.S. banks and even foreign banks and corporations. The loans, provided without oversight, were made at the risk of the solvency of the United States and the value of the dollar, and amounted to a total greater than the entire $14 trillion GDP of the U.S. It took a self-proclaimed socialist, Senator Bernie Sanders of Vermont, to call the operation what it was: "a clear case of socialism for the rich."
- A small-town bank in the Bible Belt was ordered by Federal Reserve inspectors to take down a Bible verse on its web site and remove religious symbols and literature from its office.
- Dependency has grown so great that the U.S. government sends out 88 million checks a month; more than 45.75 million Americans are on food stamps, and 50 million are on Medicaid.
- The IRS estimates Americans spend 6.6 billion uncompensated labor hours per year filling out tax forms. The National Taxpayers Union reports that American families and businesses spend over 7.5 billion hours a year complying with federal tax laws.
- Americans by the thousands are being strip-searched daily by possibly dangerous radiating scanners at airports all across the United States. The "porno scanners" produce detailed images through the clothing. The scans are supplemented by intrusive police style pat-downs. TSA agents have extended their searches to train and bus stations, and have even corralled train passengers who have already disembarked and so pose no

threat to travel. Next, the Department of Homeland Security is planning to add "genetic" pat-downs to its intrusions by taking DNA samples from travelers. And the department has pilot planning programs for the scanning of pedestrians on city streets.

- The same federal government that determines what your grandmother may or may not legally use to relieve her pain, and whether you have too much cash, also determines the mileage your car must get and regulates your washing machine, showerhead, and how much water your toilet flushes. It has now decided that you may no longer purchase incandescent lightbulbs.

What are the few things—its delegated functions—that the state has performed so well that it should now run roughshod through our daily affairs, devouring our livelihoods and passing out edicts about the ordering of our private households?

Wealth

To say that freedom creates prosperity is convenient shorthand. But to be more precise, freedom provides a conducive environment in which prosperity, the dynamic of wealth creation, can function. What is this dynamic? Where does wealth come from? We ourselves are its creators. It is the nature of man to provide himself food and shelter, to improve his circumstances, to discover, to invent, to refine, and to expand. When free to do so, he creates wealth, creates it again, and creates it anew.

The presence of petroleum was a nuisance to Pennsylvania farmers until in 1849 someone discovered how to refine kerosene. John D. Rockefeller's fortune was begun in refining kerosene, although before long a man named Thomas Edison had invented a way to light homes that was superior to kerosene lanterns. Rockefeller's business had to adjust. In much the same way, the distribution of alternating current discovered by Nikola Tesla was commercially superior to the direct current Edison built his company on and Edison Electric was forced to adapt to the new improvement.

Wealth is created by the greatest resource of all: human beings. It is people who continually discover lesser resources and put them to use in new ways. This is possible because man, out of his own nature, seeks to improve his life and is suited to do so. The hands like to be employed, the mind enjoys being engaged. And as Ralph Waldo Emerson points out, it is of our love of wonder that our science is born.

Look about at all the wealth the people have created. Buildings and homes, schools and churches, stores and places of entertainment; leisure and literacy and libraries; heating and cooling systems; bright lives of bright lights, bright colors, and stunning clothing; marvels of electronics, digital magic, and the miracle of global communications; new medical techniques, devices, and medicines; high-speed travel and stores stocked full of food, much of it fresh from around the world.

A civilization of this complexity provides all of us more and richer opportunities and caters to the satisfaction of our unique individual tastes, interests, and enthusiasms. It is in our lower natures that we are most similar. We all have bodies that must breathe, drink, and eat. We have in common our physical natures, which can be provided for with minimal means of subsistence. But it is prosperity that allows our higher natures to flourish in diversity and individuality. You like rock, I prefer Bach; you like poetry, I seek adventure; you admire the arts, I study the sciences. Our prosperity lies not just in wealth that allows us to buy endless amounts of a few limited items, but in the fact that we can indulge our uniqueness in a proliferation of options available in a sophisticated economy, with its endless array of dazzling choices. It was said that Stalin's daughter Svetlana virtually swooned on her first encounter with the—to her—dizzying range of products available at a typical American grocery store. But as we shall discover, there are collectivists like her father who prefer a dreary sameness in people, a controllable uniformity. For them the free economy is an obstacle. Such people know only too well that, despite its resilience and the richness of its blessings, the free economy is always vulnerable to the power of the state, which can be used to kick the legs of liberty out from under it.

You will have noted that freedom is often expressed in the negative: what others may not do to you—coerce, control, force. But nothing in your experience of freedom specifies what you must do with your freedom, except in the negative: you in turn may not coerce, control, or force others. In this distinction lies a hint of the return to the path of prosperity for the American people. It does not lie in legislative prescriptions, new programs, or new plans for what the state must do. Our prosperity will not be restored by some new tax-cut proposal or new spending initiative; no laws will do it; no charming candidate.

It is a point that must be reiterated. Our problem transcends any mechanical solutions or reform package. We are beyond being able to fix our problems with process tinkering, as Congressman Ron Paul has noted: "It's not a budgetary problem. The budget is a symptom of this disease." Americans have to inquire into the nature of government itself, he says. "It's a philosophy-of-government problem."

The State

It must be understood that state actions necessarily take, but never create. The state has no money that it has not first taken from someone. This era of rising gas prices should help concentrate attention on the point, because as you reach into your front pocket to fill your tank at prices that would have been thought obscene just a few years ago, the Department of Energy is taking $30 billion a year from your back pocket. And what does it do with your billions? Does it explore the remote and dangerous corners of the earth and discover any oil? Does it take enormous risks in hazardous oceans and arctic conditions and suffer substantial losses to locate energy? Recover it, refine it, and transport it to your neighborhood? Just how much gas does it put in your tank for its $30 billion?

Not a drop.

Just as the government pumps no gas, it builds no house and it grows no corn. And when it does appear to grow corn, for example, in the provision of food subsidies, it only does so by taking seeds from a man who then cannot grow his own. Because even what it appears to create is only accomplished with the labor of someone else who would have used his labor for his own preferences, or from money taken by people who are now precluded from acquiring what they prefer.

What contribution could the state have made to our prosperity? "Government is a guarantor of liberty and is compatible with liberty only if its range is adequately restricted to the preservation of economic freedom," wrote Mises. The state could have provided an environment of freedom so that prosperity could flourish, as intended. It could have stood against coercion, on watch for force and fraud. Instead, it has become a fearsome cause of coercion, and an agent of force and fraud itself.

Without instruction by the state, the American people know perfectly well how to create wealth. They do it by doing what they've always done.

They do it by going to work every day, by saving when they can, by taking pride in their work, by reading to their toddlers, by buying and selling, by coming up with new ideas around their kitchen tables, by developing good habits such as thrift and punctuality, by looking for better jobs, by looking for better products, by selling better products and ideas, and by providing fair value. There is no mystery to it. People create wealth by putting in extra time when the task calls for it, by making things that people want and making things that make the things people want, by getting up for work when the alarm goes off in the morning, even when they don't feel like it, by giving fair value, by putting off consumption today to provide for themselves tomorrow, by their ingenuity and industry. By honoring the fundamental principles of right and wrong.

The American people create wealth by keeping their word and by respecting one another's property. Financial writer Richard Maybury has identified two fundamental principles upon which civilization depends: *do all you have agreed to do* and *do not encroach on other persons or their property*. These prerequisites are met with ease in a free economy in which expectations of promises and performances become reliable, which develops means and standards of enforcing contracts so that productive business agreements can proliferate, and in which people can rely on one another. A free economy develops—all by itself—new ways for people to keep their agreements. Insurance coverage allows businesses to meet obligations and frees people to do all they have agreed to do despite risks and unforeseen circumstances. When property is free from being encroached on by others, people's time horizons grow. Long-term investments can be made; capital can flow to productive activities. Where there is a long tradition of respect for property rights, systems of title and evidence of ownership have developed, creating opportunities that have been missing among people mired in poverty in much of the world. Peruvian economist Hernando de Soto has studied the trillions of dollars in "dead capital" in poorer nations, in the statist economies of autocrats. Dead capital is wealth that can't be used as collateral, can't be used to create credit history, can't be borrowed against to send next-generation family members to college. "The poor inhabitants of these nations," he writes, "do have things, but they lack the process to represent their property and create capital. They have houses but not titles; crops but not deeds."

A free economy means property rights—the certainty that what people build and create today will still be theirs tomorrow. It therefore provides for more exchange, which means more division of labor, which allows for specialization, in turn providing for the nurturing of improved skills and methods. Its system of profits and losses inspires efficiencies and provides essential feedback so that calculation is possible and resources can go where they are most prized. The gifts of the free economy add up, multiply, and compound.

But in our contemporary experience, the state has become ravenous in directing and commandeering our productivity. As its meddling increases and its take grows greater, the farmer, the miller, and the baker who provide our bread are disheartened, their incentive drained, the results of their labor diminished. Innovation is stunted. Dependency spreads. Capital spots safer havens elsewhere. Because political connections become a more effective means of getting things done than industriousness, public policy becomes capricious. The influential use the state to protect themselves from competition, so improvements are stymied. And to make matters worse, the state corrupts the money upon which the remaining commerce depends.

A free economy means people are free to trade. Trade is the very substance of wealth. Bricks of gold in the basement would be of little value except for the willingness of others to trade for them. A bumper crop beyond what the farmer can consume himself is not worth the harvest unless he is free to exchange it for something else of value.

In a free economy the sum of human happiness increases with every act of trade, as each party gives what he values less for that which he prefers. Throughout history trade has been a means of illuminating mankind, spreading algebra and alphabets, steering discoveries in navigation, geography, and time measurement, driving transportation improvements and road construction. Trade pollinates human culture, nourishes our humanity, and inseminates our intellectual life with new foods and medicine, new ideas and arts, new inventions, technologies, and products. Trade is the measure of success as nations' fortunes ebb and flow in tides of prosperity, from Rome's rise and fall to the preeminence of the Muslim world to the Renaissance of Europe. The great French economist Frederic Bastiat noted that trade even serves to prevent war, observing that when goods don't cross borders, armies will. Indeed, mutual cooperation is the indispensable basis of trade.

Why then does the state serve as a frequent impediment to trade? Why is the trade language of the state dressed in bellicosity? It speaks of unfair trade and trade from which we need protection. If there are trade "hostilities" then trade "confrontations" are triggered. It blocks trade, erects trade barriers, and seeks to overcome them or to "retaliate." And finally there are trade "wars," which are variously described as aggressive, prolonged, destructive, and costly. They leave both "casualties" and "victims" behind. Like councils of war, trade wars require international conferences of states.

If trade contributes so much to the enrichment of human life, why is the state ceaselessly involved in impeding trade? If both parties to a simple act of exchange are made more prosperous, what good comes from trade interference? The destructive nature of state trade interventionism can be seen in the role the Smoot–Hawley tariffs—tax hikes imposed on 20,000 goods imported into the United States—played in the worldwide depression of the 1930s. In his book *The Way the World Works*, Jude Wanniski carefully tracked the legislative history of the tariff bill and concluded that although President Hoover didn't sign the law until June 1930, it cast a long shadow in advance, triggering both the 1929 stock market crash the prior October and the ensuing Great Depression. Even as the bill worked its way through Congress, foreign nations began creating retaliatory tariffs of their own directed against goods from the United States. A typical example of the consequences of this debacle unfolded when high tariffs were slapped on olive oil coming into the United States. In response, drivers of U.S.-made cars in Italy were likely to find their tires flattened and windshields broken. Before long, steep Italian duties were imposed on American cars that resulted in the shuttering of American dealerships in Italy. As the trade war spread around the globe, American exports collapsed, and contrary to the job protection that tariff supporters had promised, unemployment climbed. Although the unemployment rate had not reached double digits even in the twelve-month aftermath of the stock market crash, and in fact had eased down to 6.3 percent by the time Hoover signed Smoot–Hawley, five months later the jobless rate was 11.6 percent. And on its way to 25 percent.

By prohibiting exchanges that enrich us, the state makes us poorer. Where does the state derive the coercive power to stop free trade among free people?

People cannot be both free and prohibited from buying and selling; coercion and liberty cannot occupy the same space at the same time.

And then there is the matter of price interference. There is nothing the state does quite as incessantly as meddle in prices. And short of war, there are few things quite as destructive. It was state meddling with agricultural prices that, by the logic of the economic interventionists, made the Smoot–Hawley tariffs and its subsequent trade war inevitable. The Hoover administration, having forced domestic farm prices artificially high—even though millions of Americans desperately needed food at low prices—could only maintain those contrived prices by erecting barriers to the entry of food into the country at real-world market prices. The trade war and retaliatory measures set off by the Smoot–Hawley tariffs then destroyed the American farmers' crucial export markets. Since they convey crucial information about supply and demand, somebody once likened prices to speech. Like speech, prices need to be free to tell their tale. In the absence of the price system of a free economy, central economic planners in the Soviet Union were forced to rely upon resources like old Sears and Roebuck catalogs to infer the relative value of one product to another. Managers of Soviet industrial activities requisitioned raw materials, energy, and other resources that they did not need because they did not have to be concerned with the economizing that comes with a price system. Of course that meant that requisitioned resources they did not need were not available elsewhere to satisfy real economic demand.

When state price meddlers fix prices artificially low, it distorts the equilibrium of supply and demand and creates scarcity. It may drive important producers out of business. When the state artificially raises prices, the resulting distortion is surpluses. People who now must pay those higher prices do so at the expense of other goods and services in the economy that go unpurchased. Not only is some other need unmet, but every price received is also a price paid. In artificial price-fixing, just as in the case of trade interference, the state is favoring one citizen (or party to a transaction) over another. In taking sides it serves as both a player, acting on behalf of its preferred outcome, and a referee, charged with even handedly enforcing rules such as contract laws without favor or prejudice. It cannot do both. One might as well allow baseball umpires and basketball referees to bet on the games they officiate.

Sometimes the state attempts to fix prices to the advantage of both sides of a transaction. An individual acting at such cross-purposes would be thought mad. It is state lunacy that forces us to pay for huge agricultural price supports in the morning, making food more expensive, while in the afternoon we pay for food stamps to lower the cost of food for some. Price supports for tobacco growing come out of the taxpayers' left pocket; federal antismoking programs out of the right. Seniors looking outside the country for affordable prescriptions drugs risked federal prosecution for it, even as the government enacted a prescription drug benefit plan to lower costs, a plan that now faces a liability of $19 trillion. We go to war to protect oil supplies overseas even as we slap on import tariffs to keep cheap Brazilian ethanol from coming into the country. In one year government creates tax advantages that encourage the purchase of Hummers and huge SUVs; in another year your income taxes go to pay people to junk their gas-guzzlers and buy smaller cars. The state takes money from you to give to sugar producers, and then it takes more to nag you not to use so much sugar. The Kafkaesque absurdity of funding these mutually conflicting activities is made worse because we are impoverished by the madness along the way.

If Americans wish to reclaim their prosperity, they must embrace freedom.

That's it. Just freedom. Because by now the extent of our economic calamity should be apparent to everyone, this book isn't thick with budget numbers and fattened with projections. Instead it offers the only means of restoring our prosperity. Just freedom. And that means the state . . . must . . . JUST . . . STOP!

It must stop the big things it does that collapse our freedom. Things like price-fixing and the PATRIOT Act and endless wars of invasion and occupation and the Democrats' vote-buying Obamacare and the Republicans' vote-buying Bush drug plan. It must stop favoring the influential and politically connected by interfering with trade. It must stop the bailouts and stimulus programs of both the Republicans and Democrats. It must just stop. It must stop foreign aid and stop Ponzi schemes like Social Security. It must stop the counterproductive war on drugs just as it must stop the destruction of the monetary system by the Federal Reserve.

It must stop the endless spending of Keynesian economics, an academic pretext that has encouraged trillions in deficit spending and left America staggering down a desolate road of long-term indebtedness. The advice of British mathematician John Maynard Keynes that unemployment and recessions can be cured by creating artificial demand in the economy—that government can kick-start the economy by spending money it doesn't have or by driving down interest rates by printing money—has been the prevailing creed of Republicans and Democrats since the Great Depression. Keynes's advice failed to end the Great Depression, which didn't end until state spending collapsed after the war. It failed again in the stagflation of the 1970s when, according to the Keynesian theory, the impossible happened: the high inflation it recommended coincided with the sharp recession and rising unemployment it promised to fix. And it continues to fail today, draining our prosperity and bleeding the purchasing power of the dollar, even as it has jacked up the visible portions of the national debt from $9 trillion when the recession began in December 2007 to today's $16 trillion. Because the madness of this Keynesian statist meddling can only make our crisis worse, it cannot be allowed to continue.

The state must stop.

And not just stop the big things—the bankrupting policies and the full-frontal assaults on our freedom. It must stop little things—the constant power grabs and the death of our freedom by a thousand cuts; snooping on the web sites you view; demanding others report on your use of cash; limiting what farmers are allowed to grow; tracking the mileage you drive using GPS technology; regulating the grease in your donuts; trying to take control of the Internet; ruling who braids your hair; tracking your children's body mass index; and prying into your purchases of gold or silver.

The state must stop.

That's the formula for restoring the prosperity of the American people, for making the men and women and children of America and their families better off. Notice I don't say the formula to restore "American prosperity," as though it were all about making the state mightier. One book by a famed economist, typical of those who failed to see the meltdown calamity as it closed in on us, offers advice on restoring America's economic "superpower status." It is an unfortunate usage; the hubris betrayed by that phrase is one of the reasons that savings have been destroyed, jobs have disappeared, retirement dreams have evaporated, and the hope of a better life for your children has gone dim. Superpower status? So we can bankrupt ourselves all over again supporting the global empire, continuing to pick sides in faraway local disputes, supporting tyrants who crush the aspirations of their own people, just as we have been doing for decades while creating new generations of foreign America haters? Have we not learned yet how empires collapse?

Is it too harsh to claim that the activities of the state itself must be stopped? Experience teaches that it is too harsh to be heard from the leadership of the red and blue wings of the Washington party. To be sure, each party proposes resisting the expansion of statism, but only at the margins of its opponents' preferences. It is as though one ancient Aztec wanted to throw younger virgins into the sacrificial volcano, while his opponent argued to toss in more beautiful ones instead. But both believe in volcano sacrifice. Even among popular purported tax foes, the objective is to find the sacred rate that maximizes revenue to the state Moloch.

Will the message of freedom's restoration repel those who have been taught that the state is the sacred spring from which all blessings flow? Then the whimper of our end will be certain. This is especially undeserved for those who warned all along that bankrupting policies would produce . . . well, bankruptcy. It does seem unfair to those who resisted the destruction of our liberty. Still, deserved or undeserved, fair or not, we are all in this together. Just as we are the beneficiaries of advances in life that we personally had nothing to do with, so, too, must we share in a common fate, even if it is to be an unhappy one. But it does demand that those who have been right about our accelerating statist trajectory must intensify their efforts to arouse their slumbering fellows before it's too late—even though challenging the prerogatives of the state is always the violation of a sacred taboo.

Cries of "Treason! Treason!" arose from the floor of the Virginia legislature when revolutionary-era firebrand Patrick Henry challenged the authority of a mentally ill monarch an ocean away. In 1635 Roger Williams, a minister and founder of the Rhode Island colony, was forced to appear repeatedly before the Massachusetts General Court for his "dangerous opinions." Among his heresies was his belief that the state had no right to dictate religious ideas and practices. "Forced worship," he said, "stinks in the nostrils of God." He was banished from Massachusetts for his trouble. It was for corrupting the minds of the youth of Athens and for not believing in the gods of the state that Socrates was forced to drink the hemlock.

From ancient times, challenges to the state and its prerogatives have always been thought to be too harsh. But before you decide that my indictment is too strong, come along and judge the case on the evidence.

Sink or Swim

This book is unlike many that have been written about our national crisis, including any of a hundred that have recommended state actions to address our crisis: new initiatives, more efficient administration, better planning, new and different experts, and specific candidates; or even term limits, balanced budget amendments, campaign finance reform, and scores of other hopelessly inadequate mechanical solutions for what really is a philosophical problem. Following the Taoist principle *wu wei*, meaning "nondoing" or "nonaction," the state must just stop. Except for getting the state out of the way so that the people's natural prosperity dynamic can reassert itself, this book is empty of political prescriptions and indeed maintains that life needs to be moved from under political authority. Just as freedom is defined in negative terms, the restoration of the American dream depends on the state not doing any harm.

The thought of liberty may be disorienting to those who have been conditioned to turn to the state for solutions to every challenge. It may perturb those who fear that in the absence of the state Americans will no longer care to educate their children and will not provide for their own retirement. Such objections ring hollow in the presence of the state's failing education system, which shows students falling behind year after year. The objection that the state knows best rings empty when its retirement promises are evaporating before our eyes, leaving hanging not just the manageable few in each neighborhood or community who failed to provide for themselves, but now entire generations that find themselves unprepared for old age.

The state interventionists' agitation at the thought of liberty is like that of the man who, not having learned to swim, falls into the water and, desperate with fear, panics and thrashes about wildly, flapping and flailing and swallowing water until finally, exhausted, he sinks below the surface and drowns—all because he did not know he could float quite effortlessly. The state flails about with new deals that prolong the economic downturn. It desperately concocts money printing schemes, Soviet-style economic plans, and other boondoggles for an economy that can bob back to the surface on its own; it thrashes about with stimulus packages and bailouts, leaving in its wake a sinking currency and a nation of people succumbing to the deadweight of its debt.

Although the ranks of people who see our sinking circumstances as the product of our diminished liberty are growing—awakened by the shock of gas, grocery, and gold prices, dismal foreign adventures, the accuracy of Austrian school economists, and the few fearless champions of freedom in public life—such people are the brave few. Much larger are the ranks of unknowing statists who have never questioned the catechism of their public school years or the dogmas of the state's lapdog press. It is safe to assume that for many of them, no one has ever made an explicit case for the cause of economic freedom and its powerful engine of wealth creation. It is a case made by Murray Rothbard, who wrote:

> Production is the only method by which poverty can be wiped out.... Production must come first, and only freedom allows people to produce in the best and most efficient way possible. Force and violence may "distribute," but it cannot produce. Intervention hampers production, and socialism cannot calculate. Since production of consumer satisfactions is maximized on the free market, the free market is the only way to abolish poverty. Dictates and legislation cannot do so; in fact, they can only make things worse.

If America is not to be swallowed up in an abyss of diminished circumstances and lessened opportunity, freedom will need new supporters and able defenders.

CHAPTER TWO

The Blessings of Liberty

If a nation values anything more than freedom, it will lose its
freedom; and the irony of it is that, if it is comfort or money it
values more, it will lose that too.

—William Somerset Maugham

A History of Contempt

For years many in the public debate, libertarians and others have invoked the
U.S. Constitution as an obstacle to runaway growth of the state and the prerogatives it assumes at the expense of our self-determination. I have been
among them most of my life, from early debates in public school and as an adult
in speaking, writing, and in talk radio. Clearly the Constitution forbids the
government from broad swaths of activities—indeed, most of the things with
which it now busies itself. If the enumeration of the federal government's authority for only specific activities somehow failed to register with the governing
classes, there were always the Ninth and Tenth Amendments as reminders that
the only federal powers were those spelled out, and everything else was to be
off-limits to the general government, all other powers not enumerated in the
Constitution being lodged immutably with the people and the states.

But it began to become clear not so many years ago that those arguments
had lost their ability to move people; it was as though the Constitution itself
had become as desiccated and brittle as the old parchment original on display at the National Archives in Washington. Mention of the Constitution may

still elicit a nod of approval, but this seems merely perfunctory, like the indulgent smile with which activists dressed up in tricornered hats or carrying revolutionary-era muskets are greeted: it evokes only dim recollections of antiquarian things.

To be sure, reverence for the Constitution still rolls readily off the lips of politicians of every stripe. It is spoken of in hallowed terms at Republican Lincoln Day dinners, reverently lauded at Democratic Jefferson-Jackson day celebrations, and devoutly invoked at political conventions and Tea Party rallies. But it is just a formality. As a bulwark against the growth of the state, as an impediment to politicians with their insatiable lust for power, the Constitution has not been able to accomplish for free people what they must do for themselves.

Contempt and the Warfare State

Nowhere is the Constitution shown greater contempt—a contempt made more bitter by coming from those who have sworn to uphold it—than in going to war. Because war making is the most destructive activity of governments, it merits first place in this examination of the neglect of the Constitution. The Constitution is clear that war must be declared by Congress; the approval of the people who must pay for and die in such wars must be expressly given by their representatives. (*"The Congress shall have Power . . . To declare War . . ."*) But when it comes to seizing war-making authority, those holding the executive branch, regardless of party, give the provision the back of their hand. In this regard Presidents Clinton, Bush, and Obama have been a threesome.

Clinton took the position that decisions for war were a part of the president's foreign policy prerogatives. He rejected congressional interference with his interventions in Haiti and Somalia, insisting that "clearly the Constitution leaves the president, for good and sufficient reasons, the ultimate decision-making authority." There was no congressional declaration of war for the two months of Clinton's 1995 bombing war in Bosnia, or when he subsequently ordered the deployment of 22,000 ground troops. Similarly, on March 24, 1999, when Clinton announced that the U.S. was joining with NATO to launch air strikes against Yugoslavia, he again did so without authorization.

Rather than acquiescing, in April Congress refused to pass legislation authorizing the war. Indeed, the House specifically rejected a declaration of war on Yugoslavia by a vote of 427–2.

But the bombing continued. As it did, seventeen members of Congress, fifteen Republicans and two Democrats, filed a lawsuit against the president in federal court for violating Article 1, Section 8, Clause 11 of the U.S. Constitution by engaging in war without a declaration by Congress:

> Defendant's initiation of and continuation of an offensive military attack by United States forces against the Federal Republic of Yugoslavia, without obtaining a declaration of war or other explicit authorization from the Congress of the United States, violates Article I, Section 8, Clause 11 of the Constitution and deprived and continues to deprive the Plaintiffs of their constitutional right, opportunity, and duty to prevent, by refusing their assent, the entry of the United States into a war against the Federal Republic of Yugoslavia.

Astonishingly, a federal judge swept the issue aside by ruling that the plaintiffs did not have standing to sue. The D.C. Court of Appeals agreed and the Supreme Court chose to wash its hands of the issue as well.

The argument is made that Congress could have chosen to deny funds for a war it disapproved; just as Congress is authorized to declare war, only Congress is authorized to appropriate funds for it. Such a response is wholly inadequate. The congressional prerogative to declare war is not somehow junior to, or less explicit than, the authority to appropriate funds. The power of the legislative branch to declare war represents a necessary check on the executive branch, which has ample resources at hand to initiate war-making mischief at almost any time, even in the absence of lawful appropriations.

In his 2004 book *Plan of Attack*, Bob Woodward reported that the Bush administration secretly diverted $700 million in 2002 from appropriations made to prevent terrorism in Afghanistan, to prepare for the war in Iraq. This Bush did without notifying Congress and absent any congressional endorsement of hostilities in Iraq. Later, when Congress passed a defense appropriation bill specifically banning the construction of any permanent bases in Iraq, Bush appended a "signing statement" announcing his refusal to be bound by the act of Congress. It was, to be sure, an action of no more constitutional merit than appending a little yellow sticky note to the bill since the president's role in leg-islative enactment is also clearly specified in Article 1, Section 7. (*"Every Bill which shall have passed the House of Representatives and the Senate, shall, before it become a Law, be presented to the President of the United States; If he ap-prove he shall sign it, but if not he shall return it . . ."*) One must wonder whether the appellate court would also deny members of Congress standing to challenge Bush's novel sticky-note theory of executive authority over appropriations.

But even more important to the point about the contempt shown the Con-stitution is this: In a short span of three years the Republicans had forgotten their earlier devotion to Article 1, Section 8, Clause 11. After having sued the Democrat Clinton for waging war without a congressional declaration, all of the twelve Republicans remaining in office, except for Ron Paul, voted for the Republican George W. Bush's Iraq war "resolution." They voted to hand off their constitutional responsibility to declare war to the new president—this time a Republican—and he could decide the issue for them. One can begin to see in the subordination of the rule of law and the elevation of partisan rivalry what has happened to our liberty and our prosperity. The elected classes, sworn to uphold the Constitution, have reduced America to a sporting event: it's all about the red team versus the blue team.

Neither war—Clinton's Yugoslavia, Bush's Iraq—was a matter of hot pur-suit, a situation that might have argued against a formal war declaration to allow an immediate response to an attack. Both wars were in fact long contem-plated. Clinton and British prime minister Tony Blair were sharing war plans months before the U.S.-led bombing of Yugoslavia got under way. The attack on Iraq was more than a year and a half after the 9/11 terrorist attacks that were used as justification for the war. (Senator Bob Graham of Florida, chairman of the Intelligence Committee on 9/11, told me in a radio conversation that Gen-eral Tommy Franks, commander of U.S. forces in Afghanistan, had told him that important resources had been taken off the pursuit of Osama bin Laden and Al Qaeda leaders in Afghanistan and diverted for a planned war in Iraq—more than a year before the war began.) Even given the limitations of com-munications and travel more than seventy years ago, Congress declared war on Japan the day after the December 7, 1941, attack on Pearl Harbor, easily managing to pass a formal declaration just minutes after being asked to do so by President Roosevelt.

Long after it was widely known inside the administration that Bush was determined to initiate a war on Iraq, Bush played coy with the White House press about the prospects for war. "I haven't made up my mind yet," he said. *He* hadn't made up *his* mind? It was the sort of remark that chilled those who value the rule of law. But party loyalties prevailed. Bush dismissed the need for congressional approval with a terse response: "I don't think I need it." Perhaps it was a genetic predisposition among the Bushes. Or perhaps the younger Bush learned it from the elder, who actually bragged, "I didn't have to get permission from some old goat in the United States Congress to kick Saddam Hussein out of Kuwait."

Nor did President Obama feel the need to have any old congressional goats vote before undertaking a war with Libya, a country that had not threatened or attacked the United States. But if Congress didn't merit a vote on the war, the president thought the UN Security Council did. Perhaps Obama should have consulted with the constitutional scholar who told the *Boston Globe* in 2007, "The president does not have the power under the Constitution to unilaterally authorize a military attack in a situation that does not involve stopping an actual or imminent threat to the nation." The same scholar rebuked President Bush that year when he said, "I was a constitutional law professor, which means unlike the current president I actually respect the Constitution." That scholar's name was Barack Obama. Of course back then he was just a candidate.

That the executive branch has been permitted to usurp legislative authority for war is in part a reflection of congressional cowardice: members can always find their way to the victory banquets when the military adventure is a success, while disclaiming responsibility when things go awry. But it is not for members of Congress—cowards or no—to corrupt the lawful checks and balances among the branches. It is the Constitution itself that vests decisions to go to war with Congress, and there is no provision that allows Congress to abdicate that responsibility.

Wars of empire have hastened our economic implosion in ways that I will discuss in more detail in Chapter Nine. But there is more to calculate than the direct cost of war. Empires usher in other abuses that subvert the rule of law and thus undermine our prosperity.

The prohibitions against government in the Bill of Rights are essential to Americans who wish to go about their business peacefully and unmolested, and are a linchpin of our prosperity. During the Bush years, Democrats in

Congress were justifiably outraged when the Bush administration was discovered to have let the National Security Agency eavesdrop on Americans without court warrants, as well as the subsequent discovery that the administration was also creating a database of nearly two trillion telephone calls. (*"Amendment 4—Search and Seizure. The right of the people to be secure in their persons, houses, papers, and effects, against unreasonable searches and seizures, shall not be violated, and no Warrants shall issue, but upon probable cause, supported by Oath or affirmation, and particularly describing the place to be searched, and the persons or things to be seized."*) In the same spirit of renegade disregard, the FBI under the PATRIOT Act has issued hundreds of thousands of "National Security Letters," effectively subpoenas demanding information. That the branches of American government are divided as a check on power is meaningless when the executive is allowed to read the judicial branch out of the picture. The FBI, the CIA, and now even the Pentagon issue these demands on their own initiative without a demonstration of probable cause and without judicial oversight. Worse still, these "subpoenas" are accompanied by a gag order forbidding the recipients from telling anyone about the government's activity. This results in a truly surreal situation in which the FBI and other agencies threaten their victims with criminal charges to keep their extrajudicial activities secret, thus trampling on both the First and Fourth Amendments at the same time.

Of course in 2008, candidate Obama was opposed to "sneak and peak searches." His position at the time was spelled out in campaign documents: "There is no reason we cannot fight terrorism while maintaining our civil liberties." But in office, Obama succumbed to power's eternal lure, seeking to greatly expand his search authority, vacuuming up email addresses and even web sites the "target" has visited, all without judicial approval.

Similarly, the "state secrets" privileges candidate Obama criticized and Capitol Hill Democrats objected to during the Bush administration—a doctrine of effective immunity for criminal activities—were suddenly embraced after the votes were counted. Obama's turnaround on the issue was so complete that, in an account of a case a month after the new president was inaugurated, the *New York Times* reported that hearing again the same "state secrets" arguments the Bush administration had been making had the effect of "startling several judges on the United States Court of Appeals for the Ninth Circuit." When the court later ruled on behalf of the government, the paper called it "a major victory for the Obama administration's efforts to advance a sweeping view of executive secrecy powers."

Author and constitutional lawyer Glenn Greenwald has written at Salon .com about the use of the "state secrets" doctrine under both Bush and Obama. The Obama administration has taken a position, says Greenwald, that can be used to prevent judicial scrutiny of blatantly illegal government activities and war crimes. "They're embracing a theory that literally places government officials beyond the rule of law. No minimally honest person who criticized the Bush administration for relying on this instrument can defend the Obama administration for doing so here."

In politics the parties out of power often object to power grabs by the majority, but that is little check on the majorities, especially when the affronted minority becomes the majority. Those opposed to the omnipotent state—libertarians and champions of a free, open, and prosperous society—often join the minorities in dissent. Even so, the more experienced and wiser of them refrain from tying themselves too tightly to, or pinning their hopes on, their new political bedfellows. They have seen this dynamic at work again and again, and not just in matters of the growth of the national security state, of militarism, and of empire. Modern-day conservatives have long sung their support for fiscal responsibility as loudly as they have for the military state. Candidate Bush was happy to play the fiscal conservatives this favorite tune: "Gore offers an old and tired approach. He offers a new federal spending program to nearly every voting bloc. He expands entitlements, without reforms to sustain them. . . . Spending without discipline, spending without priorities, and spending without an end." As president, Bush said, he would save hundreds of billions of dollars by improving government efficiency and cracking down on federal spending. Soon Bush had established a new world indoor record for fiscal recklessness, becoming the biggest-spending president since Lyndon Johnson. But his record would only stand until the next president was sworn into office. (Candidate Obama: "When I'm president, I will go line-by-line to make sure that we are not spending money unwisely.")

The Republicans' financial profligacy and abuses of the Constitution become the baseline upon which Democrats heap new abuses. Likewise, assumptions by Democrats of unconstitutional powers become the foundations upon which Republicans mount their new power grabs. After Bush was allowed to assume the authority to hold U.S. citizens for years without granting them due process, it was entirely predictable that Obama would claim the right to assassinate Americans on the basis of accusations. Obama has asserted just that power in the war on terror, claiming he has the authority to carry out targeted killings far from the battlefield and without charges, trial, or due process. Clearly the presidential assumption of authority to create a "death list" for citizens, a policy that obviates the value of constitutional limitations on executive power, should create alarm among the people. Instead it has gone largely unnoticed. When Obama was sued over the assassination policy in 2010, U.S. District Court Judge John Bates tossed the case out on jurisdictional grounds. But he at least thought to wonder about the incongruity of it, writing in his opinion, "How is it that judicial approval is required when the United States decides to target a U.S. citizen overseas for electronic surveillance, but that, according to defendants, judicial scrutiny is prohibited when the United States decides to target a U.S. citizen overseas for death?" While the people sleep, the piling of new and greater abuses upon the abuses that were allowed the prior administration compounds the power of the nation-state endlessly at the expense of their liberty.

One may wonder what the power devotees of all the branches of government believe they are swearing to do when they take the oath of office. More than one member of Congress has told me how dismissive Republican House leaders were of the Constitution's requirement for a declaration of war against Iraq. Although he opposed the war itself, Congressman Ron Paul thought it important to comply with the Constitution and introduced an amendment for an explicit declaration of war. He was told by Republican Henry Hyde, chairman of the International Relations Committee, that the Constitution's requirement was "anachronistic." The question found in Shakespeare's *Julius Caesar* applies as well to our Washington kingpins: "Upon what meat doth this our Caesar feed, that he is grown so great?" Who exactly are these mighties? Where do such exalted ones find the authority to decide for themselves to which parts of the Constitution they will adhere, and which they will ignore as inconvenient and irrelevant? Are we but menials to their Caesars?

> *Why, man, he doth bestride the narrow world*
> *Like a Colossus, and we petty men*
> *Walk under his huge legs and peep about*
> *To find ourselves dishonourable graves.*

Contempt and the Welfare State

While Republicans display their eagerness to waive the Constitution on behalf of the warfare state, the Democrats are always quick to discard it in furtherance of the welfare state. House Speaker Nancy Pelosi was utterly indignant when a reporter asked what the constitutional authorization was for the mandates of the 2010 health-care bill that amounted to nationalization of seventeen percent of the U.S. economy. Pelosi could only manage to sputter, "Are you serious? Are you serious?" The Speaker's press spokesman went out of his way to scold the reporter. "You can put this on the record," he said. "That is not a serious question." The national media's neglect of that moment confirms its view: "That is not a serious question." But it should be.

An inchoate sense that fundamental questions of the sort *are* serious, coupled with a nagging intuition that their freedom was being gobbled up, may have energized the new activists and Tea Party groups in the 2010 election. The resulting new Republican House majority answered that anxiety with a ceremonial reading of the Constitution on the House floor. While some may have been grateful for the focus on the Constitution, for me it represented only a continuum of the syndrome of the state in which words replace deeds, politicians replace ideals, and state promises are irredeemable. In *The Dollar Meltdown* I used the example of the monetary system to illustrate the pattern. The earliest American coinage contained representations of liberty itself, but over the years this enduring ideal of our founding has now been supplanted by the celebration of politicians on the coins instead. Similarly the circulating dollar bills were nothing but a claim check for the real monetary commodity for which they were redeemable. Today's dollars are as irredeemable as a politician's promise. So the wary cannot be faulted for seeing in the reading of the Constitution nothing more than hollow political theater. It should have called to mind the wisdom of Jesus's admonition of the hypocrites who love to be seen praying loudly in the streets, "that they may be seen of men." Just as those hypocrites were admonished to take their prayers quietly into their closets, it would be more reassuring to believe the ceremonial Constitution readers had actually shut themselves behind closed doors and familiarized themselves with the document before they took the oath to support and defend it. As though to illustrate the futility of the stunt, just days after the public performance a reporter asked one congressman who had taken part in the reading what exactly in the Constitution authorized Obamacare's mandate that people buy health insurance. The congressman cited the "pursuit of happiness" clause. It doesn't inspire any happiness that, fresh from reading the Constitution, a member of long standing who has taken the oath personally more than a dozen times doesn't know the difference between the Declaration of Independence and the Constitution.

The growth of federal power and its costly welfare and warfare spending are proving to be the undoing of our prosperity. Neither is authorized by the Constitution, and together they are the engine of America's runaway debt. Each of the three branches bears responsibility for the riotous folly of this welfare/warfare state. For the executive branch to operate unilaterally—to make war, to oversee the issuance of its own warrants, to defy the doctrine of probable cause, to seek to immunize its own potentially criminal behavior—is an unconscionable strike at the heart of the system of checks and balances of powers upon which we have been taught to rely. By erecting entitlements and other government programs in the absence of specified authority, the legislative branch has gutted the very concept of limited government. The growth of federal power attests to the fact that relying on the courts—themselves creatures and appointees of the other branches of the government—to check the appetite of the megastate has proven a failure.

Partisan Points

Entrusting the state with the right to review and approve the legitimacy of its own actions was always a dubious proposition. The legitimacy of self-review, if there is any, is initially dependent on the evenhandedness of officeholders, and ultimately on the vigilance and fair-mindedness of the people themselves. The elected classes have demonstrated that they are not to be trusted to cry "Halt!" in the advance of government as it gobbles up new domains of state activity. This has proven particularly true when the territory involved appears to enhance their power and further their electoral prospects. Therefore the last line of defense rests with the people. But that is a defense that is only as good as they are. As anyone who has played in neighborhood ball games knows, fair play depends on the "your own man says" standard. Was the runner safe on base or thrown out? In the absence of independent officiating, the claim that "even your own man says he was out" could be determinative. (The absence of opportunities to spontaneously develop such practices of fair play, common characteristics of a free economy, is one great disadvantage of children's sports leagues and the other institutionalization of childhood activities.) The honest application of the "your own man says" standard can cultivate mutual respect and develop trust. It allows for the voluntary interdependence upon which the blessings of a complex civilization and a prosperous people depend.

But its application is not mechanical. It cannot be turned on with the flip of a switch and left to function on its own as if it were a perpetual-motion machine. As even schoolchildren soon learn, the "your own man says" rule depends on the integrity of the participants. The people are a defense against subjugation to authorities only to the extent that they are willing to place a higher value on the restraint of power than they are on the use of power to seek to live at the expense of others and to further the party that promises to help them do so. More integrity can be found among children at play—at least until they, too, have been poisoned by partisanship—than can be found in the capitals, where everything is subordinated to the concentration of power under the dome of the state.

The partisanship in modern American politics plays out within the sidelines of sound bites and sloganeering. (When the national media obsessed for days over the candidates' wearing of lapel pins during the 2008 presidential campaign, comedian Lewis Black summed it all up: "I'm not comfortable with any idea that can't be expressed in the form of men's jewelry. If it takes more than two cuff-links to say it, you lost me!") This narrow playing field of simpleminded and banal political debate keeps the contest constrained in a way that favors the perpetuation of the Washington parties and the governing classes. Those who step outside the boundaries may be ruled "offsides" by the major news enterprises and find that they are ineligible receivers of mainstream media coverage and excluded from debates. Congress throws millions of dollars at the Washington political parties to subsidize their conventions, as though the parties are the creations of the Constitution itself. But perhaps a better example of the way the political debate is strictly officiated by the Washington party is the Commission on Presidential Debates, the organization that stages the quadrennial events. It is a creation of, and jointly run by, the Republican and Democratic parties themselves. Establishment-approved candidates never challenge the consensus of the governing classes; those who do quickly find themselves benched and even denied ballot access.

Both of the 2008 presidential candidates, Obama and McCain, were at different times favored by the spotlight of the establishment media. The candidates were portrayed to the voters as ideological opposites, but on the issues that really control our liberty and prosperity—issues as fundamental as the American military empire, the Federal Reserve and its criminal destruction of the dollar, or even the national security police state—the presidential candidates were really just like practice squads, wearing different jerseys, one red and one blue, but playing on the same team. One candidate was the agent of "change." The other was the would-be maverick, always willing to buck his party. But Obama's change sure didn't mean opposing Bush's $700 billion bailout bill, while McCain was not about to buck the handout of the big bucks to the powerhouses of Wall Street.

In the moment that the bailouts were at the center of the campaign, a door of opportunity briefly opened for John McCain to win the presidency in 2008—had he been able to challenge the Washington consensus on this fundamental issue. As the mortgage meltdown accelerated, McCain dramatically suspended his campaign, putting a long-planned presidential debate with Obama on hold for a sudden White House "summit" with both candidates, congressional leaders, and President Bush. As a campaign stunt it was effective, allowing the slipping McCain campaign to briefly dominate the news cycle. But it was more politics than substance. McCain raised no objection to the bailout and really had nothing to say about it, despite having convened the summit himself. And by supporting the wildly unpopular measure, McCain missed a stunning opportunity. Calls and emails to Congress opposing the bailout ran ninety-five percent and higher. Its popularity even continued to decline after its passage, and that was without either national candidate articulating the economic case against it. The bailout sparked hundreds of demonstrations across the country; a thousand protestors descended on Wall Street. The anger ran so high that pictures of signs actually urging bankers in financial center high-rises to jump blazed across the Internet. Ron Paul supporters had turned out in Boston in 2007 for the 234th anniversary of the Boston Tea Party and commemorated the event by raising the most money any candidate had ever raised in a single day. With the Bush bailout nearly a year later, the people's burning resentment of the naked transfer of wealth and the new Tea Party movement spread like wildfire. McCain, who had tried for so long to position himself as a populist, finally had his chance, and might have been swept into office if he had had the wisdom to recognize how counterproductive the bailout would be and the harm it would do to America's solvency. He might have looked for guidance to the Republican platform on which he was running, passed at the convention only weeks earlier: "We do not support government bailouts of private institutions. Government interference in the markets exacerbates problems in the marketplace and causes the free market to take longer to correct itself." But if McCain had been capable of challenging the Washington consensus on such bedrock issues, he wouldn't have been the media darling he had become and he certainly would never have been the Republican Party's nominee.

Ironically, just two years later, when President Obama called for another stimulus package, his second, Senator McCain was highly critical, calling it "Keynes on steroids." McCain was concerned about "accumulating this incredible mounting debt on our kids and our grandkids," saying that "the economic policies have failed."

Partisan points are scored in the end zones of wedge issues and focus group-tested talking points. In this there is a hint at why such a political process cannot redeem itself. Any halfhearted Republican can point out problems among Democrats, but doing so improves Democrats very little; similarly, any run-of-the-mill Democrat can name Republicans' faults, but Republicans are not made much better for the effort. Instead, the partisans should look to clean their own houses first. A regenerated politics would require the party faithful to ruthlessly reject their own when they betray the oaths they have taken, and to reject them with the same vigor that they reject their power-grabbing opponents. Loyalists of goodwill would have to be just as vigilant in identifying the avaricious, ambitious, and self-serving members of their own party as they are exacting in finding such faults in their opponents. Of course this general principle is the very bedrock of self-responsibility in individuals, in groups, and even in nations. It is recommended in folk maxims and in wisdom traditions around the world. Christian political activists should recognize it in the admonishment to "first remove the beam from thine own eye." It is a principle fundamental to psychological maturity and yet has proven beyond the reach of most partisans. Its application would have required Republicans and other conservatives to pursue the transgressions of Bush and the officeholders of his majority with the same dogged persistence with which they went after Clinton and his misdeeds. Democrats and liberals would have had to subject the Obama presidency to the same intense scrutiny to which they subjected Bush's. This they have failed to do.

Self-Ownership

The principles discussed here—your own man says, clean up your own house first, remove the beam in your own eye—are virtues necessary to self-government, especially if it is to be steeped in partisanship. They are each the practical offspring of the Golden Rule that is found in the scriptures and wisdom traditions of the world, to "do unto others as you would have them do unto you."

They remind us (*your own* house, *your own* eye) that each one of us has quite enough of a challenge dealing with and perfecting our own self, or, in the case of a collective effort such as a team, a community, or a political party (*your own* man), correcting ourselves. We are urged thereby to the virtues of self-knowledge, self-improvement, self-responsibility, self-control, self-reliance, self-respect, and self-government.

The foundational principle of self-ownership both underlies and enables these virtues. Self-ownership is the intuitively compelling principle by which many people come to libertarianism. It is the recognition that you own your own life—and after all, if you don't own your life, who does? As history all too sadly shows, those who do not assert ownership of themselves will find others only too willing to do so. Self-ownership is not a reductionist philosophy, but rather asserts the high ground of the freedom and dignity of the individual against the deluge of mass society. It unmasks coercion in all of its appearances. And it stands as a self-evident bulwark against the claims of those who hunger for power over others.

Since self-ownership is a universal principle, it applies to all people equally. It is not just you who owns your own life, but others own their own lives as well. It is in this grant of an equal right of self-ownership to others that the principle fosters voluntary, mutual human relationships and peaceful human cooperation. Although the prominence of the term "self" might have shallow critics suggesting that there is something about self-ownership that is atomizing and isolating, to the contrary, it is a principle that is integral to all that makes social life—and civilization itself—possible.

In a delightful animated video called *The Philosophy of Liberty*, economics professor Ken Schoolland begins with a simple description of self-ownership and makes the keen observation that the basic values of life, liberty, and property can each be derived from this principle in the unfolding of time:

> You exist in time (past, present, future). This is manifest in: your life, your liberty, and the product of your life and liberty.
>
> To lose your life is to lose your future.
>
> To lose your liberty is to lose your present.
>
> And to lose the product of your life and liberty is to lose the portion of your past that produced it.
>
> A product of your life and your liberty is your property.
>
> ... To take life is murder. To take liberty is slavery. To take property is theft. It is the same whether these actions are done by one person acting alone or by the many acting against the few.

Based on the epilogue of Schoolland's book *The Adventures of Jonathan Gullible: A Free Market Odyssey, The Philosophy of Liberty* video presents the principle of self-ownership in an easily accessible form. Viewed by millions of people around the world, it is available in dozens of languages. In the early days of the 2011 Arab Spring revolution, an Arabic-language version was quickly produced for viewing throughout Egypt and the Middle East. The video can easily be found at the web site of the International Society for Individual Liberty, isil.org, or by doing an Internet search for "philosophy of liberty."

The U.S. Constitution represented the great American achievement of a new understanding of the relationship of each individual self to the state. From the earliest days of tribes and clans, under the rule of chiefs and kings, in the time of lords and masters, and during the reigns of churches, emperors, tyrants, and even democracies, each individual was thought to be the property of the tribe, master, church, city-state, or nation. Even the Magna Carta that King John of England was forced to sign in 1215 rested on the presupposition that the rights and liberties it granted were the king's; he could bestow or withhold them as he chose. In putting his seal on the "The Great Charter of the Liberties of England, and of the Liberties of the Forest," in a meadow called Runnymede along the River Thames, he chose to bestow them. Because the rebelling barons had taken London and other towns, the king soon complained that the agreement had been made under duress. He appealed to Pope Innocent III, who annulled the "shameful" document of liberties.

What was really revolutionary about the American Revolution was the change it made in this prevailing view that the liberties of other human beings were the special dominion of some person, family, group, institution, or state. The wheel of this revolution had already begun moving with ideas about natural rights and the self-evidence of inalienable rights. It was these new ideas on which the 1776 revolution turned, and not on the precedent of mere incremental additions to the cause of liberty, that might be won from time to time from some sovereign. "Our Revolution," Jefferson wrote in his last years,

> presented us an album on which we were free to write what we pleased. We had no occasion to search into musty records, to hunt up royal parchments, or to investigate the laws and institutions of a semi-barbarous ancestry. We appealed to those of nature, and found them engraved in our hearts.

These new truths were codified in the Constitution, which said nothing at all about rights hereby being conferred upon the people. The new government had no rights to bestow. Instead, the new document specified exactly what rights the government itself would be permitted: these things the general government may do, while those activities not specified, it may not. This was something new. All the ancient superstitions were overturned; the old presuppositions were stood on their heads. Henceforth rights shall be understood as lodged with human beings as individuals, prior to government. Like America's new government, other governments had been formed to provide for the common defense, to ensure domestic tranquility, and to provide for the general welfare. Those were the common objectives of many governments, ancient and modern, even tyrannical ones. But the aim that was unique, essential to the new ideal, and incorporated into the Preamble to the United States Constitution was this: to "secure the Blessings of Liberty to ourselves and our Posterity."

In case the point was overlooked, the Bill of Rights was appended to the Constitution to clarify the issue, beginning with five words reiterating who was in charge and setting the tone that followed: "Congress shall make no law . . ." In keeping with the revolutionary spirit of the Constitution, the Bill of

Rights was really a bill of "thou shalt nots" addressed to the general government. It granted no rights to the people, but presupposed as its starting point that rights belong to the people. The general government was not to "prohibit," "abridge," "infringe," or "violate" these preexisting rights.

Our constitutional government is brilliantly structured to limit power, to divide power against itself, and to otherwise check power. Certainly among the framers there were wise and learned men; great insight went into the Constitution's provisions. For example, the war-making authority was specifically delegated to the legislative branch because the authors knew that historical precedents demanded that a check be placed on heads of state, which have a proclivity to embark on unnecessary wars, as we have just experienced. But the learning and wisdom the framers brought to their creation is all for naught in our neglect of its provisions. And it is best to remember that while the Constitution incorporates compromises and mechanical processes thought to be useful, there is nothing particularly sacred about a bicameral legislature or holy about the pocket veto. It is the idea that the Constitution represents, the principle it embodies transcending mere process, which deserves to endure.

Sadly the significance of this seems lost on the American people today. One can hardly follow Internet discussions, watch news and listen to talk radio, or read letters to newspaper editors without coming across assertions such as, "The Constitution gives us the right of free speech," or "the Second Amendment gives us the right to bear arms." With that, the hard-won accomplishment of the American Revolution begins to ebb away; the old-world view begins to rise once more, that such rights are granted to the people and, if granted, as a logical extension may again be withheld.

Who Lost the Constitution?

Because the revolutionary idea embodied in the Constitution thwarts the drives and ambitions of the governing classes, it is not useful to identify them as responsible for its disappearance. It would be hopelessly naïve to have entrusted them with it to begin with. If you leave your wallet lying around at a convention of thieves, it's your own fault when it goes missing.

It is easy (and entertaining) to blame politicians for the squandering of America's prosperity and leaving little children burdened with debts they will struggle under all of their lives. And of course politicians deserve the blame for having ignored the Constitution's limitations on their authority. They have been only too willing to run riot in a system of plunder in which everyone expects something to be given to them at someone else's expense. Some want government jobs, others want to be protected from someone who may do their job better; some are military Keynesians, champions of deficit spending on warfare, who think that even if the country can't get rich building nothing but weapons, at least *they* can; some want subsidies for their farm products and pharmaceuticals; bankers want bailouts; people dependent on real estate want government-sponsored enterprises to keep house prices artificially high; some want good old-fashioned welfare; others want subsidies—welfare traveling under another name. The politicians are happy to oblige and will give anybody anything if doing so means reelection. They have turned our country into what I call the American piñata: the politicians seek office to get control of the big stick and pass it around to favored groups and supporters. Each group then gets to take a few whacks to knock loose some goodies for itself. The media plays the role of the mariachi band, keeping festive spirits high as though piñata bashing and goodie grabbing are what government should be all about. Never mind that the piñata itself is destroyed in the festivities.

The blame for the loss of the constitutional ideal can just as easily be laid at the feet of the media. The constant focus by the national media on the horse-race aspect of politics ("Coming down the stretch, candidate A is ahead by a nose, but it could be a photo finish! We'll have the latest polls tonight!") helps politicians and their partisans trivialize American politics while draining attention from the principles that should be at issue in the electoral process. But the establishment media's failure goes far beyond the campaigns. In 2002 a Bush administration task force, the White House Iraq Group, was created to sell the Iraq war to the American people. It was comprised not of sober warfare analysts, experts in assessing nuclear weapons development (or the lack thereof!), or geopolitical strategists capable of envisioning the unhappy consequences of such an invasion. It was, rather, almost all marketing experts, campaign consultants, speechwriters, spinmeisters, and PR flacks—the people who feed the lapdog press. They marketed the war like a new laundry detergent and the invasion like a soft drink. There was ample evidence before them that the case for the Iraq war was entirely contrived, but little of it was reported by the major news organizations. Network anchors, correspondents, and others have since shared numerous accounts of the corporate and political pressures to which they were subjected to sell the administration's war story. But they did not have to capitulate. Wasn't their journalistic integrity, if not their personal integrity, at stake? David Ignatius, a *Washington Post* columnist, explained the failure of the press this way: "Because there was little criticism of the war from prominent Democrats and foreign policy analysts, journalistic rules meant we shouldn't create a debate on our own." Wait a minute! He said what? Because Democrats and Washington hacks weren't questioning Republicans and Washington hacks, journalists who do so are breaking the rules? Exactly what journalistic rules are these? Does some journalism school teach these rules? Such rules are not exclusive to David Ignatius. Or to the *Washington Post.* It is plain to see that the governing classes and the corporate powers have set the boundaries of acceptable political debate for the media. But if you go to a toady's convention, and everyone there does his master's bidding, should you be surprised?

If elected officials can be blamed for their contempt for the Constitution, and if the media can be blamed for its indifference to the Constitution, what can be said about the fault of the American people? If their indignation is only aroused when the other party is at fault, their defense of their own liberties can only be described as halfhearted.

A great contributor to the advance of religious liberty in the New World was William Penn, for whom Pennsylvania is named, and who founded the city of Philadelphia, the "cradle of liberty," where the Declaration of Independence was written and the Constitution was created. It was Penn's observation that "governments, like clocks, go from the motion men give them." There is no automatic pilot that allows the passengers on the liberty ship to snooze throughout the journey; there is no perpetual-motion machine designed to preserve our freedom that can be flipped on and trusted to run forever by itself.

I lived for a time on the very edge of the jungle in Central America. The triple-canopy jungle right at my back door had to be fought back daily, or we would have soon been as overgrown with vegetation as the ancient city of Ankor Wat in Cambodia when it was first seen by Europeans, or in ruins like the lost Mayan sites. The jungle does not restrain itself, not even for a shining city on a hill. No document, no matter how inspired it may be, can protect our liberty and prosperity while we sleep.

It is true that there have been some hard-won advances in the reach of liberty since America's beginnings: the ending of slavery, the advance of women's suffrage and property rights, and the civil rights movement. These were great and indispensable accomplishments without which our ideals would be barren. But perhaps there was not enough voltage to those ideals to both maintain and extend them. Perhaps our dedication to liberty is like a river that can run wide but not deep and now is beginning to resemble a dry desert riverbed.

Americans cannot coast forever on the accomplishments of people more than 200 years ago. We can be compared today to the heirs of some great industrialist's fortune. The industry and innovation of the first generation creates something new that produces fabulous wealth. Sometimes in the second generation the fortune continues to grow, either through the momentum created from the beginning or from the hard work and foresight of members of the second generation. It may be that some members of the following generations use their inherited wealth to pursue their own particular enthusiasms. They may still endow universities and undertake other philanthropic activities. But somewhere along the line, with no new dynamic added to the original family enterprise, the fortune quits growing and begins to be depleted. Family members of several generations can still be comfortable with the trust funds left them. But eventually, even the old family estate and its grounds may be sold off to become, say, a fabulous resort and golf course. After which there is nothing left but a name.

Americans are heirs to a great enterprise in freedom, one that has made our people rich with an abundance beyond the dreams of most who have walked the earth. Like second- and third-generation heirs to great fortunes with their generous philanthropy, inheritors of this freedom have made some contributions of their own by making sure that all of our people are joint heirs to our freedom. But no new contributions to the bank of liberty itself have been made. Indeed, the reserves have been drawn down at an alarming rate. We have been free riding on the achievements of our forefathers. Perhaps much of our inheritance will be lost in the currency destruction implicit in our debt and fiat monetary system. The accomplishments of the men that gave life to the ideal of liberty on this continent are real; their names will be remembered; their place in history is secure. Is our place in history secure for entirely different reasons? Have we squandered our birthright for a mess of pottage? Inheriting so much and passing along so little, how will our names be remembered?

Can the state be contained? Can the Constitution be rebooted? Since some of its provisions are utterly ignored, it's probably not even worth asking about resetting the Constitution in its entirety. Start by looking at smaller things. Can members of Congress, who have taken an oath swearing they "will bear true faith and allegiance" to the Constitution, even be expected to have read it except out loud as a political stunt? Can we insist our courts treat entire portions of the Bill of Rights—now virtually ignored—as the law of the land that they are? Must the Tenth Amendment (*"The powers not delegated to the United States by the Constitution, nor prohibited by it to the States, are reserved to the States respectively, or to the people"*) be forever scorned by lawless officials? What stops the invasion of individual liberties when the invader is the judge of its own actions? By what means is the government held in check when the midnight promises of the minority party vanish in the ascendency of its political sun?

One conclusion of all of this is that people of indifferent standards and only situational honesty are not really capable of national self-government. They may have been fortunate enough to flourish for a time under a standard erected for a more responsible people, free riding on achievements of others for a while, while making none of their own. Seduced by the promise that they could live coercively at the expense of others, they may have finally succeeded in killing the goose that laid the golden egg of our abundance. If the conclusion is true—that through our inattention to its lies and recklessness, the centralized state eventually exhausts itself and decays—then it is a self-limiting problem. A massive decentralization can be expected to organically follow the financial and moral bankruptcy of the great central state. Attempts to resuscitate the failing central state will demand increasingly repressive measures, the proliferation of draconian laws, the demonization of whole swaths of the population, brutality on a grand scale, and perhaps foreign wars to frighten the people and justify the state's universal claim to private resources. But when the center can no longer hold, the answer is not to try to give it another go, with yet another round of more government and new elected officials with more coercive power—the answer is the minimization of the state itself.

Of course the founders already knew that. And our prosperity depends upon it. That is the case that is made in the chapters that follow.

CHAPTER THREE

The Free Economy

The sage says:
I take no action and people are reformed.
I enjoy peace and people become honest.
I use no force and people become rich.

—Lao Tzu

A Case of Mistaken Identity

Like the man who gets into a fight with his wife and then takes it out on the dog, the free economy keeps getting kicked, blamed over and over for our depressed fortune. It is blamed for the ills that come our way from influence peddling and government favoritism. It is faulted when economic policies, tax laws, and even subsidies and bailouts are handed to well-positioned corporations. The free economy is blamed for the distortions caused by regulation, licensing, tariffs, and government procurement. Even when the entire monetary policy of a nation is manipulated to favor certain insiders—often large and powerful banks—the free economy gets the blame. Why this rank abuse of government power—the creation of monopolies, wealth transfers to specific industries, extensions of state power—should be blamed on the free economy is a mystery that can only be explained by confusion on the part of politicians and those in the media. While nobody would maintain that President Obama is a free-economy enthusiast, in those ill-informed circles President Bush was said to have been one. But Bush's presidency began with special favors for the steel industry and ended with bank bailouts.

Politicians and media people don't need any help being confused about such things, but if they did they could get plenty of it from academic economists, most of whom have for generations been the tax-subsidized, ordained priests in the church of Keynesianism, the universal state religion of the governing classes, a faith much beloved by them for its devotion to deficit spending. Their responsibility for the economic destruction of the age receives more attention in the discussion of money in Chapter Eight. But members of this priesthood, so influential in the growth of statist public policy, have made confounding the people about the nature of economic freedom their special occupation.

One such academic who derides the very concept of "economic freedom" may illuminate the creed of the entire order. In what one fears is an example of the intellectual rigor of much of the profession's ministry, economics professor James K. Galbraith, author of *The Predator State*, skips down a trail of metaphysical absurdity in pursuit of "economic freedom," writing, "One might think that such a concept would refer to freedom from the compulsions of economic life; from the necessity of working in order to eat, or the choice between paying for medicine and paying the rent."

One might not think any such thing. Galbraith's suggestion—that economic freedom can only have meaning in a make-believe world, one in which means magically appear—is inane. This dismissive treatment appears to be part of an effort to avoid serious thought about economic freedom in a real world in which unlimited desires must confront limited resources. But Galbraith continues: "Nor is economic freedom akin in any way to what we normally consider to be political freedom: it is not closely related to the freedoms of speech, the press, or assembly—freedoms related to the right to participate in political life and to influence public policy."

Actually, economic freedom is contiguous with political freedom: both contemplate the state as the monopoly wielder of force. Both are about freedom from state coercion. The First Amendment is nothing if not a prohibition on state coercion: it *prohibits the state* from establishing a state religion or employing coercion against religious freedom; similarly *the state is forbidden* from employing coercion against free speech or a free press; and it *outlaws the use of state coercion* against peaceable assembly. The political freedoms that Galbraith cites are precise corollaries of economic freedom in which people are likewise free of state compulsion and coercion in their economic lives. It is worth noting that all the human rights to which Galbraith refers are manifested through economic rights to begin with. Try to imagine freedom of religion when the state controls all the gathering places and other means of its manifestation.

In the French Revolution, the clergy were made employees of the state and forced to swear loyalty to it, while church property itself was confiscated. Immediately after the fall of the tsarist government in Russia in 1917, Lenin, seeing religion as a challenge to the transcendent authority of the state, forbade the church from owning property, seizing its holdings in a campaign of violence. The churches that remained became state property and operated only at the good pleasure of the Soviet state. The Nazis ransacked and burned Jewish synagogues. In each of these cases the horrors accumulated beyond the church property involved. But the property is the visible manifestation of the religion and the center of its exercise and vitality. Minority religions are always liable to having their property rights denied and their property seized. The practice has remained widespread in our time, from practitioners of the Baha'i faith in Iran and Christians in Iraq to Jehovah's Witnesses in Russia and Falun Gong practitioners in China.

Similarly, economic freedom is indispensable to self-expression and free speech. Seizure of property by the state has always been an initial step in suppressing dissent. And one need only imagine the constraints on a free press when the state controls all the media outlets and means of communication. Publishers in third-world nations critical of their governments have had newsprint supplies, controlled by some state ministry, suddenly cut off, despite the proclaimed existence of a free press. Such was long the case in Mexico, where the state's newsprint monopoly was used to silence critics.

Controlling communications today means commanding the digital world. In Tunisia's Jasmine Revolution, where the Arab revolution of 2011 began, the government tried to disable Internet routes. Egypt responded to the uprising that eventually toppled President Hosni Mubarak by trying to shut down Twitter one day and Facebook the next, then disabling BlackBerrys and finally the entire Internet in Egypt, just as Iran had tried to do a year earlier. As the "Facebook revolution" continued, the state kleptocrats in Algeria, Syria, Libya, and Bahrain took similar steps. China has 3,000 Internet "police" trying to control what people see (and think). American libertarians are rightly alarmed by elected officials of both parties moving to take charge of the Internet. Most chilling among these power grabs is a bill by Senator Joe Lieberman bearing an official title right out of a science-fiction dystopia: the Protecting Cyberspace as a National Asset Act. It would allow the president to issue orders to, and demand that companies in the "informational infrastructure" share information with, a new agency with an equally Orwellian name: the National Center for Cybersecurity and Communications. Opponents use a more descriptive name: "the Internet kill switch." Of course the right to expression and dissent is also vulnerable to state control of locations and the policing of venues. So-called "free speech zones" became notorious during the George W. Bush presidency as the Secret Service cordoned off areas to which protestors with antiwar and anti-Bush shirts and signs were relegated. These zones were often far removed from and out of sight of the target of the protests—in one case, half a mile away—as well as invisible to other officials, event attendees, and the media.

It is clear that political rights must exist in our world—a world in which we act within the compass of material conditions. Accordingly, our political freedoms—freedom of speech, the press, religion, and assembly; and the right to be secure in our persons, houses, papers, and effects—depend on economic freedom. If these human rights are to persist, economic freedom cannot be devalued.

Shop "Till You Drop"

Having avoided a serious encounter with the concept of economic freedom, Professor Galbraith performs a remarkable act of intellectual reductionism, finally concluding that economic freedom amounts to nothing more than "the freedom to shop." Once Galbraith has fathered this flimsy straw man, he is free to ridicule his raggedy offspring. If a country like China has shopping, is it free? Did the Soviet Union vanish because it did not have shopping? Such questions are unenlightening since absolutely no one who thinks soberly shares Galbraith's disdainful definition of economic freedom. There is no need to demean economic freedom as the fantasy of a world in which wishes are horses or to belittle it as the mere "freedom to shop." Economic freedom is neither. It is the economic interaction of people in an environment free of coercion. It is voluntary, mutual, peaceful, and free of force.

But the tenets of Galbraith's creed soon become clear; his collectivist instincts bubble up on every page. The political freedoms he cites—"freedoms related to the right to participate in political life and to influence public policy"—are valued by him for their utility in *collective* policy making, while the right of individuals simply to be unmolested by that collective is neglected. The champions of economic freedom he opposes, complains Galbraith, are not interested in "mass participation in collective decision making"; they are, he says, opposed to government health care, public subsidies of the arts, and the redistribution of wealth; they want to live their economic lives "in a sphere separated from state control and therefore reserved to the interaction of private forces." But he describes social decision making as "lofty" when it is under control of the state.

If economic freedom can be reduced to the mere freedom to shop, what is Galbraith to make of the free market? The market, he begins, is an "omnipresent institution"; it is a "broker," it "presides" over our choices. With these words Galbraith appears to be describing a thing or being that can be faulted, disgraced, slandered, shamed, banished, blamed, punished, attacked, or most especially, controlled. But before long he concludes that the market is not a person, a judge, or a jury, and wonders if it is even an institution at all. In evident distress that the market frustrates his preferred apparatus of state coercion, Galbraith concludes that the market is a "negation." It is the "nonstate," and applies to transactions so long as they are not directed by the dictates of the state.

Intending this as a pejorative, Galbraith has come close to what, for any would-be state economic orchestrator, is an uncomfortable truth. The market simply refers to the multiplicity of the innumerable voluntary exchanges that take place between individuals and their agents. Since such interactions go on continuously, the market is best understood as a process. A free market is one in which this process is noncoercive; individuals are free to express their own values and preferences by making or not making such exchanges, as they deem desirable. A command economy is the opposite, involving the widespread suppression of human choice, often by means of the most extreme brutality. The state in some form—boards, bodies, bureaucrats, and others—controls human economic activities. Whatever individual volition exists does so only at the good pleasure of the state. In a world of limits and scarcity in which trade-offs have to be made, how are your preferences to be ordered? By you, yourself, or by someone with the power to command you? Will you be ordered about as a mere unit in an economic aggregate, a statistical unit forced to conform to a standard demographic projection? Or will you be left free to make such subjective choices you deem suitable and advantageous within the framework of your own values and goals? Of course freedom means that you can still relinquish your own choice and have it exercised for you by another, if you wish. You are free to let someone else order off life's menu for you, but you are not free to order for others without their permission. It might seem self-evident that peaceful and voluntary human interactions are to be preferred to those initiated by the use of force, but for those who wield power over the decisions and activities of their fellow human beings—or hope to—force has its irresistible allure.

Most people would love freedom for its own sake—the right to be sovereigns over their own lives, to make choices and decisions for themselves, even if there were no reward beyond that right of self-determination. But the evidence is abundant—North and South Korea come to mind again, as does the example of East and West Germany—that liberty is accompanied along the way by prosperity. It should not be a surprise that this is so. A simple example illustrates the way human satisfaction is increased by the interaction of participants in a free economy.

Imagine you and I live in a closed community in which I grow wheat while you prefer to fish. It would be a poor world indeed where I had to subsist only on bread and you on fish. No doubt we would soon grow weary of the monotony and agree to trade, say, five loaves for two fish, the terms resulting from our subjective valuations of both commodities. In trading freely we are both enriched, having given up something we then and there value less ("Not another loaf of bread for dinner again tonight!") for that which we prefer more ("If I could just once have something to eat besides fish!"). The trade improves both of our circumstances, while neither of us has been impoverished or deprived by it. And although no additional goods have entered the equation, the sum total of human happiness in our community has increased by our little miracle of fish and loaves.

While the joy of a man consigned to an eternal diet of bread who suddenly finds fish added to his menu knows no bounds, such a free-market exchange has improved the lives of only the parties to the trade; for mankind as a whole the change is imperceptible. But add in networks upon networks of free-market exchanges, overlaid one upon another, all mutually benefiting the parties to them, all allowing for the division of labor and specialization, all interworking with one another in countless unforeseeable ways. Uncoil the power of human creativity, unleash endeavor in this way, set free invention for millions of human beings seeking to improve their own circumstances by finding some way to serve their fellows, with each producing some good or service that is valued by others, as a means of enabling them to achieve the satisfaction of their desires. Allow for unplanned improvements, fortuitous discoveries, and ideas that manifest in new ways that no priesthood of economic planners can foretell, and the lot of mankind is improved exponentially. This is the field of freedom in which human creativity grows. This is the way mankind prospers. This is the experience of economic freedom.

The Price System

The academic dogmas of my student years were as openly hostile to economic freedom as today's. The fashionable collectivist arguments of the period were generally a variation of a catechism that claimed economic freedom might have been fine for simpler times or for agrarian economies, but society was now too large and complex to do without economic decision making centralized and handed down from on high by the state. As a young man fresh out of school and starting out in life I spent a fair amount of time in the company of politicians, some with national reputations. Among those with positions or platforms friendly to a free economy I made the topic a common line of conversation: How did they respond to this objection of scale and complexity? How was the statist argument best refuted? None were able to respond satisfactorily.

Of course the answer is that in the functioning of a society of greater size and complexity, economic freedom becomes much more productive and even more imperative than in a smaller one. It is at least conceivable that in our example of a small, closed society, say, an island of just one farmer and one fisherman, some island chieftain might be able to direct the disposition of a fixed supply of bread and fish in a way that, if not reflective of the valuations of the producers involved, still manages to see bread and fish exchanged at some arbitrary ratio—after the chieftain has skimmed off his take.

But the world turns and life is change. What happens when someone is born or someone dies? When the oceans change and fish are scarce? Or more abundant? What happens when one party has an unrestrained appetite and consumes more calories than the other? When the soil is depleted or erodes and the grain crops disappoint? What happens when the fisherman develops allergies and must adopt a gluten-free diet? When a new food supply is discovered? When a castaway washes ashore?

What happens when something changes?

How is an island chieftain expected to keep up? Any valuation he sets is bound to fail to reflect the changing conditions of the next moment. His economic dictates are necessarily arbitrary and must be unfair to at least one party to the transaction. Otherwise the exchange would have been made naturally, the result of mutual agreement between farmer and fisherman. One party to a trade at a mandated rate or price is virtually certain to be an unwilling participant. So coerced, he will feel he has been taken. In the command economy such exploitation by coercion is ubiquitous; attempting to mastermind the exploitation is the very life's work of the collectivist academic. Half the parties to such exchanges are plundered by acts great and small. Never mind the material blessings absent in the statist economy, and overlook even the drab life it delivers. Is this constant bleeding of half the population a social lubricant, or is it social dynamite?

So far we are considering a closed society of only a few economic actors. Multiply them by a hundred million for the nation, or by billions of economic participants in a global economy. At this level the pretenses of central planners are laughable. But factor in as well the exponential complexity of not just trading in bread and fish, but the products and consumables of a modern and sophisticated world, and suddenly the affectations of these national and global chieftains become pathological. In a world that is inexpressibly complex, the problem of centralized management of raw materials and producer and consumer goods soon spirals out of control; each step of production, manufacturing, distribution, and marketing is dependent on tens of thousands of other products that must be at hand before the work can progress; each of these products consisting of resources, processes, and other products which are dependent on still others, which in turn are themselves dependent upon . . .

Reflecting on this endless dependency is like looking at the mirrored walls in a barber shop that regress endlessly. At each step along the way, in each process, millions of people are involved in the availability of the simplest of each of these products that will be used in ways in which they, the providers, are quite unaware. In the modern world each of those people depends upon foods of increasing sophistication from a menu of choices that reflect global complexity; transportation for the goods involved and the people themselves; each meal and every item of clothing; the delivery of power and water; homes modest and magnificent. All are the provision of millions of people working in their own specialties or at their local tasks for the achievement of their own ends. None can imagine all the far-flung end users of their labor or how their efforts sustain others involved in economic activities vital to the achievement of yet other objectives that in turn affect and improve the lives of millions.

This kind of activity is far too complex and fast changing for command and control management by tribal chieftains, academic economists, or power wielders. In *The Origin of Wealth*, Eric Beinhocker estimates that there are somewhere in the order of tens of billions of distinct products and service items (SKUs, stock-keeping units) that businesses sell just in the city of New York. Only a madman would think himself equal to the task of directing all these activities. How then are all these economic interactions orchestrated? How can something ever-changing and of such immense complexity possibly be coordinated? The answer is at hand everywhere and every day. Only the devoted statist can fail to see it; only the power hungry can resist it. All of it is coordinated effortlessly by the free economy.

It is the price system of the free economy that draws human ingenuity and labor to where it is needed and rewarded. It is the free movement of prices that directs resources to applications where they are prized, instead of being left to pile up in mountains of waste in government warehouses. It is in the bidding by consumers with what they are willing to pay that producers are driven to meet their needs. It is prices free to move higher that speed goods and services to fill the vacuum of shortages, just as it is lower prices that disperse surpluses to where they can be usefully employed. One can argue with free prices in a free economy—a seller insisting that they are too low and a buyer that they are too high. But they reflect reality as reliably as the weather. One can curse the rain on the day of the picnic or lament the lack of snow for the ski holiday, but reality can't be lamented away or cursed into changing. Besides, for those unhappy with prevailing prices, remember what Mark Twain said about the weather in New England: wait a while and it will change. Wait a while and the feedback system of a free economy soon deals with prices that are either too high or too low. If prices of a product are too high, additional producers and more resources will soon be diverted to the profit opportunity those high prices represent. Consumers respond to price signals as well, foregoing overpriced goods and finding substitutes; as supplies then rise and demand falls, prices head down. Similarly when goods or services are priced too low, producers find their efforts poorly rewarded and seek more profitable opportunities elsewhere. Consumers, attracted by low prices, load up. In the face of reduced supplies and increased demand, prices head up. This is a typical dynamic in a free economy: rising and falling; systolic and diastolic; expanding and contracting; living and breathing; inhaling and exhaling. It is like the interplay of yin and yang. It is the self-regulating process of life—simple, efficient, and effortless—and it takes place without state interference.

Self-Organizing Systems

All of these market activities, Galbraith complains, take place without "the procedures or rules or limitations" of the state. Such remarks betray a preference for the command economy and obliviousness to the unwritten rules and customs that arise in a free economy. The real and lasting practices that facilitate peaceful social relations are not handed down from on high; they are not the offspring of legislators, but arise spontaneously from the living experience of people through time. It is these customs and traditions that allow for expectations to be made by the parties about the duties involved in commercial and social interactions.

To the extent that such expectations are reliable, the term "rule of law" is applicable to a state or culture, and a prosperity-generating economy is possible. On the other hand, in a state which is, as C. S. Lewis says, "incessantly engaged in legislating" or one in which bureaucracies have proliferated, standards become capricious, arbitrary, ever-changing, and unforeseeable. In such soil prosperity seldom takes root.

It is hard *not* to see the efficient functioning of cooperative and self-regulating interaction, the outcome of commercial and social relationships governed by consent without mandates of the state. They are rich with procedures and rules and limitations, Galbraith notwithstanding. Indeed, they are so ubiquitous and plentiful, in matters great and small, that this enormous everyday spectrum can only be missed willfully.

- The Internet has enabled a proliferation of human collaboration in new and productive ways, such as free and open-source software. Thousands of programmers have contributed to Linux, the leading server operating system, which is used by cities and stock exchanges, Amazon and ATMs, schools and courts, and major companies all around the world. Desktop applications of Linux include the popular Mozilla Firefox web browser. The world's most successful smartphone platform, the Android operating system, is based on a modified Linux version, and is itself open-source, free software. By early 2011, 350,000 new Android devices were being activated every day.

- The man who replaces the storm-damaged tiles on my roof wants half the payment in advance. That way he is at no risk in ordering the materials involved; I don't pay the other half until I've inspected the work.

- Billions of dollars of foreign currencies trade daily on a phone call; billions more in financial assets change hands on the floors of the financial exchanges every day on nothing more than eye contact and a hand gesture. Commodity markets have developed spontaneously over thousands of years to meet the needs of users and producers, evolving their own standards of quality, clearing, and delivery. Today commodity trading amounts to trillions of dollars a year.

- eBay and other online auction web sites host millions of participants buying and selling billions of dollars worth of collectibles, clothing, electronics, industrial equipment, art, services, and more. Even the original "Hollywood" sign sold on eBay for $450,000. The companies have developed and continue to refine payment and customer rating systems. To ensure customer confidence, participants take great pains to protect their reputations. Some may be genuinely concerned for their personal integrity, but all are concerned with the profit opportunity that relies on ensuring customer confidence.

- When I make a reservation with the trendy restaurant and give my phone number, they know instantly whether I have honored my reservations in the past and whether to hold a table for me if I'm late on a busy Saturday night.

- Wikipedia is a free and collaborative online encyclopedia. Its 18 million articles are submitted and edited by volunteers around the world and

reflect a diversity of interests and expertise. It enables one to find everything from Lindsay Lohan's birthday (born July 2, 1986, in New York City)
to the woefully inadequate 2002 cost estimate for the Iraq war that got Bush
administration economist Lawrence Lindsay fired for being an alarmist
($100–$200 billion, he suggested). Nonhierarchical, self-organizing systems such as Wikipedia have their own internal rules, procedures, and
limitations customized to their own needs.

- When competing forms of currency are in use in an economy, people tend
  to spend and pass along the inferior currency but hold on to and hoard a
  currency of evident superiority. Even when gold and silver have served as
  currency side by side, if a fixed exchange rate is mandated, one will tend
  to be overvalued relative to the other, since supply and demand are not
  fixed. Thus the more valuable metal will tend to disappear from circula-
  tion, while the other is passed along. This unlegislated human economic
  behavior is enacted so dependably in all places at all times that it has even
  been given a name: Gresham's law.

For Galbraith, all of this is "vaporous." It is not like "government—a tangible decision making process that actually exists," he says. But spontaneous
self-organizing systems like markets are consistent with people's real-world
experience—the things they have found useful, and the productive outcomes
they seek. They are, says eighteenth-century philosopher Adam Ferguson, "the
products of human action but not human design." It is from the traditions of
customary law and the general principles of common law, as Nobel Prize winner Friedrich Hayek points out, that the law of liberty arises. Legislation can
only have merit to the extent that it reflects the shared ground of common
experience of the people. But legislated laws that do not arise out of the common sense of the people are often ignored or resented, and are, as essayist
Joseph Sobran noted, obeyed rather than observed.

If the free economy, emerging spontaneously, can be called "vaporous,"
one might as well say that human language is "wispy" because it, too, arises
naturally from human usage, and yet it enables us to communicate richly and
be understood about things both simple and complex. Although the gram-
matical rules of language and the meanings of words have developed in a spontaneous and self-organizing way, as Hayek has pointed out, languages are the

product of social cooperation and can only be done damage by Galbraith's "government—a tangible decision making process that actually exists."

Understanding the economic order in this manner—that it evolves in a living and organic way, rather than as a mechanically constructed artifice; that it arises spontaneously and by consent, rather than through coercion—forces an unwelcome humility on reformers and master planners, schemers, and world improvers. It demands that they rely on persuasion rather than coercion. The economic arrangements they champion must have merit and functionality and therefore, like language, be willingly adopted and not forced. Governments that employ language police force their linguistic wares with destructive economic effects. Companies large and small fled Quebec when the language police showed up in the 1970s, taking thousands of jobs with them. L'Office québécois went after delicatessens for stocking imported "kosher for Passover" products that did not have labeling in French, while one plumber was fined for an illegal apostrophe in his sign. On a smaller scale, in France the language police are busy resisting the contamination of the mother tongue by the usage of individual foreign terms like "blog" and "podcasting."

More serious than the nuisance of the state trying to prevent the adoption of foreign words is the economic meddling that statists encourage at almost every turn, which represents a continuous drain on our prosperity. One need not peer too closely to see that legislated law in the United States has increasingly become a rich mine for the extraction of government largesse, as influential bailout beneficiaries, stimulus recipients, and others dig deeply into Treasury vaults. But in a free economy troubled companies are bailed out only by willing creditors who risk their own money for business reasons—reasons in which they have faith. No faith, no credit. Likewise, stimulus spending is provided only by the patronage of satisfied customers. No satisfaction, no spending. Stripped of politics—that is, the absence of influence peddling, special interests, connections, favoritism, and even bribery—would anyone extend capital to a company that inspires no faith? Or whip and drive customers like cattle to a business that produces no satisfaction? In a command economy, what provides economic enterprises the feedback to know that they are not serving their clients well? (Or to care? That is why dealing with government offices, government-protected monopolies, and bureaucrats is so often frustrating. Your satisfaction can be a matter of utter indifference to them.) Where do the signals arise to change the practices of such businesses to meet changing conditions? Galbraith may be right, that government is "a tangible decision making process that actually exists," but it is also one that breaks the feedback circuit that propels improvement and progress. And thus a vital economy becomes rigid, arthritic, crippled, ossified, moribund—and finally dies.

One might well understand the frustration tribal chieftains, academic economists, and world improvers feel in the presence of the free economy. The bottlenecks they create are unwelcome. The improvements they have pigeonholed have been noted, and the progress that they are unprepared to assimilate into their plans becomes evident when contrasted with the free economy. The surpluses and shortages they create are seen to be wasteful and unnecessary. They themselves are superfluous. In a charitable spirit one wishes them Godspeed as they return to their private affairs.

James Galbraith has the perfect pedigree of such a statist. His father, John Kenneth Galbraith, was also a celebrated academic economist, a Harvard professor for many years, a faithful Keynesian, and the champion of something he called "new socialism." Just as the son served in government as the director of a congressional economic committee, the father had been a top bureaucrat in the Office of Price Administration during World War II, and afterward remained a believer in the implementation of permanent government price controls, certainly one of the most disastrous of all economic misadventures. The elder Galbraith's praises of the Russian and Chinese communist states read like embarrassing anachronisms in light of the Soviet collapse and China's post-Mao prosperity. So great was his fealty to the state that he insisted that public authority be put to the task of uplifting the tastes of the people and serving as the custodian of aesthetics by, for example, teaching people how to use their leisure. When John Kenneth Galbraith passed away in 2006, William L. Anderson summed up his work, pointing out that "to the very end, Galbraith was a socialist impersonating an economist."

The point is not that statist, collectivist thinking runs in families, but that it has run seemingly unimpeded for generations on college and university campuses and in the halls of government power. Of course there are squabbles among such academics, but they are generally at the margin of state power. The Galbraiths may want the Federal Reserve to serve one policy; their ideological opponents prefer another. As an example, the monetarists, a school of economics that is James Galbraith's bête noire, support central banking—just as do Galbraith's Keynesians. It is the levers of economic authority in the hands of the state that underlie every policy prescription. There is bickering among politicians, but it is generally over questions of magnitude: one party wants the minimum wage set a few cents higher or lower than the other, but the debate in the marble halls is seldom about the state's right to interfere in such private commercial arrangements to begin with. One party wants more foreign aid for one cause, the other for a different recipient. The authority to take money from Americans to give to foreign governments is presumed by both the red and the blue parties.

On the key issue of the state versus the individual, they are bees of a common hive that never sting one another. The state is paramount. That is the starting point for political discourse. Policy positions begin with this assumption. It is about such unexamined presuppositions that Socrates taught us to beware. And it is only within the grip of this presupposition that the dominant media entertains debate. No matter how they may squabble over academic issues, no matter how pitched the political battles, implicit within most contemporary economic debates and the starting point of politicians left and right is the unquestioned preeminence of the state and the subordination of the individual to the collective.

The prevalence of this presupposition dims our economic prospects. But there is more at stake than just our prosperity. Collectivism as a universal presupposition says something about the future trajectory of humankind as well. In the television and motion picture series *Star Trek*, anyone in the path of the Borg, a vast galactic cybermachine, was warned to "prepare to be assimilated." Collectivist economics and the subordination of the individual to the state is the social order that ultimately promises the assimilation of each individual into the machine of the state and its hive mind. Indeed, the Borg intended to assimilate the earth itself.

"Resistance," it announced, "is futile."

CHAPTER FOUR

Property Rights

If historical experience could teach us anything, it would be that
private property is inextricably linked with civilization.

—Ludwig von Mises

Worth the Effort

The right to own property is a necessity of human life, and just like life and
liberty, with which it is often linked, it is prior to law. From the time of the
earliest hunters and gatherers, the satisfaction of life's demands required the
expenditure of human effort. Even the "noble savage," man in a supposed state
of nature and a fanciful ideal in the eighteenth century still occasionally encountered in the enthusiasms of modern environmentalists, had to gather
wood and carry water. In the storied abundance of the world's gardens of par-
adise, the fruits of the trees had to be picked. Even when manna fell like rain
from heaven, Exodus tells us that each morning it had to be collected. It is this
expenditure of human energy that gave birth to property and to law itself.

From the dawn of civilization human progress has depended on property, with the attendant assumption that energy expended would be worth the
effort. The earliest people spent time fashioning tools in the expectation of
being able to use them; crops were planted, fields were worked, orchards were
tended—all with the expectation of the right to the harvest. The consequences
of subverting property rights are dire in every corner of human activity. But

because human beings are completely dependent on the need to eat, the consequences are most immediately visible and grave in their impact on the food supply.

A classic account that should be a part of America's national memory and reflected upon each Thanksgiving comes from the history of the Pilgrims, who arrived on the *Mayflower* and settled at Plymouth in 1620. Within five months, half the company had died of sickness and starvation. The sponsors of the enterprise had insisted that for the first seven years the colony would have "all things in common." This communal organization exacerbated the settlement's woes. Governor Bradford wrote that men complained about working for other men's wives and children without being compensated while the wives thought it a form of slavery "to be commanded to do service for other men, as dressing their meat, washing their clothes, etc.; they deemed it a kind of slavery, neither could many husbands well brook it." Altogether the experience of communal property "was found to breed much confusion and discontent and retard much employment that would have been to their benefit and comfort."

Eventually it was decided, wrote Bradford, that each family would be assigned its own parcel of land so "that they should set corn every man for his own particular, and in that regard trust to themselves." The result of the new arrangement was predictable. After one year Bradford reported,

> This had very good success, for it made all hands very industrious, so as much more corn was planted than otherwise would have been. . . . The women now went willingly into the field, and took their little ones with them to set corn; which before would allege weakness and inability; whom to have compelled would have been thought great tyranny and oppression.

We all are the beneficiaries of property rights, even of property we do not own ourselves. Economist Thomas Sowell points out that although few of us are farmers or own any agricultural land, we have better food in greater variety and abundance available to us than in places where there are no agricultural property rights. Though of little consolation for the human suffering that it entailed, the experience of the Soviet Union nevertheless provided a multigenerational laboratory in absent property rights. Sowell tells of the encounter of a delegation of American farmers with collectivized Soviet agriculture:

They were appalled at the way various agricultural produce was shipped, carelessly packed and with spoiled fruit or vegetables left to spread the spoilage to other fruits and vegetables in the same sack or boxes. Coming from a country where individuals owned agricultural produce as their private property, American farmers had no experience with such gross carelessness and waste, which would have caused someone to lose much money needlessly in the United States.

Sowell makes the additional point that the tragedy of this rampant waste was compounded by the fact that Soviet life was often characterized by food shortages. Meanwhile the apologists who seek to avoid acknowledging statism's dysfunctionality quickly scurry to the retort that all can be fixed with improved management or a more powerful state; the solution to a problem simply requires a proliferation of bureaucrats, new regulations, or closer monitoring of procedures. Even if this were effective, Sowell reminds us, such measures are not free. They can only be provided at the expense of other demands for the resources devoured in supporting stepped-up bureaucracies, while property rights on their own create self-monitoring that is both less costly and more effective.

The Tragedies

Implicit in the Soviet model and in all socialist statism is the confrontation with what has been called "the tragedy of the commons," the inescapable conclusion that that which everybody owns, nobody owns. The dilemma of the commons is often illustrated by the example of the seventeenth-century villagers who grazed livestock on community or "common" town property. Predictably, each was eager to get the maximum benefit of the commons. While care was exercised that their private pastures were not overused and remained productive, the villagers had no such incentive in the use of the commons, which would be left depleted from overgrazing. What everybody owns, nobody owns. Each user imposes costs, as it were, on the other users of the property. It is a condition so widespread that workers in every kind of business will be familiar with it. While your own microwave oven and refrigerator at home are likely to be clean, we have all seen the microwaves in the office and workplace kitchens that are encrusted with the remains of a mess, while the break room refrigerator is cluttered with long-forgotten mystery meals. What everybody owns, nobody owns.

This "commons" analysis can be applied to understanding the debt of the U.S. government as well. Because membership has its privileges, imagine that you and every other citizen carries a national credit card. Call it the American MasterVisa. Everyone has the same charge account with the same account number. No one leaves home without the American MasterVisa since all your purchases can be charged to it. Now at the end of the year, the total bill for everything purchased is divided equally among all 310 million cardholder citizens. Whether you personally charged a great deal or a little—or even nothing at all—on the American MasterVisa, you are responsible for paying 1/310 millionth of total federal spending.

In fiscal year 2010 the federal government spent $3.720 trillion. Your bill for 1/310 millionth of that is $12,000. Why should you be restrained in your spending? You will be billed for $12,000 in any case, even if you purchased nothing, so you can be expected, like most people, to charge all you can to the American MasterVisa to be sure that you at least get your money's worth. Many cardholders will want to get more than their money's worth and will spend on anything that can possibly be construed as a benefit: welfare and warfare, bailouts and subsidies, retirement programs, loan guarantees, corporate handouts, "stimulus" measures, foreign aid, health benefits, and transfer payments. Everyone in the country goes on a shopping spree! This is of course a commons problem. The bill for this spending can only be paid by private capital that has been made public. When government takes private capital and attempts (or pretends) to provide specific benefits to specific beneficiaries, a commons tragedy results. It is a collective scheme in which each citizen is allowed to impose costs on the others. Like the Soviet agriculture nightmare, it is accompanied by waste; like the village pasture, it is overused; and like the communal kitchen, it suffers neglect. Enabling people to vote themselves largesse from the public purse, directly or indirectly, leads to certain collapse and the ruins of bankruptcy. It might be called "the tragedy of the public debt."

But the ruinous spending is not driven just by the demands of recipients; if anything, those dispensing government handouts act even more recklessly. Indeed, their very calling involves whetting the appetites of potential beneficiaries with the sweet taste of something for nothing. Individual voters may win a perk here and a giveaway there—a small government rebate or promise of a future benefit for their votes. But on the scale of today's political racketeering, they sell their votes too cheaply. The governing classes and elected officials buy the goodwill and indebtedness of likely donors and supporters in influential industries and companies with big money. While individual voters can be bribed for a few thousands, purchasing the affection of favored corporations and important financial institutions is measured in billions. The last few years of banker bailouts and war spending have provided us with case studies of the reckless abandon with which bureaucrats spend money—as long as it is not their own.

Bailouts and Bags of Cash

Two years after the Bush administration's $700 billion bailout program, Neil Barofsky, the special inspector general of the Troubled Asset Relief Program (TARP), issued a scathing report on the program's performance. TARP had not increased bank lending as promised. In fact, the report points out that two years on, bank lending had continued to contract, despite hundreds of billions of dollars provided to banks specifically for increased lending. Similarly, unemployment was higher after two years than when the program began. And preserving home ownership—the rationale used to try to win public support for the bailout bill to begin with—had "fallen woefully short." The report details other predictable failures, including increased concentration in the financial industry. "The biggest banks are bigger than ever, fueled by Government support and taxpayer-assisted mergers and acquisitions," it said, while these larger "too big to fail" banks were now the beneficiaries of the competitive advantage of enhanced credit ratings, thanks to repeated assurances that the government would stand behind them as favored institutions. But most revealing of the purposes for which the program was really created was the report's reminder that the Treasury used the program to "compensate American International Group, Inc.'s [AIG] counterparties 100 cents on the dollar for securities worth less than half that amount."

While these outrages richly deserve to be recounted in a book dealing with the causes of America's waning prosperity, our purpose in this section is to highlight the differing treatment of private property and "the commons," contrasting the stewardship private interests receive with the indifferent treatment of public or socialized interests. Bush's $700 billion bailout was driven by Treasury secretary Henry Paulson and overseen by his Treasury sidekick Neel

Kashkari. An expenditure of such magnitude certainly merited special diligence from responsible officials at the highest levels, and Wall Street had bequeathed its best and brightest technocrats to Washington: Paulson with a Harvard MBA, Kashkari with an MBA from Wharton; Paulson a recent Goldman Sachs chairman and CEO, Kashkari his former Goldman Sachs colleague. Clearly, $700 billion was a precise number for a carefully drawn, specific plan arrived at after detailed calculations involving analysts, risk managers, statisticians, and banking regulators burning the midnight oil at the Treasury to study financial statements and balance sheets.

Actually not. Instead, it was so haphazard as to dispel any pretense of governmental competence and lay bare the conceit that the economy can somehow be managed by Wall Street's finest—or by government at all. Watching Paulson lurch from one iteration of the "Paulson plan" to the next had some observers wondering whether it was really just a bait-and-switch operation to get the bailout appropriation through Congress. One day Paulson favored buying distressed assets from the banks, arguing that injecting capital into the banks hadn't worked for Japan. The next he was presenting leading banks a "take it or take it" offer to sell the government preferred shares.

If the plan for the expenditure was uncertain, the amount of wealth to be transferred was certainly formulated with the deep regard due the American people whose money it was. Well . . . actually, no again. The aptly named Kashkari did the math right on his BlackBerry. "Seven hundred billion was a number out of the air," he later admitted. When Paulson told him he couldn't get a trillion dollars, Kashkari put his investment banking skills to work in earnest. "We have $11 trillion residential mortgages, $3 trillion commercial mortgages. Total $14 trillion. Five percent of that is $700 billion. A nice round number."

A nice round number, indeed, although one can be sure that Kashkari and Paulson would not be quite so cavalier if someone offered to back the truck up to their personal bank accounts. Most people put more forethought into spending a few thousand dollars of their own money on a new car, or even a few hundred dollars on a new phone than bureaucrats put into expending billions of tax dollars—other people's money.

The bailout program sent $10 billion Goldman Sachs' way, providing the money on terms far less favorable than those Warren Buffett had won from Goldman Sachs just a month earlier. Of Paulson's deal to buy preferred shares of his former company, Bloomberg News reported, "While he invested $10 billion in Goldman Sachs in October, twice as much as Buffett did the month before, Paulson gained certificates worth one-fourth as much as the billionaire." But Buffett was using his money; Paulson was using yours.

Observers were quick to identify the transaction as "a really bad deal," "a gimmick," and "egregious." According to Nobel Prize–winning economist Joseph Stiglitz, Paulson claimed he needed to make the deals attractive to the banks, "which is code for 'I'm going to give money away.'" Stiglitz made clear that the terms the taxpayers, represented by Paulson, ended up with were not what any self-respecting investment banker would have gotten for his private clients, saying that "if Paulson was still an employee of Goldman Sachs and he'd done this deal, he would have been fired."

Bailout money moved around faster than the pea in a shell game on Broadway. While Goldman Sachs eventually paid back the TARP money, it didn't hurt that the New York Federal Reserve Bank under president Tim Geithner and the Treasury under Paulson made $122.8 billion available to AIG as it teetered on the edge of bankruptcy. It was this public money that allowed the insurance giant to repay Goldman Sachs $12.9 billion, paying par for assets that could have ended up worthless or at least deeply discounted. As previously noted by TARP's special inspector general, Paulson struck a deal compensating AIG's counterparties twice what the securities were worth.

There was more sleight of hand in the bailout than in a three-card monte game in Times Square. Both Federal Reserve Chairman Ben Bernanke and Tim Geithner, at the time president of the New York Fed, assured senators in their April 2008 banking committee testimony that the assets assumed by the Fed in its bailout of Bear Stearns were "investment grade." In loading its own balance sheet with unprecedented credit risk, the Fed not only made the American people guarantors of toxic paper—and placed the value of the dollar at greater risk—it materially misrepresented the quality of the securities involved. While credit quality and credit risk were at the heart of the unfolding banking crisis, the Fed was claiming that $30 billion in collateral it assumed consisted of only currently performing investment-grade assets. But the collateralized debt obligations and mortgage-backed bonds involved had already been downgraded at the time they provided that testimony.

In the face of Fed stonewalling, Bloomberg News had to go to federal court to get documents in the transaction released to the light of day. Finally in 2010 Bloomberg News was able to report that the government "became the owner of

$16 billion of credit-default swaps, and taxpayers wound up guaranteeing high-yield, high-risk junk bonds." Senate Banking Committee member Richard Shelby told Bloomberg News that despite his efforts to discover the quality of the assets during the 2008 testimony, "It is apparent that the Fed withheld from the Congress and the public material information about the condition of these securities."

Other People's Money

It is clear that when authorities play fast and loose in these matters it is because what they are playing with is other people's money. With their own money, it's another matter. Upon making the move to Washington, Paulson was able to sell his Goldman Sachs stock—some $500 million worth—and take advantage of a special exemption as a federal appointee that by some accounts saved him $200 million in capital gains taxes. He could get all his eggs out of the Goldman Sachs basket, move them elsewhere, and only pay taxes if and when they are realized later. Geithner, his successor as Treasury secretary, was found at his Senate confirmation hearing to have made "careless" and "unintentional" errors in his own IRS filings. Needless to say, the error involved underpaying, not overpaying, his taxes. Although it is a rich irony that a Treasury secretary can be befuddled by the tax laws he is charged with enforcing, it can happen to anyone. And Paulson is entitled to take advantage of his tax exemption. It is only to be expected that both exercise more care holding on to their own money than that of other people.

This syndrome, "the tragedy of the public debt," can be found wherever the state is at work. In pushing Obamacare, the bill to nationalize seventeen percent of the entire economy, Speaker of the House Nancy Pelosi claimed that "we have to pass the bill so that you can find out what is in it." And so it passed—all 2,400 unread, indecipherable pages. Can a gentle fate await those governed by such deranged neglect?

On September 10, 2001, a day before the 9/11 attacks on the World Trade Center and the Pentagon, Defense Secretary Donald Rumsfeld admitted that the Defense Department could not track $2.3 trillion dollars in department transactions. That's $7,500 for every man, woman, and child in America, virtually all of whom would have been acutely aware if $7,500 of their own money had gone missing. But $2.3 trillion unaccounted for is business as usual in the tragedy of the public debt.

The Pentagon has special expertise in recklessness with money. For more than a year immediately following the U.S. invasion of Iraq, U.S. Air Force C-130 cargo planes began flying into Baghdad carrying cash from the Federal Reserve Bank of New York: washing machine–sized pallets of hundred-dollar bills. Pallets of shrink-wrapped cold, hard cash, at least $12 billion, although the speaker of Iraq's parliament says it was more than $18.7 billion altogether, shipped to Iraq between April 2003 and June 2004. The money went directly to the Coalition Provisional Authority (CPA) run by Paul Bremer, who reported to Rumsfeld. And from there it went . . .

Well, from there, no one really knows. Virtually unmonitored and unaccounted for, the cash disappeared into the hands of American contracting companies created virtually overnight to do things they had no experience doing. It went to Iraqi officials for reasons that aren't clear. It paid the salaries of thousands of "ghost" employees—people who didn't exist for work that wasn't done. It went into the back of pickup trucks; it disappeared into hidey-holes and rat holes; it went into gunnysacks, duffel bags, and footlockers. It just went. In an October 2007 *Vanity Fair* piece, "Billions over Baghdad," the Pulitzer Prize–winning investigative reporting team of Donald Barlett and James Steele concluded, "The US government never did care about accounting for those Iraqi billions and it doesn't care now. It cares only about ensuring that an accounting does not occur."

The money was said to be Iraq's, some that had been frozen in U.S. banks, some from Iraq oil revenue under control of the United Nations, and still more that represented seized Iraq assets. The disdain for accounting for the cash and its dispersal was voiced most clearly in a BBC documentary interview when retired admiral David Oliver, head of finance for the CPA, was asked where the money went:

Oliver: I have no idea—I can't tell you whether or not the money went to the right things or didn't—nor do I actually think it's important.

Q: Not important?

Oliver: No. The coalition—and I think it was between 300 and 600 people, civilians—and you want to bring in 3,000 auditors to make sure money's being spent?

Q: Yes, but the fact is that billions of dollars have disappeared without a trace.

Oliver: Of their money. Billions of dollars of their money, yeah, I understand. I'm saying what difference does it make?

It wasn't his money. It was *their* money. Maybe it could be called the tragedy of other people's money. But it should have made a difference, no matter whose money it was. How much of the undocumented cash found its way to funding sectarian violence in Iraq? To Ba'athists and their supporters? To Muqtada al-Sadr and the Mahdi army? Shortly after the cash airlifts began, Bremer disbanded the Iraqi army, leaving 400,000 soldiers unemployed. Did any of the unaccounted billions find its way into their idle hands? How many IEDs and acts of terrorism did it buy? How much of it underwrote the torture of detainees by Iraqi security forces? How much went to drive four million Iraqi refugees from their homes, more than two million fleeing the country? We will never know.

"I'm saying what difference does it make?"

But history repeats itself. From 2001 to 2010 the U.S. spent $55 billion "rebuilding" Afghanistan. The special investigator general for Afghanistan Reconstruction can't figure out where it all went. But in October 2010, the same month he issued his report, Afghan president Hamid Karzai admitted he had been getting "bags of money" from Washington. Karzai has multiple benefactors. Several times a year Karzai gets large plastic bags full of cash from Iran as well. "We are grateful to the Iranians for this," he said. "Patriotism has a price."

At least it's their money.

By what right is money taken from the American people and secretly handed off by the bagful to foreign officials? The right of people to their earnings, savings, and wealth is a property right. Are property rights secure when their money is taken from them under threat of criminal charges and given to failed investment banks and mismanaged insurance companies? How can people's right to the rewards of their labor be subordinated to a bureaucracy that loses track of their earnings by the trillions? How can such a system last, much less provide the grounds for prosperity to flourish? We know from experience that we get more of economic activities that are subsidized, just as we get less of activities that are penalized. As the governing classes subsidize reckless financial institutions and penalize productive and industrious people, which behaviors can we expect more of? Which less?

Plunder

It is when property rights are secure that people work and save for the future instead of toiling only for what can be consumed today. It is property rights that allow these savings—capital—to come together and do large things: to create railroad lines then and airlines now; to lay transatlantic cable then and erect antenna towers now; to manufacture cell phones and fuel cells; to build industrial parks and theme parks, oil tankers, and cruise ships. Property rights allow those with capital to take chances, to fund ideas sound and risky, large and small, at no cost to the skeptical or the unwilling. It is property that funds wonderful and inventive means of production designed to serve consumer needs and make our lives richer and easier.

But always, lurking in the shadows, is the threat of plunder. Because in addition to production—growing, building, saving, inventing, improving, exchanging, discovering, and the other creative means of producing prosperity—wealth can also be acquired by theft. By property rights I mean the right of humans to be free of expropriation by the stronger man, the roving gang, the invading army, the robust corporate state, or the collectivist tyranny. Just as it is a widening recognition of property rights that has allowed mankind to devote lesser portions of its energy defending what it has produced and more in creative efforts and the production of abundance, it is plunder that sets prosperity back. Predation forced many of our ancestors to abandon fertile valleys to scratch out a rude existence in harsh terrain; to build homes high up on inhospitable cliff walls for defensive purposes; to abandon permanent dwellings and towns built at the cost of years of toil for a rough nomadic existence.

It is threats to life, liberty, and property that had people come together to create laws and form rudimentary governments. But granting the state a monopoly on the use of violence to suppress and resist theft and coercion by others has not prevented the state from being an agent of plunder itself. While bands of thieves in the night represent a constant threat to property, they pale next to the large-scale systemic plunder that is the primary occupation of the efficient modern state.

But is the political expropriation of property somehow less destructive of prosperity? Economist Murray Rothbard's answer is "no." The peaceful means of production and exchange are the natural path to man's survival and prosperity, in which resources are multiplied enormously, while coercive means are a prosperity sinkhole,

> for instead of adding to production, it subtracts from it. The "political means" siphons production off to a parasitic and destructive individual or group; and this siphoning not only subtracts from the number producing, but also lowers the producer's incentive to produce beyond his own subsistence. In the long run, the robber destroys his own subsistence by dwindling or eliminating the source of his own supply.

There are two kinds of plunder, observed nineteenth-century French assemblyman and political philosopher Frederic Bastiat: legal and illegal. Ordinarily each person can choose the services he performs and receives, declining one service and preferring another. "The true and just rule for mankind is the *voluntary exchange of service for service.* Plunder consists in prohibiting, by force or fraud, freedom of exchange, in order to receive a service without rendering one in return." Bastiat warned that legal plunder can be recognized quite simply:

> See if the law takes from some persons what belongs to them, and gives it to other persons to whom it does not belong. See if the law benefits one citizen at the expense of another by doing what the citizen himself cannot do without committing a crime.
>
> Then abolish this law without delay, for it is not only an evil itself, but also a fertile source for further evils. . . . If such a law—which may be an isolated case—is not abolished immediately, it will spread, multiply, and develop into a system. . . .
>
> This question of legal plunder must be settled once and for all and there are only three ways to settle it:

1. The few plunder the many.
2. Everybody plunders everybody.
3. Nobody plunders anybody.

It demands more enlightenment than people possess, wrote Bastiat, for the plundered classes, upon assuming power themselves, to refrain from instituting their own regime of plunder instead of abolishing legal plunder. Are we, 165 years later, any more enlightened or must we suffer "a cruel retribution—some for their evilness, and some for their lack of understanding" before a reign of justice appears, in which nobody plunders anybody?

Taking

One of the most flagrant assaults on property rights was enabled by the Supreme Court's 2005 *Kelo v. City of New London* decision. The city of New London, Connecticut, had authorized a bureaucracy to condemn and then acquire, for a private real estate development that was expected to accommodate a $300 million Pfizer pharmaceutical facility, the property of home owners who were unwilling to sell their property. Home owners whose land was targeted for takeover by the development include Wilhelmina Dery, who had lived all her life in the house where she was born in 1918, along with her husband, Charles, who had lived there with her since they were married sixty years earlier; and Susette Kelo, who had a condemnation letter stuck on her door by the sheriff the day before Thanksgiving.

The city relied on the "takings clause" of the Fifth Amendment: "*nor shall private property be taken for public use, without just compensation.*" It argued that the taking of land, even taking developed land from one party to give to another private party, was a "public use," just like eminent domain, which is used to acquire land to build a public road or a public building. In its 2005 ruling, the Supreme Court held that New London's rationale that the new owner would create more jobs and tax revenue for the city was sufficient to satisfy the public use clause of the Fifth Amendment.

Although the court had clearly been increasingly finding against private property rights for years, the ruling by Justices Stevens, Kennedy, Souter, Ginsburg, and Breyer left no doubt that property rights were now subordinated to the state and hostage to politicians, without apology. Justice O'Connor wrote in the dissenting opinion that the decision eliminates "any distinction between private and public use of property—and thereby effectively delete[s] the words 'for public use' from the Takings Clause of the Fifth Amendment." If the subversion of property rights alone wasn't enough, the added indignity of the interpretation that "a man's home is his castle" until, that is, a powerful multinational corporation wants it was enough to set off populist outrage against the decision.

The outrage provoked by the *Kelo* decision was so great because it represented a frontal attack on hearth and home. The heat was such that even President George W. Bush responded with a toothless executive order instructing that federal eminent domain must not be "merely for the purpose of advancing the economic interest of private parties." But of course Bush made his fortune when eminent domain was used to force unwilling sellers to surrender their land for a baseball stadium for his team—a stadium that was built largely with tax dollars.

Stadium stories such as this have been repeated many times in many places, illustrating that the practice the Supreme Court enshrined in *Kelo*—the taking of private property for private benefit—has become a mainstay of modern government. The pretense that tax money is for public purposes—the common defense against force and fraud, courts, even roads—has long since been dropped. Property in the form of money is quite blatantly taken for no other purpose than to give it to others. Even the development project that was the subject of the *Kelo* case had been funded by a wealth transfer of $2 million in federal money to begin with. So Susette Kelo and the other soon-to-be-dispossessed home owners were themselves paying taxes that were used to seed a private development that would require their homes of them. Such wealth transfers are so common as to go unremarked. It is by conditioning that money itself—people's earnings and savings—has been accorded a property status that says "it's mine until the state wishes to give it to someone else." Perhaps after a few generations of conditioning, people will become accustomed to viewing their homes as their property only so long as such is the good pleasure of the state.

This has been the multigenerational track of American government. Taxation is the process by which private property is converted to collective ownership, and collective ownership is characterized by overuse of the commons, waste, and neglect. What everybody owns, nobody owns. For a country that would be prosperous, private property is the remedy. And while it is true that private owners can sometimes be wastrels as well, such is generally the exception, and a self-liquidating problem: their property is destined for other hands, for they are the fools who are soon parted from their money.

Just as fools who lose their property rights are parted from prosperity.

SECTION II
THE STATE

CHAPTER FIVE

Central Planning

A centipede was happy quite,
Until a frog in fun
Said, "Pray tell which leg comes after which?"
This raised her mind to such a pitch,
She lay distracted in a ditch,
Considering how to run.

—Anonymous

Planning to Fail

Borders, as noted at the beginning of the book, can tell a story. Crossing them makes the story more clear.

In 1999, legendary investor Jim Rogers set out to drive around the world—again. He had done so by motorcycle some ten years earlier but this time went by Mercedes, a car he knew he would be able to get serviced even in remote and backward countries ("Every dictator and Mafioso in the world drives a Mercedes," he wrote). The three-year journey, described in his book *Adventure Capitalist*, took him 152,000 miles and through 116 countries. Always alert for investment opportunities, Rogers paid special attention to the borders. Crossing into one country, he noted that the border guards would not accept their own currency for the minor fees involved. Nor would the soldiers manning the government toll road. "There is nothing like crossing outlying borders for gaining insight into a country."

In an experience that confirmed his assessment of Mexico's grim economic prospects at the time, Rogers described a three-hour border ordeal just trying to get out of Mexico, a process that involved three different offices, not all of them located on the border—"one of them requiring us to backtrack fifteen miles"—and even required that he purchase a tourist license just to leave the country. He recounted the story of a truck carrying 340 school desks donated from the United States that Mexican customs officials refused to allow into the country without payment of a high duty charge. Eventually, because individual desks were duty-free, several hundred Mexican schoolchildren went to the border and dragged the desks across the border one at a time.

Such interferences, from petty to grand, are evidence of centralized economic planning by the state. On the petty scale of minor border tyrants it fosters bribery and corruption, and is often the result of the patronage-driven proliferation of bureaucrats and self-important officials. Always and everywhere it is rooted in regulatory regimes. On a large scale, it springs from state policies with such grandiose names as "national industrial policy," "new economic planning," and "national economic policy." Industrial policy usually involves the targeting of sectors of the economy and specific industries for special favoritism. That treatment can involve taxpayer-funded subsidies, protection from both foreign and domestic competition, and tax favoritism. This centralized economic planning is much more than just the nuisance one encounters crossing such a state's borders; it is incompatible with a free economy and destructive of prosperity.

At first the light of prosperity flickers and dims with economic interventionism by the state. But eventually the light goes out completely, snuffed by the economic chaos of the planned economy. One need only look at what central planning did in the last century to two of the world's largest countries, China and Russia—and continues to do in the planned economies of Cuba and North Korea.

Despite this all-too-evident record of failure, the hubris of central economic planners goes unchecked. Just as its state economic planners thought it best for Japan to avoid the automobile and consumer electronics industries, Washington's central economic wizards inflated America's real estate bubble with artificial, centrally planned credit conditions and top-down, strong-arm interference in mortgage lending.

The ruling trend of American economic life is this centralization of decision making in the hands of the state. The right of individuals to make decisions for themselves is rapidly being diminished by government, from the relatively minor state dictates about personal things like the toilets, lightbulbs, and vitamins we can buy to the full-blown state decisions about entire industries that are favored and subsidized by the state, ranging from banking and insurance to automotive and energy to food and health care. Control over our economic choices is being narrowed and directed as though we were not capable of learning even from recent history.

The Twentieth Century

That the great central plan is the enthusiasm of the state only stands to reason: why pursue power if it cannot be used to an end? New means of communication such as radio and television, and of transportation—automobiles, railways, and airplanes—allowed for the consolidation of the nation-state in the twentieth century. The state was "the greatest gainer" as well as "the central failure" of the century, according to British historian Paul Johnson. Not only did it consume resources in an unprecedented way, proving itself "an insatiable spender" and "an unrivalled waster," it had become the greatest killer in human history. Along the way, politics even replaced religion and became the primary agent of zealotry in service to the central plan of the state:

> To archetypes of the new class, such as Lenin, Hitler, and Mao Tse-tung, politics—by which they meant the engineering of society for lofty purposes—was the one legitimate form of moral activity, the only sure means of improving humanity. This view, which would have struck an earlier age as fantastic, became to some extent the orthodoxy everywhere: diluted in the West, in virulent form behind the Iron Curtain and in the Third World. At the democratic end of the spectrum, the political zealot offered New Deals, Great Societies, and Welfare States; at the totalitarian end, cultural revolutions; always and everywhere, Plans.

One of the great untold stories of the last hundred years concerns the admiration the heads of the later-warring states of World War II had for one another and their emulation of one another's collectivist objectives. Fascists often sprang from communist roots; before he was the head of state, Mussolini had been a man of the hard Left, one of Italy's leading socialists; it is no secret that Mussolini's fascism was an early inspiration for Hitler. Less known was Hitler's admiration of Stalin, while Stalin no less admired Hitler, whom he thought "a genius." Mussolini was pleased that Stalin had actually created a form of what he called "Slavonic fascism." And there was socialism all around. Nazis were members of the National *Socialist* German Workers' Party, while the Soviet Union was the Union of Soviet *Socialist* Republics.

Sharing their statist ambitions (perhaps diluted as Johnson suggested above, although one wonders what would have served as a brake on Franklin Delano Roosevelt's ambitions if he had succeeded in his scheme to pack the Supreme Court), the heads of democratic states often applauded the means and methods of both fascists and communists. FDR's interventionism and corporate statism was enough to have Italian commentators widely applauding him as a fascist, while Mussolini praised FDR's *Looking Forward*, the book the new president wrote for his inauguration, a chapter of which was titled "Need for Economic Planning." "Reminiscent of fascism," said Il Duce of the book's interventionist economic principles. It was the same in Germany, where the Nazi press recognized the principles of National Socialism in the New Deal.

The economic system of Hitler's Germany differed from the Russian communist one, observed Ludwig von Mises, only to the extent that Germany retained the terminology and labels of a free economy. But in reality it was all managed by a ministry with a hierarchy of führers from which, wrote Mises,

> came all the orders to every enterprise: what to produce in what quantity, where to get the raw materials and what to pay for them. The workers got the order to work in a definite factory, and they received wages which the government decreed. The whole economic system was now regulated in every detail by the government. . . .
>
> And while this was going on in Germany, Great Britain—during the Second World War—did precisely what Germany did; starting with the price control of some commodities only, the British government began, step by step (in the same way Hitler had done in peacetime, even before the start of the war) to control more and more of the economy until, by the time the war ended, they had reached something that was almost pure socialism.

It was not, Mises explained, the Labour government, which took power in the closing weeks of World War II, that brought ruinous socialism to Britain in 1945; Britain became socialist during the war under the government of Prime Minister Winston Churchill.

In the United States FDR insinuated the central planners of the New Deal into every nook and cranny of the economy—and needlessly dragged the pain of the Depression out for years. With the help of Congress, which appropriated billions for the effort, Roosevelt let gush forth an alphabet soup of new regulatory agencies, authorities, and administrators. Among them were AAA, CAA, CCC, CWA, EBA, FAP, FCA, FCC, FDIC, FERA, FHA, FLA, FMP, FSA, FSRC, FTP, FWA, FWP, FLSA, HOLC, NIRA, NLRB, NRA, PRRA, PWA, RA, REA, SEC, SSB, TVA, USHA, USMC, and WPA.

Chief in the proliferation of bureaucracies was the NRA, the National Recovery Administration. It was the spearhead of the assault on the free economy. If the letters of the alphabet agencies alone don't spell out the reach of the central planners, it can be calculated in the appalling numbers of the NRA's activities: 550 codes with 200 supplementary regulations; 4,000 to 5,000 business practices prohibited; 11,000 administrative orders; 10 million pages of rules; 2.3 million employers impacted; 16 million workers affected.

This NRA bureaucracy, the crowning achievement of the New Dealers, was really a Medusa's head, a writhing, tangled monstrosity of serpents capable of turning a free economy to stone. The entire operation is captured in the microcosm of one tale that can only be told with disdain. It is the story of a forty-nine-year-old desperado, a Polish immigrant and father of four, a malefactor named Jacob Maged.

The NRA, created on June 16, 1933, wasted no time in going about the people's business. Before the end of the year it had rounded up 150 errant dry cleaners who were summoned to Washington for the crime of discounting their services. Within months, topping off their victory, the long arm of the law was able to apprehend the villainous Maged, proprietor of a tailor shop in Jersey City, New Jersey. Maged, who had been pressing men's pants for twenty-two years, was found out for having charged thirty-five cents to press a suit when the NRA's dry-cleaning code specified the task was to be performed for the lawful price of forty cents.

The defiant Maged was even discovered to have uttered these words of impudence: "You can't tell me how to run my business." But the desperado was forced to reconsider when he found himself on the receiving end of state justice for his thuggish ways: a fine of $100 and a thirty-day jail sentence. Those who minister to men's souls often claim that no man is beyond redemption, and perhaps it is true, for this outlaw is said to have seen the error of his ways and agreed to take down the sign advertising the pressing of suits for thirty-five cents and replace it with the symbol of the NRA, a vigilant blue eagle, wings spread aloft and bearing an industrial gearwheel in one talon—appearing to remind us that we are all cogs in a machine—and fearsome lightning bolts in the other, reminding us of the state's power to imprison dangerous scofflaws.

Upon Maged's repentance, a kindly black-robed judge remitted the fine and terminated the sentence after a mere three days of incarceration. In doing so, His Honor gently reproved the errant tailor, instructing him, "You must conduct your business in the right way, however, or your competitors will complain. You may not know it but you owe your trouble to complaints made by competitors who said they were losing business because of your action."

And with that Maged was freed from the jailhouse and returned to his home, his family, and the humble pursuits of a now law-abiding tailor. The *New York Times* memorialized the transformation in these words: "Maged, if not quite so ruggedly individualistic as formerly, was a free man once more."

The *New York Herald Tribune* noted the point that I have been making in this chapter: to find the likes of the Maged case, one would have to look to "the Fascist or Communist states of Europe."

Maged's woeful tale is representative of smaller businesses across the land, the providers of most of America's jobs, who were forbidden by the law from competing by offering lower prices than the favored cartels. The impact on a people suffering widespread unemployment and impoverishment, people who desperately needed lower prices, was like the impact of New Deal agricultural policies on people who didn't have enough to eat, as the administration ordered crops plowed under and farm animals destroyed.

Lawrence Reed of the Foundation for Economic Education has noted that the NRA raised the cost of doing business by an average of forty percent and had other predictable consequences:

> In the five months leading up to the act's passage, signs of recovery were evident: factory employment and payrolls had increased by 23

and 35 percent, respectively. Then came the NRA, shortening hours of work, raising wages arbitrarily and imposing other new costs on enterprise. In the six months after the law took effect, industrial production dropped 25 percent.

The real impact of the NRA, and the entire philosophy of the New Deal, was the application of political criteria to the evaluation of business, financial, and economic conditions. It empowered the administration and thus empowered corporations that supported the administration as it fixed prices and curtailed production, throttled competition, and fostered monopolies on a broad scale. All in all, Roosevelt's policies prompted Mussolini to tell a *New York Times* writer, "Your plan for coordination of industry follows precisely our lines of cooperation."

World War II is responsible for the unexamined presupposition that our opponents represented views of the nature of man and his relationship to the state that were somehow the polar opposite of our own. But the similarity of the allegiance of both sides to centralized state planning should have been alarming. None were stalwarts of economic freedom; all supported the subordination of the individual to the collective. The tune was played in several different keys, but for all it was the great whirling dance of statism.

The dance continued throughout the twentieth century. Johnson has chronicled it thus:

> across the decades and the hemispheres; mountebanks, charismatics, *exaltés*, secular saints, mass murderers, united by their belief that politics was the cure for human ills: Sun Yat-sen and Ataturk, Stalin and Mussolini, Khrushchev, Ho Chi Minh, Pol Pot, Castro, Nehru, U Nu and Sukarno, Peron and Allende, Nkrumah and Nyerere, Nasser, Shah Pahlevi and Gadafy, usually bringing death and poverty in their train.

The orchestrators of the state have not left the world stage; their musicians have not laid down their instruments. Today they play for the new millennium. *"Always and everywhere, Plans."*

The Knowledge Deficit

At first glance, a critic of central planning may arouse skepticism. The software on the laptop that I am using to write this didn't just create itself. Somebody had to plan how it would work and how it would interface with hardware and other programs, what new features would create a demand for it, how it would be tested, how it would be marketed, and so on. But it is not a question, as Friedrich Hayek writes in *The Use of Knowledge in Society*, of whether or not economic plans are made. Of course they are. It is a question of who does the planning. As it turns out, it is a question that matters a great deal. Hayek says the choices are three:

1. Central planning, which means the direction of the whole economic system by the state in a single, unified plan.
2. The free economy, which means decentralized planning by many separate persons.
3. The halfway house between the two, the delegation of planning to organized industries, or, in other words, monopoly.

In the first instance the economy is organized by force; the second is the free economy in which economic activities are voluntary. Because Hayek's third case of delegated planning, or state monopolies, is also characterized by coercion—it's hard to imagine an economic act that is half free and half mandatory; even economic acts that are undertaken grudgingly or because there are no better alternatives remain voluntary unless they are entered upon "at gunpoint"—I shall deal only with 1 and 2 here, although I shall have more to say about state monopolies in the following chapter on corporatism and crony capitalism.

Hayek asks how knowledge, which is dispersed among all people so that some possess advantages in some things and others have special knowledge about other things, is best communicated so that it can be used most efficiently. The central planners of the state are indifferent to this dispersal of knowledge, focused as they are on statistics of production and consumption, aggregate numbers that displace the individual, who is anonymous and insignificant. Human beings with their constant changes and the richness of their variety can be a nuisance to these economic manipulators who wish only to direct the state to change an input factor here and measure an output there in a mechanical fashion.

But it is not just human beings that change. Because everything changes, Hayek argues that rapid adaptation to changing conditions is key to society's economic functioning. The flow of goods and services upon which prosperity rests depends on people free to adjust: substituting resources; changing work, production, and delivery schedules; adjusting prices; adding and dropping suppliers; changing specifications; determining to meet one customer's needs at the expense of another and anticipating the consequences; and a thousand other adaptations to unforeseeable change. Furthermore, Hayek points out even where there is stability in the performance of statistical aggregates, that stability exists thanks to these constant adjustments to local conditions and specific circumstances by individual economic actors, a process that goes virtually unnoticed at the level of state planning and aggregates. What is being described applies not only to large industrial or manufacturing enterprises, but to the everyday life of every economic actor—and that means all of us. The owner of a sports bar who caters to fans of a specific team knows to order more beer when the team is having a winning season. A truck driver who dropped out of high school will know more about the viability of roads in his territory during different weather conditions than a senior transportation official in a state office with a PhD. In the town of my childhood, merchants knew that if it snowed before Thanksgiving, they would likely sell out of snow tires and snowblowers. If the first snowfall came later in the year, probably not. Merchants in towns with different weather patterns have different experiences.

We cannot possibly expect unorganized knowledge of ceaselessly changing local conditions to be somehow painstakingly gathered from people aware of those conditions in an economy of almost unbelievable interdependency and complexity and communicated to centralized authorities, who, upon assimilating it, will make wise decisions. By the time they issue their orders, conditions will have changed, and like the centipede that tries to centralize a function that worked spontaneously of itself, prosperity is run into a ditch.

In the conceit of his endeavor, the state planner, if he is the least bit serious about his role, must soon be swept away in a torrent of information, an unending but somehow never adequate flood of data about the smallest details of economic life in his constant struggle to avoid being faulted for his inevitable failure. (Nor does this even take into consideration the internal political pressures to which the bureaucrat can respond, issues having to do with only his own personal incentives and career advancement, however inimical they may be to the public good.) But still, in the absence of the state central planner, whatever his shortcomings, how is all the information that he was charged with providing for—information about surpluses and shortages, about labor and skills, about priorities and trade-offs between limited resources, about the means of production, about time preferences, and about new improvements and failures—how is the need for all such information from far-flung activities possibly met in a world of constant change?

Hayek answers that the knowledge the central planners lack is indeed known; it is available and communicated to every economic actor in a free economy to the extent that he needs it. Although almost anything anywhere can have an impact on the decisions he must make, he need not be entangled in the minutiae that hopelessly confuse central planners. He need not know about the drought in Agraria, mines flooded in Brazuela, or labor conditions in Caspiar. That bandwidth leasing rates are higher or lower; that skilled labor is more readily available at one plant than another; or that concrete pipes are more readily available and PVC pipes are less; all these things are effortlessly communicated to him in efficient form, says Hayek:

> All that is significant for him is how much more or less difficult to pro-
> cure they have become compared with other things with which he is
> also concerned, or how much more or less urgently wanted are the
> alternative things he produces or uses.
>
> The most significant fact about this system is the economy of
> knowledge with which it operates, or how little the individual par-
> ticipants need to know in order to be able to take the right action. In
> abbreviated form, by a kind of symbol, only the most essential infor-
> mation is passed on and passed on only to those concerned. It is more
> than a metaphor to describe the price system as a kind of machinery
> for registering change, or a system of telecommunications which en-
> ables individual producers to watch merely the movement of a few
> pointers, as an engineer might watch the hands of a few dials, in order
> to adjust their activities to changes of which they may never know
> more than is reflected in the price movement.

Hayek is correct in calling this system a marvel. Consider, for example, the sudden scarcity of one raw material. The reasons for it may be known to no more than a few, and in fact it doesn't matter whether the scarcity is the result of a new use for the material or a diminished source. Suddenly thousands, or even millions of users, their individual identities quite unknown, begin to economize in its use. "They move in the right direction," says Hayek. More astonishing is that they move in the right direction *at a pace exactly in keeping with the needs of their individual circumstances*, some faster, some slower. In similar circumstances the central planner, once the facts of a new scarcity are known to him, is reduced to issuing one-size-fits-all dictates, ordering all users to cut back by a fixed percentage. In this way the planner needlessly enforces changes both where they can be more readily adapted and where they cause far-reaching economic havoc. On the other hand, if the mechanism of a free economy in which people are guided by price changes to respond to conditions far beyond their sphere of knowledge; if such a system in which people adapt to circumstances of which they know nothing; if such a process were the result of human invention, says Hayek, it would be regarded as one of the greatest triumphs of the human mind.

Instead it is just one more way in which the blessings of liberty provide for our prosperity.

The Road to Serfdom

Born in 1899, Hayek came of age just in time to experience the economic madness of the twentieth century, wild in its enthusiasm for central state planning. At about the time Hayek reached his majority, that enthusiasm had reached a global pitch, coinciding with the Russian Revolution and the end of World War I, a war in which Hayek served. By 1974, when he was awarded the Nobel Prize for economics—the first free-market economist so honored—Hayek had long shined his light into the dark corners of the century, clearly and patiently making the intellectual case for a free and open society. He continued to do so until his death in 1992 at the age of ninety-two.

But it was in the middle of his life, in 1944 as World War II neared its end, that his most well-known work, *The Road to Serfdom*, was published. It was in his later work that Hayek demonstrated that the knowledge deficit of central planners was dysfunctional and impoverishing. But with *The Road to Serfdom* he told the story in a different way, describing why state economic planning must destroy human freedom.

Hayek's objective was to warn the British that despite years of war with Nazi Germany, a totalitarian outcome could await them even in victory; that fascism and communism were just variants of the centrally planned command economy they were furiously implementing. To make his position clear, he dedicated the book to "the socialists of all parties."

Hayek acknowledges the contributions of classical antiquity and Christianity to Western civilization's developing respect for the individual, and his entitlement to his life—that the individual is the ultimate judge of his own ends, to decide what is more and what is less important to him within his own sphere. It must then be understood that each individual has his own plans. The more the state plans, the more certain it is that individuals will find their own plans prohibited. Ultimately the enforcement of its plan requires the state to go to war with its own people.

It is rightly an abhorrent idea to some statists and central planners that their objectives may have to be accomplished by the brutal methods mankind has witnessed so often. But Hayek observes that "if the policy is to be pursued, totalitarian forces will get the upper hand." It is no less dangerous that "socialism can only be put into practice by methods of which most socialists disapprove." Ruthlessness must ensue.

Is there a kinder, gentler statism? Can the grim outcome Hayek observed and analyzed throughout the century be dispelled by democracy? But even if the central direction of the economy were an objective arrived at by some democratic means, personal freedom can still be destroyed. The conferral of power by democracy—which is merely a mechanism or a process and not to be confused with freedom itself—is not a guarantee against power used in an arbitrary and destructive manner. It is the limitation of power, Hayek makes clear, regardless of its source or authority, that provides for freedom. Because the implementation of large-scale state plans demands the most effective instrument of coercion, planning becomes the pathway to dictatorship no matter how the central plan itself is selected.

With the passage of time, the practice of socialism has come to have more to do with the redistribution of wealth through taxation and the growth of the welfare state than at the time Hayek first wrote, when control of the means of production was emphasized. Under these newer circumstances, Hayek wrote for a later edition of the book, the outcomes he described come about more slowly and indirectly, although the consequence tends to be very much the same. Furthermore, and important in assessing the prospects for our own immediate future, Hayek observes that while it may take a couple of generations to unfold, the growth of government control changes the character and psychology of a people:

> This means, among other things, that even a strong tradition of political liberty is no safeguard if the danger is precisely that new institutions and policies will gradually undermine and destroy that spirit. The consequences can of course be averted if that spirit reasserts itself in time and the people . . . recognize the nature of the danger and resolutely change their course.

The U.S.A. Today

Planning, when undertaken by the individual, even when he makes mistakes, provides him with crucial feedback. Success and failure both inform the individual's subsequent plans and allow him to assess and correct, to persist or desist in a way harmonious with his individual nature. And while the damage from an individual's poor planning of his own affairs is generally limited, this is not so when the central planner—the board, body, or bureaucrat—makes a mistake. Their calamities are systemic. When damage on the wide scale of their planning authority takes place, countless individuals with no complicity in the affair can be victimized and forced to make painful adjustments to circumstances not of their own making. But as our recent experience shows, the central planners themselves generally escape consequences.

Did any Federal Reserve chairmen lose their jobs or personal fortunes for blowing up the dot-com bubble or for taking the whole country down with the reckless centrally planned artificial credit and housing bust? The answer is no: their salaries and retirements are quite secure, as are their fleet of private jets, luxury automobiles and drivers, and retirement consulting and speaking fees. Meanwhile millions of Americans lost their homes, their jobs, their insurance, and much more in the debacle.

The Federal Reserve wasn't the only central planning institution in on the housing bust. Fannie Mae, the creation of a congressionally approved central plan to expand the mortgage market, dates back to the halcyon days of state economic management, the New Deal. As he was helping to blow up the real estate bubble, Fannie Mae chairman Franklin Raines received millions in below-market-rate mortgage loans from Countrywide Financial. Fannie Mae was of course the biggest buyer of Countrywide Financial mortgages. Meanwhile, the American people have been put on the hook for the $5 trillion in mortgage-backed securities and debt held by Fannie Mae and Freddie Mac. In June 2010, both Fannie Mae and Freddie Mac were delisted from the New York Stock Exchange. As for Franklin Raines (*Franklin Delano* Raines, ironically enough), the central planner made more than $90 million during his five years as Fannie Mae chairman.

As the state burdens the free economy with the costs of its monetary duplicity and foolhardy fiscal conduct—the billions in bailout giveaways and trillions in taxes taken and spent, the state plans that no one can decipher in legislation that no one can decode—still, even as the load grows day by day, under the reign of Republicans and the tenure of Democrats, and as the burden grows brick by regulatory brick, despite it all . . .

. . . somehow the free economy struggles to get its legs under it, manages to rise to its feet, still staggering.

The least regulated parts of the economy, those furthest from the central planners and the compounding tangle of their regulators, perform best. They innovate, improve performance, and lower costs year after year. But it is only because these industries are moving too fast for the much slower-witted state to catch up that they have managed to escape some of the ill effects of the regulatory impulse. You might have spent thousands on a flat-panel plasma TV only a few years ago. Today a bigger flat-screen TV with better picture quality, of lighter weight, consuming less power, and generating less heat is yours for a fraction of the price of the old ones. Your smartphone has more computing power than your old laptop, which is faster and has more memory than the desktop you used just a few years before. Now you can use your phone to charge a purchase, watch videos, surf the Internet, play games, check your location, find a business and get directions, dictate notes, take pictures, shoot video, and hundreds of other things in a way that was impossible only a few years ago, and yet is now affordable to millions. Oh, and it makes calls, too!

Similarly, some medical procedures far from the oversight of the state are the exception to the relentlessly rising costs of medical care. Lasik and other corrective eye surgeries are generally elective procedures not covered by the state-driven health insurance industry or by Medicare. Predictably, corrective-vision technology improves every year and the cost of the procedures has fallen dramatically.

Contrast these examples of efficiency and consumer satisfaction with some of the most visible activities of the state—activities, not coincidentally, with high consumer complaints: the airport security bureaucracy, health care, and public education. A 2010 maintenance record review showed that TSA airport full-body scans were emitting radiation at ten times the expected levels. At the same time the federal authorities were mismanaging their own activities and irradiating air travelers in this way, the government was clamoring for more control of the medical industry—in which case, its demonstrable misman-agement of radiation levels should distress future X–ray candidates. The TSA explained the elevated radiation by attributing it to misreading information and math mistakes. Which could well be a reflection on the state's education system.

The Regulatory Imperative

The cry for state regulation has seemingly become the automatic response of the American mind to every problem and failure in business and economic relations. It has the quality of a meme, an unthinking, widely shared autonomic response, which, when viewed through libertarian eyes, is quite misplaced. So deep-seated is this conditioning—that every need demands a regulatory response—that it can be dislodged only with some practice in seeing the world in a new way. But at least a few paragraphs of refutation must be offered. Since food and its provision have been a recurrent thread here, interventionism in the industry may as well serve as a stand-in for state regulation as a whole.

A friend of mine, a stand-up comedian, has a funny line about solving the actuarial problems of Social Security and Medicare by ending the state's "in-trusive inspection of meat." It gets a big laugh, but provokes an important question: what would happen if the state did not inspect meat—or other food products?

Kroger and Safeway are the nation's largest and second-largest grocery store chains, with revenue of $82 billion and $41 billion, respectively. Both have stores in our neighborhood; we shop in both. Competition between them and among the other grocery chains where we live is fierce in a business in which profit margins are generally very low to begin with. Both companies spend enormous amounts of money to make their stores inviting and to win our business. Their selections are enormous, with meat counters marvelous in their quality and produce departments that are simply breathtaking with their array of familiar as well as exotic fresh foods. Their employees are generally friendly and helpful and will even order specialty items for us if they can. No doubt some executive at each chain knows exactly how much it costs, on average, to bring shoppers like us into their stores and to keep us as loyal customers.

With all they spend and do to win our business, I have to ask if it's all a pretense. Do they really not care about the incremental spending my family and others like ours bring to their stores? In the absence of federal meat inspection, would they really be willing to spend all that money to bring us into their stores, only to kill us all with adulterated beef? Would one of them be willing to stand by flat-footed while its competitors advertise the rigorous and independent meat inspections it employs? How long would such a business persist in having no similar safety measures? Would its insurance carriers continue to renew the stores' liability policies? Would their executives mind the loss of their positions and careers and their shareholders the loss of their investment when the stores begin selling contaminated pork? It seems unlikely. Perhaps the regulatory state provides businesses a means of shifting responsibilities? But such responsibilities are better left not in the hands of the state, but in the hands of those who are rewarded when they perform them well and who find it costly when they do not.

An E. coli outbreak in Washington State in 1993 claimed four lives. The tragedy cost Jack in the Box restaurants $160 million in settlements and lost business, and although, according to the company, the contaminated beef was traced to one slaughterhouse where U.S. Department of Agriculture inspections were already in place, those inspections were later deemed to have been inadequate. What we do know for sure is that Jack in the Box did not independently require its supplier to test the meat it provided. After all, meat inspection is the business of the USDA.

Central planning in public safety is fraught with the same shortcomings as central planning elsewhere in the economy. It stifles progress and innovation, drives up costs, and protects powerful interests from competition. These

are not just the shortcomings of regulation; they are the intended consequences. Economist George Stigler, a Nobel laureate, has made the case that
state regulation is designed to provide special privileges to regulated industries, protect them, and raise prices on their behalf. Of course this "regulatory
capture" in which the regulators actually serve their industries is exactly the
opposite of what the governing classes promise the public. Instead, regulating
agencies restrict competition in ways that actually victimize the public. Stigler
has suggested that "every industry or occupation that has enough political
power to utilize the state will seek to control entry."

After the discovery of bovine spongiform encephalopathy (BSE), better
known as mad cow disease, in the U.S. in 2003, Japan halted the importation
of American beef. Motivated by a desire to resume selling to Japan, Creekstone
Farms in Kansas invested heavily and built a testing lab so that it could inde-
pendently test all of its cattle. This was a challenge to the USDA, which, captured by the food industry it regulates, supports only random testing. It should
go without saying that large U.S. meatpackers opposed Creekstone's effort to
pioneer new and improved testing protocols. A meat industry spokesman insisted that any testing should take place only under government oversight. In
2006 Creekstone was forced to sue the USDA for refusing it permission to test
all of its cattle. In 2008 a U.S. Court of Appeals overturned a lower court ruling
that would have allowed Creekstone to proceed. "We owe the USDA a considerable degree of deference," wrote a judge in the case.

What would replace the "intrusive inspection of meat" in the absence of
the state? Has the state even been doing a good job in its inspections? That is a
question that can only be answered by asking "compared to what?" Would the
"poke and sniff" method of feeling and smelling meat—the mainstay of USDA
inspections for almost a hundred years but one that cannot detect pathogenic
bacteria and microbes like E. coli—have been improved on many years earlier
than it was by innovators in a free economy looking for better ways of doing
the job? It is impossible to say. Would one uniform standard of inspection have
emerged, so clearly superior that it would go unchallenged? Or would there be
many means of testing for food safety, each one offering greater thoroughness
and more efficient costs than the next? It is impossible to know until creative
minds attack the problem, a prospect that is sharply reduced in the presence
of the state's monopoly. If there were a widespread outbreak of mad cow disease, how many would suffer needlessly because regulatory capture blocked

new advances in testing? Innovations that never see the light of day, held back by the regulatory state, cannot be known. But in a free economy it is foolish to think that people wanting wholesome food will flounder about and go unsatisfied in the absence of the state.

Lighten the Load

Commerce strains and the economy groans under a growing regulatory load that can be lifted at little cost. We have become utterly inured to the burden that America's productive people bear, but it is massive. According to the 2010 annual report by the Competitive Enterprise Institute, *Ten Thousand Commandments: An Annual Snapshot of the Federal Regulatory State*, businesses spent $1.187 trillion on federal regulatory compliance in 2009. The lion's share, seventy percent, is the cost of economic regulation, consisting of non-environmental restrictions and incentives on businesses; things like price supports, import restrictions, and other wealth "transfer costs"; and tax compliance.

That doesn't include the $54.3 billion the bureaucracy itself spent enforcing those regulations. The $1.24 trillion total works out to a regulatory burden of $16,000 for a family of four.

For one not familiar with it, the extent of federal regulation can be stupefying, as can be quickly discovered by looking in the Federal Register. Running roughly 80,000 pages a year, the Federal Register publishes all actions taken by federal agencies, including proposed rules and regulations, final and changed rules, and notices of meetings and proceedings. From a typical day, March 16, 2011, here is an excerpt from just one entry—selected only because it was the first one on that day's table of contents. It details a final rule making about grapes from the Agricultural Marketing Service of the Department of Agriculture. It simply has to be read to be believed.

> SUMMARY: This rule revises the requirements under the Export Grape and Plum Act. This rule changes the minimum bunch weight requirement for grapes exported to Japan, Europe, and Greenland from one-half pound to one-quarter pound.... This action was recommended by the California Grape and Tree Fruit League (League)....

Section 35.11 of the regulations establishes minimum size and quality requirements for export shipments of any variety of vinifera species table grapes. Currently, such grapes shipped to Japan, Europe, or Greenland must meet a minimum grade of U.S. Fancy Table as specified in the U.S. Standards for Grades of Table Grapes (U.S. Standards) (7CFR part 51, Sec. 51.880-51.992), with the additional requirement that bunches must each weigh at least one-half pound.

This final rule revises Sec. 35.11(a) of the order's administrative rules and regulations by changing the minimum bunch weight requirement for grapes exported to Japan, Europe, and Greenland from one-half pound to one-quarter pound.

The entry goes on in this manner for a full three pages of eye-crossing, mind-numbing bureaucratic jargon. Actually, at three pages it is a rather diminutive rule as these things go. But finally we get to the heart of the matter, the reason for all the citing, revising, and specifying:

There has been an increasing retail demand for table grapes packaged in plastic clamshells, particularly for export markets. One of the most popular package sizes is the 500 gram (approximately 1.1 pounds) clamshell. However, shippers find it difficult to fit two larger (minimum one-half pound) grape bunches into the 500 gram clamshell. This change allows shippers to use smaller (minimum one-quarter pound) bunches to fill the smaller clamshell packages. This change offers shippers greater flexibility in packaging and allows them to pack a greater portion of the crop into the clamshell packages that are popular in the marketplace. The League believes this change positions shippers and exporters to better meet market demand while maintaining pack quality.

In lieu of asking where federal authority for the Export Grape and Plum Act originates, we'll note only the obvious: that in a free economy grape growers, exporters, and shippers are quite capable of determining the bunch weights and package sizes the market demands. If the market is clamoring for clamshells, why must a bunch of grape growers get federal approval to do something about it? If there is an "increasing retail demand" for "popular" packaging, why should meeting that demand require a ten-month process involving departments of tax-consuming bureaucrats with plum jobs? Do you suppose China, the world's largest grape producer, demands that its producers endure prolonged processes before adapting to the simple packaging needs of their customers? The entire episode seems a little silly until you note that the cost of the federal regulatory load is equal to 8.7 percent of the U.S. gross domestic product. That's serious money.

Talk about a stimulus package! Lift this regulatory load—do we really need federal agents snooping on Amish farmers for fear someone is drinking organic milk?—and watch an American *Wirtschaftswunder*, an "economic miracle." And unlike the Republican and Democrat boondoggles, it wouldn't explode the debt. Athletes intentionally burden themselves with weights strapped to their arms and legs, but only for training. Removal of the load leads to a higher level of performance in competition. And Americans badly need to be freed to run a more competitive race.

CHAPTER SIX

Fascism and Crony Capitalism

The law locks up the man or woman
Who steals the goose from off the common
But leaves the greater villain loose
Who steals the common from under the goose.

—Anonymous

Phony Capitalism

In his autobiography, *The Age of Turbulence*, former Federal Reserve chairman Alan Greenspan offered a description of crony capitalism: "When a government's leaders routinely seek out private-sector individuals or businesses and, in exchange for political support, bestow favors on them, the country is said to be in the grip of 'crony capitalism.'" Greenspan was describing Indonesia, Russia, and Mexico, but he could easily have offered up the example of the United States. That's what *Rolling Stone* journalist Matt Taibbi did.

In prose not as dry as the chairman's, Taibbi famously called the investment bank Goldman Sachs "a great vampire squid wrapped around the face of humanity, relentlessly jamming its blood funnel into anything that smells like money." The imagery suggested a useful new taxonomy for the entire genus of corporate statism, in which political authorities and state policies quite transparently function in the service of powerful corporate interests. Crony capitalism is but one aspect of the corporate state. Prominent among the characteristics of crony capitalism is that it subsists on the government's provision of market protection and monopoly status, bailouts, subsidies, regulatory favoritism, special tax treatment, and influence peddling; and similar to the drinking habits of the vampire from which Taibbi's colorful description is drawn, it drains the prosperity of the people.

While crony capitalism has nothing to do with a free economy, the long-standing practice of crony capitalism is so repugnant in the minds of thoughtful people that the very word "capitalism" has been tainted by it. For that reason I have written instead about the free economy in these pages, having long ago abandoned the word "capitalism," which has become unalterably linked in the public mind to the image of the Monopoly man—the top-hatted, cane-carrying cartoon figure of the board game. It is a word that conjures up images of state capitalists: plutocrats and war profiteers, banksters and Wall Street barons who trade on political connections.

While deferred consumption, capital, is the mighty fuel of economic growth, even people without capital generally prefer to be free; and championing economic freedom against ubiquitous state interventionism is demanding enough without having to rehabilitate a word along the way. But there is a perfectly serviceable word for such corporate statism or corporatism that is the subject of this chapter: fascism.

Fascism

Why the language of politics and economics should be controlled by Marx and Stalin and the like, who apply terms that suit the objectives of their propaganda—usages that the rest of us should then be obligated to use—has never been made clear. "Capitalism" was propelled into usage in the works of Marx as a pejorative, while Stalin, trying to save his own brand, gave orders that the word "socialist" be dropped when referring to competing totalitarians. Stalin insisted on the use of "fascist" for his adversaries, including Germany's National Socialists. The distinction may have spared socialism itself from being forever stained by the Nazis' crimes.

Spotting fascists is something of an evergreen industry in the publishing business, with titles from both the Left and the Right identifying fascists among the authors' ideological opponents. There are, of course, books of merit from both sides of the ideological divide. Both conservatives and liberals have described incipient threats and real dangers to our freedom and prosperity, but they generally do so only when they detect the authoritarian features of their opposite numbers in the face of the state. Where their own political enthusiasms prevail, they can exhibit a remarkable psychological blindness.

From the Right, *National Review Online* editor Jonah Goldberg's 2007 *Liberal Fascism* is most useful in identifying the genealogy the Wilsonian progressives and the New Dealers share with European fascism. But while his definition of fascism identifies it as totalitarian and a religion of the state, he conspicuously says nothing specific about its militarized and police-state nature, a characteristic of fascism one strains to miss. It is a curious blind spot because even late in the book, when he proposes to undertake an examination of the fascist tendencies of the American Right, the charges of militarism and expansion of the police state that were unavoidable during the Bush years (during which Goldberg wrote) not only go without rebuttal, they are conspicuously absent. Similarly, when Goldberg, who was a cheerleader for the Iraq war, describes the threat of American life being "frittered away for a bag of magic beans called security," he means only the welfare state and, overlooking the warfare state, is quick to exclude the Bush administration and the war on terror. And when he throws his support behind the Bush "democracy agenda," he doesn't bother to distance himself from unauthorized wiretaps, waterboarding, Abu Ghraib, Guantánamo, or the secret transfer of innocent people to be tortured in fascist proxy states like Libya, Syria, and Egypt.

Chris Hedges, a former *New York Times* war correspondent, approaches fascism from his perspective on the Left. He targets the Christian Right in his 2006 book *American Fascists: The Christian Right and the War on America.* Hedges focuses from the outset on Christian dominionists, "an ideology that calls on the radical church to take political power." The types Hedges describes are common enough in public view, and although he doesn't say it, appear to be followers of a well-muscled and avenging Jesus—a savior who bears a better resemblance to Thor, the hammer-wielding Norse god of thunder, than to the Prince of Peace who delivered the Beatitudes. Traditional fundamentalism, says Hedges, "has never attempted to impose its belief system on the rest of the nation." But under the dominionism he describes, with its militant biblicism, America must become an agent of God, and those who then dissent from its leaders must be considered agents of Satan. It is a philosophy that would return us to the divine right of rulers and the infallibility of the state.

The radical Christian Right, Hedges says, "bears within it a Christian fascism." In the event of an economic calamity or other crisis, it stands ready to manipulate fear and chaos to reshape America accordingly.

Hedges, a socialist, is candid in faulting the Democratic Party for being like the Republican Party in its support for imperial wars and the national security state and doing the bidding of corporations. But his books leave one wondering why, for all their descriptions of the willingness of people to fall in with intolerant movements and to be duped by the state's needless wars, socialists should persist in favoring economic organization concentrated in "public" hands—practically speaking, the hands of the state. When by his own convincing description authoritarians are ever at hand and totalitarians are closer than breathing, why encourage the pooling of economic might in collectivist hands (often referred to benignly as "community") with the irresistible lure those concentrations have for the power hungry?

Like a Rorschach test, one-sided descriptions say more about the peculiar psychology of both the American Left and the Right than about fascism itself, for without its famous police states and its militarism, fascism simply wouldn't be fascism, just as it is only collectivism that makes possible a religion of the state with its mass rituals, holy regalia, and idolatry of leaders.

Another book that addresses fascism in America deserves mention because the author displays more balance than one generally expects from the Left or the Right. Published in 2007, *The End of America: Letter of Warning to a Young Patriot* is by Naomi Wolf, a liberal. Alarmed at "echoes" of mid-twentieth-century fascism in current events, Wolf lists ten specific political developments that warn of fascism's approach and provides details of the state's enactment of each. Among them are the surveillance of citizens, restrictions on and intimidation of the press, infiltration of citizen groups, the characterization of dissent as subversion and treason, and the establishment of secret prisons.

Wolf demonstrates a real appreciation of the political characteristics of fascism and has recently surprised some of her colleagues on the Left by praising the Tea Party as an important counter to undue corporate and military power in the U.S. and as a check on executive power and the Fed. At its best, says Wolf, the Tea Party movement is an overdue constitutionalist movement. Americans, she told an interviewer, can't "sit around waiting for the two corrupted established parties to restore the Constitution or the Republic."

Readers of these books can't fail to note that the economics of fascism are given short shrift. But economics are central to journalist John T. Flynn's 1944 book *As We Go Marching,* which chronicled the rise of fascism in Europe and its ominous parallels as they developed in the United States. As Flynn tells it, in distinguishing fascism from socialism Mussolini described the "usefulness" of capitalism, and blasted the ruinous socialist policy of state ownership. Hitler's outlook was much the same. When asked about his intentions for Krupp, the giant German munitions and steel manufacturer—was it to be nationalized?—Hitler answered that he would leave it alone. "Do you think I am crazy enough to ruin Germany's greatest industry?"

It is not ownership of the means of production that matters to the fascists—which in any event generates the kind of resistance that communism encounters in much of the West—but control. Flynn specifies objectives of fascist economics that are familiar to us today:

- An economic system in which production and distribution are carried out by private owners but in accordance with plans made by the state directly or under its immediate supervision.
- These plans involve control of all the instruments of production and distribution through great government bureaus, which have the power to make regulations or directives with the force of law.
- They involve also the comprehensive integration of government and private finances, under which investment is directed and regimented by the government, so that while ownership is private and production is carried on by private owners, there is a type of socialization of investment, of the financial aspects of production. By this means the state, which by law and by regulation can exercise a powerful control over industry, can enormously expand and complete that control by assuming the role of banker and partner.
- They involve also the device of creating streams of purchasing power by federal government borrowing and spending as a permanent institution.

For their part, the corporations that have been involved in the appearance of fascism see the state as a way to fix prices, limit production, and eliminate risk and competition. Having spliced together the DNA of the state and corporations in this way, fascism has bequeathed to us its reproduction of monopolies, monopoly capitalism, and collective monopolies or cartels, all in compliance with Mussolini's dictum: "Everything within the State, nothing outside the State, nothing against the State." Prominent among the offspring of fascism's steaming, bubbling corporate/state gene pool is crony capitalism.

Crony Capitalism

Crony capitalists, like all corporate statists, have a symbiotic relationship with the state and cannot exist apart from the state. Politicians, of course, receive campaign contributions for their favors, but a glance reveals that the tentacles of crony capitalism reach far beyond simple support of candidates. (This is one of the reasons that campaign finance reform is a hopelessly feeble means of cleaning up politics.) The methods of crony capitalists can be likened to the production of goods in the economy. Just as the entire production and manufacturing process is aimed at the end outcome of consumer goods, so, too, does the long chain of means available to crony capitalists in their "manufacturing" process serve the growth of the state as a means of producing the "consumer goods" the cronies have in mind for themselves—wealth! The raw materials they employ—statist ideas, programs, proposals—are first turned into producer goods—public policy, legislation, and electoral victories. It is from this that the objective of the entire process is realized: wealth transfers, protection from competition, bailouts, handouts, government contracts, defense contract procurement, and subsidies of all kinds—ill-gotten gains provided by the hand of the state and at the expense of the people. Corporate statists and crony capitalists don't limit themselves, then, to electoral politics; they work with the governing classes and the media resources of the state's enablers throughout this entire production process.

A Pentagon propaganda program ramped up to coincide with the launch of the Iraq war illustrates one side of such an operation. Retired senior military officials on the payroll of defense contractors also became cable and television network analysts and commentators, what the Pentagon called "message force multipliers," to deliver administration talking points on the war. The *New York Times* story on the affair reported that "most of the analysts have ties to military contractors vested in the very war policies they are asked to assess on air," and that those financial ties, representing 150 different war contractors, generally went undisclosed. The propaganda program provided the "analysts" with "hundreds of private briefings with senior military leaders, including officials with significant influence over contracting and budget matters." The appearance of having special insight and inside knowledge created a demand for these Pentagon propagandists as news commentators. Although it had nothing to do with electoral politics, it was a program designed to help manufacture consent for the administration's war policies, policies that were profitable for the war contractors. Some participants later expressed regret at being used in a propaganda effort. As the war went on, a commentator for NBC News described a gap between what they had been told by the Pentagon and what subsequent events revealed. "Night and day," he said. "I felt we'd been hosed."

The Wormhole Express

Like the stars in the sky, the opportunities to influence state policy are without number. Among them are contributions to think tanks and the endowment of university chairs as a means of advancing careers and shaping the public debate. But no means of impacting state policy is more efficient than the revolving door of corporate business and government appointments. Like a science-fiction wormhole between galaxies, Goldman Sachs has a New York–Washington passageway that seems to defy space and time.

There's Robert Rubin, who made the transit from New York to Washington and back again. Rubin was cochairman of Goldman Sachs before becoming President Clinton's Treasury secretary. After leaving Washington he went back to New York and Wall Street and joined banking giant Citigroup as a senior official and director. In that capacity Rubin encouraged more risk taking by the bank, and take more risk it did. When it inevitably collapsed, Citigroup not only took almost $50 billion in bailout money, the government guaranteed $306 billion of the bank's toxic assets. Although the share price shriveled, from $55 to $1, Rubin made $115 million in the years he was there.

Citigroup was a major creditor of Enron Corporation, a company that was itself a textbook example of crony capitalism. In 2001, as Enron was crumbling and just two years after leaving his post as Treasury secretary, Rubin tried to intervene with his former department back in Washington. He wanted the Treasury to exert influence on the bond-rating agencies to refrain from downgrading Enron's debt, a downgrade that was already long overdue.

Efficient crony capitalism is a nonpartisan operation. Just as Goldman Sachs provided Clinton's Treasury secretary, it provided George W. Bush one as well. Josh Bolten, a Goldman Sachs veteran himself, was Bush's chief of staff.

He recruited Henry Paulson, the chairman and CEO of Goldman Sachs, to take the Wormhole Express from the financial capital to the political capital. It was Paulson as Treasury secretary who arranged the $700 billion Bush bailouts in the fall of 2008, including that astonishing bailout for Rubin's company, Citigroup. Also instrumental in the deal was Timothy Geithner, then president of the New York Federal Reserve Bank. Geithner, who became Obama's Treasury secretary, once worked for Rubin at the Treasury Department. Less well known is that in the 1980s, Barack Obama's mother was employed by the Ford Foundation in Indonesia, where she worked for Timothy Geithner's father, who headed up some of the foundation's Asian operations. For many who questioned Geithner's performance as Treasury secretary, especially as he presided over the loss of America's AAA bond rating, only that crony connection seemed to explain his appointment.

The chairman of the New York Federal Reserve Bank, under whom Geithner served as president, was Stephen Friedman. Friedman is another former Goldman Sachs cochairman and CEO and remained a board member there even as the New York Fed was in a regulatory capacity over Goldman Sachs. Friedman was able to get a waiver to prevent him from having to sell his Goldman Sachs stock. In fact, rather than selling his shares during his tenure at the Fed, as Wall Street was being bailed out, he bought *more* shares in the company despite his position with the Fed.

Merrill Lynch, the largest retail stock brokerage firm, was losing billions in the subprime crisis (it lost $58.1 billion in one twelve-month period). As it neared collapse, Bank of America, which had already taken over Countrywide Financial, was pressured by Paulson and Fed chairman Ben Bernanke to take over the stock brokerage house as well. John Thain, chairman and CEO of Merrill Lynch, was another Goldman Sachs veteran.

So far this account hasn't even begun to scratch the surface of Goldman Sachs' New York to Washington wormhole. Other players in the creation or management of TARP, the $700 billion bailout, include Goldman Sachs veterans Edward Forst, Karthik Ramanathan, and Neel Kashkari, whose role was described earlier. Edward Liddy was a Goldman Sachs board member when Paulson named him to run American International Group (AIG), which was crucial in Goldman Sachs' fortunes, as we shall see.

Cronyism comes at a price and Goldman Sachs has been willing to pay it.

The company has forty-one lobbyists on the payroll and additionally retains thirteen firms to do its work. Presidential candidate Obama received more than $1 million from Goldman Sachs employees. And speaking of paying the price, Goldman Sachs paid Larry Summers, the man who succeeded Robert Rubin in the Clinton Treasury, $135,000 for a speech in 2008. Jon Corzine is willing to pay the price, too. Corzine spent $62 million of his own money getting elected to the U.S. Senate in 2000. In 2005 he spent another $60 million running for governor of New Jersey. Corzine is another former Goldman Sachs chairman and CEO. It should not surprise anyone that Geithner's chief of staff at the Treasury, Mark Patterson, was a Goldman Sachs vice president or that Geithner was succeeded as president of the New York Fed by William C. Dudley, yet another Goldman Sachs veteran.

In a story that should be familiar by now, during the real estate bubble Goldman Sachs bundled mortgages together into packages known as collateralized debt obligations (CDOs) or mortgage-backed securities (MBS). While it was operating a "conveyor belt" that fed these instruments into the markets, Goldman Sachs had a different view of the risks of the mortgage securities it was selling to others. The company made billions shorting them—taking a market position against the mortgage instruments that was profitable as the value of the securities sank.

AIG was the world's largest insurance company. It sold insurance on the kinds of CDOs that Goldman Sachs was creating, instruments called credit default swaps. As the mortgage market melted down, AIG, which had insured hundreds of billions of dollars' worth of these risky subprime mortgage CDOs, could not meet its obligations and teetered on the edge of bankruptcy. Once again the taxpayers, whipped and driven like an unwilling mule, rode to the rescue, forking over an initial $85 billion to back the company up, an amount that soon rose to $182 billion, and $12.9 billion of the money that AIG got went straight to Goldman Sachs; Merrill Lynch got $6.8 billion.

The unmistakable stench of crony capitalism is present in an event recounted earlier: Goldman Sachs, the largest counterparty, and other AIG counterparties that stood to get nothing in the insurance giant's collapse, were paid full value—100 cents on the dollar—for securities that had a market value of half that or less due to AIG's insolvency. The special inspector general for TARP, the Bush bailout program, said, "The very design of the federal assistance to AIG was that tens of billions of dollars of government money was funneled inexorably and directly to AIG's counterparties."

It was Geithner who arranged the meetings at his New York Fed offices, where the AIG bailout deal was struck. Oddly enough, Lloyd Blankfein, chairman and CEO of Goldman Sachs, was among those present at the September 15, 2008, meeting. His company's stock price (in 2010 Blankfein owned 3.37 million shares) had been in virtual free fall for almost a year, from nearly $250 in late 2007 to less than $50 by fall 2008, so Goldman Sachs' executives must have welcomed the AIG windfall.

Geithner was instrumental in the other Bush bailouts that Paulson orchestrated. It was somebody at Geithner's New York Fed who urged AIG to withhold information about the recipients and amounts of payments from AIG. The most obvious reason for officials to keep what some have called "backdoor bailouts" confidential is the volatility of the issue, with much of the public angered over the giveaways. The inspector general's 2010 report said, "This Administration is institutionalizing a culture that ignores the American people's right to know and their call for more transparency in government."

That criticism of the Obama administration is well justified. Of course when rule bending, favoritism, trading on influence, and profiteering at the public expense are the order of the day, secrecy is at a premium. But to reiterate a key theme, such criticism applies to the Republican Bush administration as well. During the mortgage meltdown in September 2008, after it took over Countrywide Financial, Bank of America's chairman Ken Lewis was looking for relief from Federal Reserve capital requirements so that the bank wouldn't have to cut dividends to its shareholders. Lewis turned to Treasury secretary Paulson, expecting a wink from him and a nod from Fed chairman Bernanke, especially because Paulson thought Lewis might be willing to take over Lehman Brothers. While the pretext for the establishment of capital requirements is to protect consumers, the incident sweeps the pretext aside. In an environment radioactive with risk for consumers, Paulsen's willingness to pull strings for special treatment of one large financial institution is but one example of the malady of corporatism in which favored—and sometimes failed—businesses are protected by government and excused from the very feedback that investors and others need to adjust to dynamic economic and market conditions.

Indeed, the securities laws and the very existence of the Securities and

Exchange Commission (SEC) are predicated on the right of investors to full disclosure of facts that have a material impact on their investments. But different rules prevail if it is the state that has disclosures to make. In an attempt to prop up the stock market, the Treasury and the Fed pressured the SEC in 2008 to ban the short-selling of the stock of hundreds of financial companies. But short-selling is an essential part of the market's function of price discovery, in this case alerting investors to toxic mortgage risks held by financial companies. Should the state's regulators have tried to conceal from the public the real condition of Bear Stearns or, a few years earlier, the calamity of Enron's stock by banning short-selling? These are risks investors should be allowed to know about, free of the state's interference.

For one telling the story of crony capitalism, the events of 2008 are too good to be true: the popping of the bubble and the bailouts, stimulus, and spending that followed; the officials and their secrecy; the Masters of the Universe who got richer despite their losses, and yet even richer still once taxpayer money uncorked the bonus bottle; the wealth for Wall Street and the poverty for the people. Its kind will never be seen again because it somehow manages to tell everything. It is the archetypal account. It illustrates every point.

Nothing like it has ever happened before or since.

Except it has. Before.

In 1994 Mexico suffered a financial meltdown, devaluing the peso. The Mexican government had been borrowing enormous amounts of money by issuing bonds payable not in pesos but in U.S. dollars. Reflecting the risk involved, Mexican interest rates were sharply higher than other rates, with short-term rates that ran from six to sixteen percent higher than U.S. treasuries during the 1993–94 period. These Mexican bonds, *tesebonos*, were essentially junk bonds. Having devalued the peso, Mexico was taxing its people and accumulating foreign exchange in its now cheaper currency, and at the new exchange rate was unable to pay the dollar-denominated *tesebonos* as they came due. Ten billion dollars in *tesebonos* came due in the first quarter of 1995, another $19 billion by year's end. But Mexico's reserves amounted to only about $6 billion.

In January 1995 the U.S. government committed $9 billion to a Mexico bailout. As the situation south of the border continued to deteriorate, the Clinton administration proposed giving Mexico $40 billion in U.S. government guarantees, essentially putting U.S. taxpayers on the hook for Mexican junk bonds. In detail the plan called for Wall Street firms to issue about $40 billion in U.S. insured bonds (a nice chunk of bond business in itself). The proceeds would go to the Mexican government, which would repay the *tesebonos* that came due. As with the Bush 2008 bailout, the Mexico bailout was immediately and enormously unpopular. Pat Buchanan began calling it "Goldman Sachs-onomics," while a *Los Angeles Times* poll found that eighty-one percent of Americans disapproved of the giveaway.

It is material at this point to note that Goldman Sachs was Mexico's investment bank. And in fact, the point man handling the Mexican account at Goldman Sachs was Robert Rubin. Now, as Treasury secretary, Rubin was the chief architect of the Mexican bailout plan. And a bailout plan it was. It would bail out Goldman Sachs and its clients who were holding potentially worthless Mexican bonds (information is hard to come by; the company was private until 1999, but one account has claimed that Goldman had $5 billion of the Mexican bonds in its own portfolio).

It soon became clear that Congress was unwilling to approve Rubin's wealth transfer plan. If Goldman Sachs, its clients, and others who had purchased Mexican bonds were to avoid losses in the billions, the administration had to come up with another angle, one that would circumvent Congress. So the administration next proposed a package of $20 billion in direct loans from the United States, along with $18 billion from the International Monetary Fund and $13 billion from the Bank for International Settlements and other banks. To bypass Congress, the U.S. share would come from the Exchange Stabilization Fund. In a move of ironic bipartisanship, House Speaker Newt Gingrich wrote a letter to Clinton endorsing this attempt to do an end run around the opposition of his own newly elected congressional majority.

Incidentally, Geithner worked at the Treasury under Rubin and Summers on the Mexican bailout.

More Than Meets the Eye

Apologists for the state and the governing classes who supported the Bush bailout are now fulsome in their praise for its success. The *Washington Post* applauded the "legislators who courageously supported it" and offered the conventional statist wisdom that "TARP helped save the United States from an economic collapse . . ." From elsewhere in the Beltway, a Politico.com piece said it "succeeded far beyond expectations."

Not so fast. Aside from the rather sizable stumbling block that home prices have continued to fall since 2008 (by February 2011 prices had fallen to their lowest level in nine years; eight million home owners were a month or more behind on mortgage payments or in foreclosure), has everyone in Washington forgotten that the bailout was sold under the guise of reinflating the housing market and that the program's supporters made no suggestion that double-digit real unemployment would persist for years? Other than failing to achieve its intended purpose is the small issue of the other side of the balance sheet: the costs. Of course the program is a success from the perspective of those who got the money; that is a foregone conclusion and shouldn't merit celebration by the state's journalistic footmen. But a hard reckoning of the price paid has yet to be made. This is what the classical liberal Frederic Bastiat tried to teach us in the mid-nineteenth century: "There is only one difference between a bad economist and a good one: the bad economist confines himself to the visible effect; the good economist takes into account both the effect that can be seen and those effects that must be foreseen."

Crony capitalists make good use of what is seen. It is certainly true that financial institutions that might otherwise have gone under have been saved. But even this "seen" effect may not actually be a good thing. These giants of finance and insurance have now been given a market advantage over those that were prudent and suffered through the downturn with their own resources. In the meantime the fiscally alert must shiver, considering the long-term consequences of firms utterly incapable of managing their own affairs and surviving only to continue advising millions of Americans about their personal financial and retirement plans. It calls to mind the parable of the man who has been faithful in small things being given charge over great things. These institutions are manifestly reckless in great things; are they to be trusted with the small? They cannot manage their own finances; should they be trusted with yours?

The long-term consequences of bailouts and stimulus spending don't go away simply because they are unseen today or obscured in complexity. In 2009 the TARP inspector general reported that the government and the Federal Reserve had potential liabilities including the cost of the bailout, agency liabilities, and other guarantees of almost $24 trillion. Guaranteeing the solvency of the banks will prove to have been accomplished at the expense of the monetary stability of the United States, shredding the very fabric of our culture and resulting in damage that will be far more costly to the long-term prosperity of the American people than the failure of even the biggest financial institutions. And while disclosures are hard-won from the Fed, what little we have been able to find out suggests an operation so brazen that it is clear why the Fed prefers secrecy.

For while the *Washington Post* editorial cheers the billions paid back, the question is what secret financial assistance the banks may have gotten from the Fed. How exactly were the money center banks able to begin paying back the bailout cash? Banks make money by lending money, but in the months after the meltdown nobody reported a sudden surge in bank lending. That would have meant a surge in hiring, less unemployment, rising household incomes, and fewer foreclosures. Well, where did the banks get the money, then? Some pointed to the banks' cozy deal that allows them to borrow money from the Fed through the "discount window" for zero percent interest, only to turn around and loan it to the Treasury at higher rates. That would be a risk-free and profitable transaction for the banks, and enable the Treasury to fund its voracious borrowing appetite along the way. But as usual, it's not so good for the people, since first, the banks don't have to find real business borrowers who can actually use the money for productive activities—and hire people along the way as well. Second, any money the Fed lends to the banks is "magic" money, created out of thin air. And since there is no such thing as magic, the cost of this sleight of hand will eventually have to be borne by the people in inflation.

Years later, and piece by piece, more details are beginning to emerge. Because it came with caps on executive compensation, Goldman Sachs was eager to repay the TARP funds it received, according to Eric Fry, editor of the investment newsletter *The Daily Reckoning*:

> On June 17, 2009, Goldman finally got its wish, thanks to some timely, undisclosed assistance from the Federal Reserve. Goldman repaid its $10 billion TARP loan. But just six days before this announcement, Goldman sold $11 billion of MBS to the Fed. In other words, Goldman "repaid" the Treasury by secretly selling illiquid assets to the Fed.

One month later, Goldman's CEO Lloyd Blankfein beamed, "We

are grateful for the government efforts and are pleased that [the monies we repaid] can be used by the government to revitalize the economy, a priority in which we all have a common stake."

As it turns out, the government continued to "revitalize" that small sliver of the economy known as Goldman Sachs. During the three months following Goldman's re-payment of its $10 billion TARP loan, the Fed purchased $27 billion of MBS from Goldman. In all, the Fed would purchase more than $100 billion of MBS from Goldman during the 12 months that followed Goldman's TARP re-payment.

In a onetime partial audit that the Federal Reserve resisted mightily, the Government Accounting Office found that from December 1, 2007, through July 21, 2010, the Federal Reserve provided more than $16 trillion—a sum equal to America's entire visible national debt—in secret loans to some of the world's most politically powerful banks and companies. Among the major recipients of the windfall were Citigroup, Morgan Stanley, Merrill Lynch, Bank of America, Bear Stearns, and Goldman Sachs. But the beneficiaries weren't just American financial institutions. The Fed was acting as central banker to the world. In fact at one point, in October 2008, seventy percent of Fed loans were to foreign banks. Foreign recipients of the windfall included powerful European banks: Barclays, Royal Bank of Scotland, Deutsche Bank, UBS, Credit Suisse, and others. Among the disclosures the Fed was forced to make is that it extended seventy-three separate loans for an aggregate $35 billion to Arab Bank Corp., owned in substantial part by the Central Bank of Libya.

Sixteen trillion dollars is big money, but the odor of cronyism is hard to miss even in the lesser costs of administration of those secret loans, a mere $660 million in fees paid to banks, mostly awarded without bids, and even to banks that were themselves Fed loan recipients.

But there is still more. The Federal Reserve's secret activities went on even in the case of clear conflicts among those with formal and influential authority within the Fed who stood to benefit from its loans. A statement by Vermont senator Bernie Sanders cited two such cases:

For example, the CEO of JP Morgan Chase served on the New York Fed's board of directors at the same time that his bank received more than $390 billion in financial assistance from the Fed. Moreover, JP

Morgan Chase served as one of the clearing banks for the Fed's emergency lending programs.

In another disturbing finding, the GAO said that on Sept. 19, 2008, William Dudley, who is now the New York Fed president, was granted a waiver to let him keep investments in AIG and General Electric at the same time AIG and GE were given bailout funds. One reason the Fed did not make Dudley sell his holdings, according to the audit, was that it might have created the appearance of a conflict of interest.

With the limited disclosures the Fed has been forced to make, we are getting a peek at what has been going on behind the curtain of the Great and Powerful Oz. It looks like an elaborate carnival tent show, the kind created to empty the pockets of the clueless. Just how much of this has gone on we do not yet know, but the Fed's operations are fat with opportunities to transfer wealth to the money center banks, those that created the Fed to serve their interests in the first place. The discount window, bond purchasing, the primary dealer system and pricing structure, currency and gold swaps and repurchase agreements, Open Market Committee operations with foreign banks—all of these dark corners of the Fed and its friends are hidden from public view. That is why the Federal Reserve must be subjected to the full disinfecting sunlight of public disclosure and undergo the thorough and complete audit it has so long resisted.

Chicken Little Called and Wants Your Money

Just as the growth of the state is driven by fear, crony capitalists often preach that the sky will fall if they aren't given title to other people's money. But the truth is, the sky may fall anyway; they just want to be sure it doesn't fall on them. The effectiveness of the technique can be measured in the dollars that change hands. But for the Fed's intervention, we are told, and trillions of dollars thrown around, the entire economy would collapse! What a poor weakling the free economy must be! Capable of producing all this wealth, and yet utterly inferior to the skill of the state in sorting it all out. And what does this say about the investment banker's art? One can only conclude that the billing rates for the services of the elite firms should collapse now and for all time as we are forced to the realization that, while they have dazzled us with their fancy financial footwork, they are incapable of sorting the financial wheat from the chaff in the aftermath of the meltdown. We are told that banks with whole floors of risk managers, valuation experts, financial modelers, analysts of every kind, and deal makers in every industry, could never have picked through the rubble of firms like Bear Stearns, Lehman Brothers, and any other troubled portfolio, sort the worthwhile from the worthless assets, pay a reasonable amount for what promised profitability, and bid adieu to the rest. But what they could *not* do collectively in a free marketplace, Bernanke, Paulson, and Geithner *could* do sitting around a table with Kashkari while he did simple arithmetic on his BlackBerry.

In the face of the claim that the sky would fall if the national credit card wasn't handed over, one can only offer up the objection that the economic wizards who made that claim hadn't ever gotten much of anything right. Geithner threatened that the sky would fall if Bear Stearns wasn't bailed out. It was bailed out and the sky fell anyway. Bernanke, as chairman of the President's Council of Economic Advisers, told Congress in October 2005 that he wasn't concerned about a housing bubble. By March 2007, a year and a half later, Bernanke was Fed chairman and the mortgage meltdown was well under way. Bernanke testified then that the subprime market was "contained." It wasn't. Greenspan missed it, too, saying later that he "didn't get it." One Fed economist may have been trying to call Greenspan's attention to the market bubbling over in late 2005. At an Open Market Committee meeting he pointed out that there was a new television series on the Discovery Channel called *Flip That House*. Everybody had a good laugh. But if the anecdotal evidence didn't get the chairman's attention, it's hard to explain how he could have missed the numbers: mortgage debt had grown from $1.8 trillion to $8 trillion on his watch.

After the bailout events, what the Politico.com piece called "the apocalypse avoided," the usual suspects went to work finalizing the crony capitalist case. In a 2010 paper Alan Blinder, a former Fed vice chairman, and Mark Zandi, the chief economist at Moody's Analytics, concluded that but for the interventionism, lower employment, and a collapse in GDP, another Great Depression would have ensued. But they both had somehow managed to miss the housing bubble as it frothed up. How good was their economic modeling when they couldn't foresee the greatest financial calamity since the Great Depression as it began boiling over?

"Everybody missed it," said Greenspan.

Not so fast. Is it not clear that, like a midnight chorus after closing time, those singing the praises of the bailouts are those who have drunk deeply from the Keynesians' well of deficit spending? That those who failed to notice the house-flipping frenzy are almost universally those who have imbibed most deeply in the statist doctrines? When the state's consensus-school economists all join in the same off-key tune, and miss something so big, it's time to take a sober second look at the school of thought itself. Statist economists and Keynesians missed the housing bubble. Econometric modeling of the sort Blinder and Zandi used—based on statist and Keynesian assumptions—missed it. Clearly those assumptions need to be checked. Because, Greenspan notwithstanding, not everyone shared the intoxication. Not everyone missed it.

Those who understand the free economy didn't miss the housing bubble. The Austrian school economists, and those who employ their insights, didn't miss it. The scholars at the Mises Institute didn't miss it. Perhaps the most visible exponent of Austrian economics, Congressman Ron Paul, didn't miss it. His 2005 speech on the floor of the House of Representatives described in advance and with an uncanny precision the way the housing bubble would unfold. And as he said later, when the bailouts passed, the problems had merely been shifted from the banks at the cost of destroying the dollar itself. "Long term, this is disastrous," said the congressman in 2008. "This is going to destroy the dollar—that's what you should be concerned about. If you destroy the dollar you're going to destroy a worldwide economy and that's what we're on the verge of doing." Uncanny precision.

But still the peddlers of crony capitalism have been able to sell their wares for a very long time. Bastiat satirized the use of state interventionism in an 1845 piece titled "The Candlemakers' Petition."

The French manufacturers of candles, tapers, lanterns, candlesticks, street lamps, and similar goods petition their chamber of deputies, seeking state intervention against ruinous competition they are suffering from a foreign rival that is flooding the domestic market with incredibly low prices. The candle makers point out that if the state will intervene on their behalf, welcome economic results will follow. As France consumes more tallow—the stuff of candles—there will be more cattle and sheep, and therefore more meat, wool, leather, and even valuable manure; as France consumes more oil, there will be an increase in the cultivation of poppies, olives, and rapeseed; and there will be thousands of new vessels engaged in whaling for oil, all to the greater glory of France. Therefore since this rival,

> which is none other than the sun, is waging war on us so mercilessly... we ask you to be so good as to pass a law requiring the closing of all windows, dormers, skylights, inside and outside shutters, curtains... in short, all openings, holes, chinks, and fissures, through which the light of the sun is wont to enter houses, to the detriment of the fair industries with which we have endowed the country...

Bastiat points out that the lawmakers cannot object that the consumer has an interest in natural light, because producers have a stake in its blockage. American consumers have an interest in keeping their own money. They have an interest in a debt-free state, since they and their children will be burdened by the debt, but bailout recipients have a stake in their windfall. And just as in Bastiat's France, so, too, in America: the state has long since admitted the principle of intervention on behalf of well-positioned cronies to the detriment of consumers.

That's just parody, some may object. Very well, how about an equally absurd real-life case of crony capitalism? About his experience touring Japan, where rice prices are many times higher than in the United States, Jim Rogers noted the influence of rich Japanese rice farmers. Japanese rationales for this real state of affairs rival Bastiat's parody:

> They will tell you that Japanese rice is protected because Japanese rice is different from other rice, that the Japanese digestive system is therefore different, and that therefore the country's plumbing system is different. If everybody started eating foreign rice, they will go on to explain, not only will the nation's health collapse, but its plumbing would collapse as well.

They aren't holding toilet flushing hostage (Congress, which took on legislating toilet specifications in 1992, has already contributed to that obstruction), but American sugar cronies, much like the rice cronies of Japan, have succeeded in costing the American consumer as much as $4 billion a year,

forcing them to pay almost twice the world sugar price to protect a few ineffi-
cient sugar beet and cane growers and some agribusiness operators. Typical of
state economic interference, things really get byzantine because the government mandate of artificially high sugar prices has hurt American sugar refiners, who can't export refined sugar if they are paying twice the world market
price for raw sugar. Similarly, American manufacturers of products containing
sugar are priced out of world markets by their uncompetitive high prices. So
the United States Department of Agriculture's Foreign Agricultural Service
had to create sugar reexport programs, including the Refined Sugar Re-Export
Program, which allows a refiner to export domestically produced refined sugar
and later import world raw sugar under license, and the Sugar Containing
Products Re-Export Program so that manufacturers can buy world-priced
sugar for use in products that will be exported to the world market. Thus the
bureaucracy flourishes, and it's all just to make sure that the American consumer pays artificially high prices. Which creates a sweet deal for a handful of
cronies.

At the same time the resulting artificially high sugar prices drive demand
for substitutes like high-fructose corn syrup, which adds to the demand for
corn. Meanwhile, federal ethanol mandates and programs plump with billions
in subsidies and tax breaks drive that demand higher still. Heading into 2011,
President Obama signed a bill extending a forty-five cents per gallon tax credit
and a fifty-four cents tariff for ethanol for another year. American agribusiness
cronies' victories include ethanol mandates that now account for as much as
forty percent of U.S. demand for corn. In a free economy, high prices will tend
to moderate demand, but these government mandates are fixed and so have an
inordinate impact on corn production. As more arable land is converted from
other crops to corn and feed costs rise, food prices spike. This contributes to
world food shortages and riots from Algeria and Bangladesh to China, Haiti,
and India to Senegal and Tunisia—all thanks to distorted agriculture policies
that are driven by politicians and plutocrats instead of by economic reality. In
behavior that is termed clinical when exhibited by an individual, the left hand
of the state creates countless programs to provide food to people of limited
means, even as the right hand, driven by crony capitalism, pushes food prices
beyond their reach.

The game of crony capitalism stops at nothing. If it takes defense contractors located in almost every congressional district in the land to ensure con-

gressional support and approval of subsidized weapons sales to foreign despots who will use them to start regional conflagrations or shoot their own citizens, then let the sales begin, even if it makes enemies around the world for unsuspecting Americans.

Plan Colombia, the $1.3 billion Clinton-era bonanza, ignited a heated battle for more than $300 million in helicopters to be provided to the Colombian police and military. Would the windfall go to United Technologies for Blackhawks or Bell Helicopter Textron for Hueys? Democratic senators Chris Dodd and Joe Lieberman, both representing United Technologies' home state of Connecticut, received enormous contributions from that company. Meanwhile, Republican House members from Texas, home of Bell Helicopter Textron, were generously supported by Textron, and fought vigorously for Hueys. Eventually the purchases were divided and the plan easily passed with support from both camps: United Technologies got $208 million and Textron got $120 million.

Just as one should ask if the Bush bailout was about rescuing the housing market, as advertised, or stovepiping cash to influential banks, and whether the Mexican bailout was about saving Mexico or channeling money to wealthy bond investors who had made a bad bet, it should also be asked if Plan Colombia was about Colombia or about funneling money to defense contractors. These are questions that can be answered quite simply by answering a question: who got the money? Those who got the money were those who were intended to get the money. When Plan Colombia was first in discussion, Colombian president Andrés Pastrana told President Clinton that he was seeking U.S. help for human development. "I can't help you with that," Clinton told him. "What I can get for you out of Congress is weapons and military supplies."

All Cronies Great and Small

It's not just foreign aid to subsidize merchants of death, fat deals for agribusiness, or bailouts for billionaires. Crony capitalism has taken root in every state and in counties and towns across the land. Here are some typical examples from just one major metropolitan area, Phoenix, Arizona, including deals for retailers, automobile dealers, developers, and sports teams.

In rapid succession two Phoenix-area communities forfeited $100 million in tax revenue to secure two mega–sporting goods stores. Although the development partners had assets of more than $4.5 billion, the city of Mesa agreed to provide $84 million in tax breaks for a development project featuring a Bass Pro Shop. One city councilman said it would take sixty-eight years for the store to generate the millions in tax revenue equal to the taxpayers' costs to bring it to town. Across the metropolitan area, Glendale gave Cabela's sporting goods $16.7 million to open a store.

The pitch to city officials for these tax abatement favors—one that Cabela's has made in towns across the country—is that the stores will bring millions of visitors. If true, there would be additional demand for city infrastructure and services, costs not borne by the new centerpiece retailers but by existing businesses. Meanwhile the Phoenix market was already spending $1 billion a year on sporting goods, so taxpaying retailers, generally family-owned and regional businesses, faced the prospect of having their customer base cannibalized by competitors subsidized with sweetheart tax deals.

In 2004 President Bush and Vice President Cheney campaigned at Cabela's locations. Apparently neither found time in their talks to comment on the corporate socialism of their host.

Wal-Mart, Target, and other chains help themselves to special tax treatment in the same way.

Columnist George Will has called the Phoenix metro city of Glendale "less a community with professional sports facilities than a sports enterprise with a community held hostage." Despite the fact that the National Hockey League's Coyotes had never made a profit since moving to Phoenix in 1996, when the team went looking for a new arena, the adjacent city of Glendale decided to step up to the puck. Although wiser voices warned against it, the city spent $180 million on an arena. The team moved into its new taxpayer-funded facility and after a few years—and despite hockey legend Wayne Gretzky as head coach— the Coyotes declared bankruptcy. This spelled trouble for Glendale, which was dependent on the team as a tenant to pay its arena debt.

Things went from bad to worse for Glendale, which then guaranteed the team's funding in 2010–11, costing another $25 million. That was followed by another $25 million guarantee for the 2011–12 season. Digging itself in deeper, it offered to borrow $100 million in the bond market to give to a potential buyer for the team, as well as offering to pay the team another $97 million to operate the arena. The city, with a 2010 population under 227,000, was willing to put itself on the hook for $362 million or more for a team *Forbes.com* rates as only worth $134 million. All because Glendale officials wanted taxpayers to give millionaire owners a place to play.

Scottsdale, one of the wealthiest communities in Arizona, was hit with a crony capitalist attack by some of its car dealers. This was an area dealership group that recently had $1.25 billion in annual sales. The Chevrolet dealer in the group of cronies was owned by the ninth-largest dealership corporation in the country, with annual sales of $2.4 billion. The Infinity dealership involved ranked fourth nationally with annual sales of $5.6 billion. Four Scottsdale dealerships in the group were owned by the nation's second-largest dealer corporation, with annual sales of $8.6 billion. Also among those set to siphon off a little something from the people was the largest dealer in the nation, with $19.3 billion in sales. The Scottsdale City Council agreed that struggling single mothers and working-class fathers of the town should pay taxes to fund a $1.5 million advertising campaign for this group of automotive plutocrats.

The city of Phoenix offered a $97.4 million subsidy to a high-end retail development called CityNorth in one of the most affluent areas in the valley. The deal gave the developers half of the sales tax collected at the $1.8 billion project, money that was ostensibly for the construction of a parking garage. As if, without the hand out, there would be no parking? Of course, it's absurd to think that the developer of a prime retail facility would expect to attract the upscale tenants it needed if those customers did not have places to park. On behalf of six small businesses the Goldwater Institute, a public policy organization, challenged the wealth transfer, calling the parking garage a "smokescreen." The Arizona Supreme Court agreed. Applying its ruling prospectively, it let the CityNorth deal stand, although Goldwater Institute litigation director Clint Bolick said, "That development has proved to be such a disaster that it's doubtful taxpayer money will ever change hands. CityNorth will stand as a monument to government folly."

Arizona's taxpayers and its visitors shouldered a $1.8 billion tax burden centered around the construction of a new stadium for the NFL Arizona Cardinals. Team owners fought a protracted battle to have a new stadium constructed in the flight path of Phoenix Sky Harbor airport, despite the prospect that flights involving 200,000 air passengers a day might have to be diverted to make room for the stately football dome. Finally, when air traffic controllers and pilots objected, the site was moved. What was the attraction of the site near the airport? A local paper reported that development rights adjacent to the location were controlled by the team owners and that there was a quiet plan to favor them with additional millions of dollars in property-tax abatement. By some estimates team owners saw their personal net worth grow by more than $300 million thanks to the construction of a taxpayer-funded stadium.

It's one thing for ticket holders and other fans to pay the salaries of millionaire players. But it is something else entirely when exorbitant player salaries and incredible owner net worth is made possible because the taxpayers are forced to pay the cost of their places of work.

By now the real essence of crony capitalism should be apparent. It is a system designed to privatize profits and socialize losses. When the banking cartel, agribusiness consortium, or sports oligarch makes a profit, there is no need to peer into your mailbox to find a dividend check. When there is a loss (or sometimes a new capital expense to be encountered), expect to pay for it. How does rampant cronyism large and small affect our prosperity? People struggling to get by, to provide for themselves and their families, to save and prepare for the future are stripped of wealth throughout their lives subsidizing the crony classes. The American living standard has gone down at the same time the income disparity between rich and poor continues to grow. In the year of our bicentennial, 1976, the richest one percent of Americans took home nine percent of total income; now it's up to twenty-four percent. The richest one percent now control forty percent of the wealth in the country. In 1980, the year Ronald Reagan was elected, the CEOs of America's largest companies had earnings forty-two times that of the average worker; by 2010 it was 343 times as much.

The favoritism shown the politically connected quashes innovation, initiative, and industry. This is dramatically portrayed in Ayn Rand's classic novel *Atlas Shrugged*, and explains the book's renewed popularity. It contrasts the innovative and productive character Hank Reardon, who develops a steel substitute that is both stronger and less expensive to produce, with the steel executive Orren Boyle, a "looter" whose success is dependent on influence peddling and garnering special government measures to protect him from having to compete. The book is art imitating our economic plight. We have failed investment houses, failed insurance companies, failed banks, and failed automobile manufacturers for whose failures people who have managed their businesses and personal affairs prudently are forced to pay. But take it as a rule of economics: what you subsidize you get more of. What you penalize you get less of. You can see where this is going. Crony capitalism subsidizes failure and penalizes success. More failure, less success. It is a simple formula that outlines America's prospects.

There are more bitter consequences of tolerating crony capitalism in our civic life than just a declining standard of living. Resentment over taxpayer-paid windfalls for plutocrats whose skill consists in manipulating politicians is fundamental to today's grassroots political disenchantment. While the parties to every exchange in a free economy benefit from it (one man's gain is another man's gain or the exchange wouldn't be made), the interventionist state and its coercive economic relationships necessarily mean that one group or class reaps benefits at the expense of another. This results in a simmering resentment which, given the right conditions, can spill over into the streets, as we have seen recently from the kleptocracies of the Middle East to the financial capitals of the industrialized world.

Conditions are especially volatile in an environment of economic decline, when the lines dividing the privileged from those who pay for those privileges become battle lines. The beginning of this chapter described the cauldron in which the state/corporate hybrid is brought to life as fascism. It is a word with ugly associations and, in the full boil of an economic crisis, a practice as destructive as the images the word evokes. It represents an existential threat to humane and open societies and can only be neutralized by a return to a free economy. Whether or not that is America's likely trajectory is examined in the next chapter.

CHAPTER SEVEN

The Enemies of Prosperity

[The founders] knew the Constitution alone could not restrain the power lusts of Certain Types and warned that we needed eternal vigilance—but they could only give us the Constitution, not the vigilance. Alas!

—Robert Anton Wilson

The Weapon of Poverty

Despite the evidence that freedom works, it must be acknowledged that a great number of our fellow citizens have rejected freedom, and therefore prosperity, either consciously or unconsciously and that they are enough in number and in influence to have the body politic accelerating on its statist course. Even as it is clear that much of the rest of the world, especially the heretofore deprived, desires prosperity and is incrementally embracing freedom in order to get it, it should be equally clear that America as a state endeavor has charted a different course. And while a complete detailing of those who reject the merits of freedom and prosperity is worthy of its own book, it is useful to at least identify here some of the leading types, the patterns of their activities, and the pretexts they employ in the assimilation of the individual into the collective.

There are of course the minimalists in our midst who desire for themselves a greater simplicity of life and who enjoy the challenges of independence and self-sufficiency. To the extent that they are true individualists, these can be an admirable type whose choices affect only themselves. A free society is perfectly accommodating to those who observe the wisdom of the ancient Greek maxim "moderation in all things," just as it allows for the free exercise of personal choice by radical minimalists. Indeed, it is far easier for the renunciate in a prosperous culture to ratchet down his lifestyle than it is for the self-indulgent to raise his standard of living in a culture governed by the principles of poverty. To the extent that minimalists like Thoreau encourage examination of the presuppositions of mass society, they can serve as an exception to the general rule that all opponents of prosperity are also enemies of freedom. It is only those who seek to use the instrument of the state to force others to adopt their enthusiasms who are indistinguishable from any other petty tyrants.

At times the destruction of prosperity has been useful to those seeking to create dependence on the state. At other times poverty has been a punitive measure deployed against resistance to the state and state tyranny. In yet other cases it has simply been the predictable collateral damage of the command economy.

State dependency was on display during the U.S.-driven United Nations sanctions on Iraq between the first Gulf War and the 2003 invasion. It was one of the most comprehensive and cruel sanctions programs in the modern era, and while it impoverished the Iraqi people, in doing so it only increased their dependency on Saddam Hussein, who became the nation's subsistence provider. Although his power base had been seriously eroded by long and costly wars, the sanctions made the Iraqi people dependent on food rationed and distributed by the regime, strengthening Hussein's hold on the state and weakening any opposition.

Stalin's terror famine against Ukrainians in 1932–33 was the culmination of the forced collectivization of Soviet agriculture and a brutal example of the use of poverty for punitive purposes. People in Ukraine, "the breadbasket of Europe," were viewed as troublesomely independent and an impediment to the imposition of totalitarian control by Russia. Targeted for their resistance to Soviet collectivization, armed detachments were sent into the Ukrainian countryside to take whatever food could be found. Millions were sent to forced labor camps, and seven to ten million died of starvation. Still, Stalin had enough grain on hand during the famine for export to earn foreign exchange; and it was said that a train traveler through Ukraine could look out the window and see gaunt children eating grass even as Soviet butter was exported to the capitals of Europe.

In China, farming was collectivized by Mao Tse-tung during the Great Leap Forward. Typical of such grandiose state planning, it proved to be the Great Leap into the Abyss. The Chinese famine during the years 1958 to 1961 followed the earlier famine of 1956. Mao's command economy authored this suffering by starvation in innumerable ways. Food rationing was instituted in 1955, and by 1958 private farming was prohibited. The government decreed the adoption of untested and new (quack) agricultural theories. If one farmer or even a neighborhood of farmers adopts foolish theories or experiments with ultimately unsuccessful methods, the damage is limited and the failed practices are rejected by others. But the Chinese experience warns of the dangerous ambitions of state central planners everywhere. Because the dictates of command economies are universal, the institutionalized agricultural failures in China were national in scale and affected millions. Government bureaucrats lied about production levels to meet quotas demanded of them by other bureaucrats further up the food chain. What food was produced was distributed according to the mandates of long-standing and unrealistic political plans, rather than responsive to market signals that would have determined where it was most needed and valued. Even as farming was increasingly collectivized, the "people's communes" were also expected to deliver on another of Mao's enthusiasms: steel production. Backyard steel furnaces were built in urban neighborhoods and in communes across the land. Agricultural workers were requisitioned for the project. Farm machinery and agricultural implements were thrown into the fires of the mills to help meet government steel production quotas. It is hard to say whether farming or the new steel industry was the bigger failure. What can be said is that people can live without steel, but agriculture is indispensable, and so as many as forty million people perished. One government official who saw corpses pile up across the countryside disputed reports that dogs were eating the bodies. Not true, he said—the dogs had long since been eaten by the people.

In any case, whether poverty is a tool used to breed state dependency, as a punitive measure to enforce state control, or as the unavoidable consequence of tyranny, it is the dependable result of an environment deprived of the oxygen of freedom.

Your Freedom at Their Feet

The universal fetish of the enemies of freedom is the raw, naked lust for power. This is the primary motivating force of tyrants throughout time, as they and their parties seek power for its own sake. Often the ancient rulers, such as the Roman emperor Caligula, contented themselves largely with their own private debaucheries. Indeed, Mao in China, Stalin's chief of secret police Lavrenty Beria in Moscow, and Saddam Hussein's son Uday in Baghdad were all known to abduct teenage girls from the streets to rape in their private quarters. But in the modern era this criminality and appetite for power is found cloaked in ideology. The regimes of Mao, Stalin, and Saddam thought it necessary to package their nightmarish deeds in an intellectually contrived vision—a philosophy of the state. Such schemes usually resemble the organization of the anthill or the hive and promise the reordering of society and the redesign of the very nature of mankind itself—always at the cost of the utter subordination of individual freedom. The great leader of the enterprise links the success of his chosen historical vision to a desire to achieve a lasting impact and perhaps even a sense of his own immortality; thus armed, he can become increasingly fanatical in seeing his designs implemented. But autocrats and oligarchs, especially in the modern era of widespread literacy and modern communications, cannot come to power or maintain it without the help of an intellectual class of servitors to advance the cause, justify the actions, and conceal the crimes of the rulers.

We may call this modern class of freedom's opponents and state apologists "Procrusteans" after the robber of Greek mythology. Procrustes bound his victims to an iron bed. He cut off the legs of those who were too tall for the bed, while those who were too short he stretched on a rack until they conformed. Modern-day Procrusteans demand a uniformity of thought—directed by themselves, of course—and find inequality of conditions offensive. They prefer a common poverty to the inequality that always appears in the circumstances of free humans. Like Procrustes, they are robbers of the rich diversity of gifts, industry, and preferences that distinguish one human being from another. Although often cloaked in the language of fairness and equality, it is not hard to discover that envy, one of the most destructive of human emotions, is the dynamic that drives the Procrusteans. This is not the emotion of admiring or even desiring the advantages of others, a characteristic common to all of us; it is the destructive emotion of the spurned who throws acid in the face of his lover, preferring to destroy beauty if he cannot have it for himself. It is the sickness of the mother who, in the midst of a divorce with her children wrenched from her custody, chooses to kill them all rather than lose them. In its political manifestation this envy propagates poverty by means of the universal leveling employed by communists, fascists, and other statists in every corner of the earth. It is betrayed by a devotion to uniformity among the people: uniformity in education, homogeneity in purpose, sameness in outlook, work, entertainment, and leisure, lifestyle, and even in dress.

The purposes of these state levelers and grandiose world reformers have been insightfully explored in great works of literature. One of the most spellbinding accounts is found in Dostoyevsky's *The Brothers Karamazov* as Ivan tells his bother Alyosha the tale of the Grand Inquisitor. During the Spanish Inquisition, Christ returns. He walks the streets silently, healing the sick and restoring sight to the blind. Observing this, the Grand Inquisitor has his guards abduct Christ and lock him in a gloomy prison of the Holy Inquisition. Late that night, the Grand Inquisitor visits Christ in the prison and tells him, "Tomorrow I shall condemn thee and burn thee at the stake as the worst of heretics. And the very people who have today kissed thy feet, tomorrow at the faintest sign from me will rush to heap up the embers of thy fire."

The Grand Inquisitor cites the temptation of Jesus in the wilderness, but he and his kind have made a different response to those temptations and in so doing have relieved man's burden. We have corrected your work, he says. We have vanquished freedom, and by doing so have at last made men happy. People "have brought their freedom to us and laid it humbly at our feet."

> Then we shall give them the quiet humble happiness of weak creatures such as they are by nature. Oh, we shall persuade them at last not to be proud, for Thou didst lift them up and thereby taught them to be proud. We shall show them that they are weak, that they are only pitiful children, but that childlike happiness is the sweetest of all. They will become timid and look to us and huddle close to us in fear, as chicks to the hen. They will marvel at us and be awe stricken before us, and will be proud at our being so powerful and clever, that we have

been able to subdue such a turbulent flock of thousands of millions. They will tremble impotently before our wrath, their minds will grow fearful. . . .

They shall submit to us gladly, he says, for we shall spare them "the great anxiety and terrible agony of making free decisions for themselves." And then they will be happy.

"I have joined the ranks of those who have corrected thy work," the Grand Inquisitor concludes, saying, "Tomorrow I shall burn thee at the stake for coming to hinder us."

Aldous Huxley's prescient novel *Brave New World* repaints in modern hues Dostoyevsky's portrait of the grandiose world reformers who have taken the freedom of mankind on themselves. John, the so-called "savage" from the Indian reservation in New Mexico, finds himself in the "civilization" of this brave new world, with its populace indoctrinated, controlled, and constantly subjected to conditioning, even as they sleep; a mechanized society without nobility or heroism of any kind; highly centralized and collectivized, with all remnants of individualism suppressed, thanks to universal dependence on a mood-stabilizing drug, soma.

In despair, and disillusioned with this world and confronted with the squalor and empty lives of its citizens, John takes matters into his own hands, proclaiming, "Don't you want to be free and men? Don't you even understand what manhood and freedom are? . . . I'll teach you. I'll make you be free whether you want to or not."

When John creates a public spectacle, throwing a hospital's supply of soma out of a window, he is arrested and as both a curiosity and a celebrity outsider is brought before the "Resident World Controller."

In John's encounter with the World Controller there is none of the brutality of heretics burned at the stake. Rather, the meeting is characterized by good-natured politeness. This is, after all, a world of social stability in which people are programmed from birth and chemically tranquilized. Politely addressing John as "Mr. Savage," the World Controller defends the civilization he has helped engineer.

The world's stable now. People are happy; they get what they want, and they never want what they can't get. They're well off; they're safe;

they're never ill; they're not afraid of death; they're blissfully ignorant of passion and old age; they're plagued with no mothers or fathers; they've got no wives, or children, or lovers to feel strongly about; they're so conditioned that they practically can't help behaving as they ought to behave. And if anything should go wrong, there's soma.

Dostoyevsky's Grand Inquisitor, Huxley's World Controller, and the intellectual class they represent approve of liberty only to the extent that it empowers them to remake the world according to their own design at the expense of everyone else's liberty. But surely these are reformers who, if they do ill, are simply deluded in their naïve worldview. They are well-meaning fellows whose children love them, who make good neighbors, and who let someone with just a few items ahead of them in a busy checkout line. Their intentions are for the greater good of all, and their Procrustean state policies, more foolish than cruel, surely don't extend to the executions and reeducation centers of the totalitarian state.

The Worst Get on Top

Nobel Prize winner Friedrich Hayek gives this dangerously naïve view the dismissal it deserves. In a chapter of *The Road to Serfdom* called "Why the Worst Get on Top," Hayek explains the totalitarian inevitability of the socialist or collectivist state. In such a state a person only has value to the extent he is a member of the collective and works for its common ends. In collectivist ethics, the supreme moral norm is "the good of the whole." The holder of any individual objectives that are at variance with the state becomes an enemy of "the greater good" and must be dealt with accordingly. Indeed, the existence of a state plan implies its implementation at whatever cost—else why have a central plan? A central plan without ruthlessness is no plan at all. It withers away. In such a state, the leadership's demand for the complete allegiance of the masses provides it with increasing power to deal as it must with every impediment to the plans of the state.

The enablers of such a state, those who serve as its brawn, cannot be drawn from those with moral convictions of their own. They must be "completely unprincipled and literally capable of everything," says Hayek. The moral ideals of Western civilization have little attraction for people who have no ideals of their own; for such people, the totalitarian state beckons. If some people's limbs must be chopped off to fit Procrustes' bed, if millions must starve to death, then so be it. As *New York Times* reporter Walter Duranty, a Stalin apologist, said in justification of the Ukraine famine," You can't make an omelet without breaking eggs," thus illustrating Hayek's observation that the able servitor of the totalitarian state must be prepared to accept "specious justification of vile deeds." It is just such amoral service to central authority that is rewarded in the totalitarian state.

In literature, as in life, we discover that absolutism can be born of many narratives: religion, race, insistence on order, an eye to plunder, overvaluation of efficiency, scientific or philosophical hubris. But it is always undergirded by the urge to power. "The only tastes which are satisfied," says Hayek, "are the taste for power as such and the pleasure of being obeyed and of being part of a well-functioning and immensely powerful machine to which everything else must give way."

In dressing the power drive in the robe of the national security police state or some secular Utopia, the academics and the intellectual classes are enlisted as the state's brains and propagandists. The ruthless depend on the Walter Durantys of the day. The Soviet regime, said Solzhenitsyn, "could stand and grow due to the enthusiastic support from an enormous number of Western intellectuals who felt a kinship and refused to see communism's crimes. And when they no longer could do so, they tried to justify them." It is to the rationale of Dostoyevsky's Grand Inquisitor and Huxley's World Controller that the state propagandists turn: that people must be systematically controlled by rulers who must take on the burden of their freedom; that the state must provide order according to scientific principles. For members of the intelligentsia, it is a self-serving narrative: the affairs of mankind must be managed; there are decisions to be made, and who better than we, equipped with training and gifts of the mind, to take on the task? While such a narrative appeals to the vanity of the intellectual classes, for the state itself the collectivist narrative is indispensable. It is at once a means of state organization and a suppression of individualism's potential challenge to the state at its earliest appearance. While smothering dangerous dissent, the state's totalist narrative also masks its essential brutality and that of its agents. Whatever the prevailing state narrative, it is for this cause that the court intellectuals are only too willing to put their cleverness on display, hideously contorting themselves to justify as noble and progressive what George Orwell called "a boot stamping on a human face—forever."

That line is from Orwell's *1984*, which strips away the thin veneer of the intelligentsia's narrative to address quite candidly the state's underlying intoxication with power. It is during his prolonged torture and "re-education" that Winston Smith, the tale's protagonist, is told the truth about the party's motivations. Desperately trying to give his tormentor an acceptable answer to the question about what drives the party's pursuit of power, Smith offers the politically correct response: You are ruling over us for our own good, he ventures; it is for the good of the majority; human beings are not fit to govern themselves.

Not so! Smith isn't dealing with an ordinary state propagandist. Because of his "thoughtcrimes," he has penetrated to the very core of the state apparatus. His interrogator, O'Brien, is an Inner Party functionary who has no need for the empty sloganeering that is ground out by the party for mass consumption:

> The party seeks power entirely for its own sake. We are not interested in the good of others; we are interested solely in power. Not wealth or luxury or long life or happiness; only power, pure power.... We know that no one ever seizes power with the intention of relinquishing it. Power is not a means, it is an end. One does not establish a dictatorship in order to safeguard a revolution; one makes the revolution in order to establish the dictatorship.

Always there is the intoxication of power, he explains. "The object of persecution is persecution. The object of torture is torture. The object of power is power."

The State Taboo

But what do old works of literature (*The Brothers Karamazov* was published in 1880, *Brave New World* in 1932, and *1984* in 1949) have to do with modern times such as ours? The answer is that, as inspired works often do, each has tapped into powerful archetypes of human experience. It is the portrayals of these motifs repeated in ever new forms that make each of these books endure, as the archetypes they depict speak to the experience of current generations. Today, for example, few are susceptible to the idea of the divine right of kings (which was itself an updated retelling of the even older myths of the immortal god rulers who once walked the earth), but the ageless archetype persists in modern form in the idea of the sovereign and infallible state.

One challenges these deep-seated archetypes at considerable risk. The emotional reaction provoked among the masses by the violation of state taboos is unmistakable. It is characterized by a religious fervor and can be accompanied by death threats, as those who challenge the mythic state and its bogus and ruinous wars—for example, former U.S. diplomat Joe Wilson and even the Dixie Chicks—or those who tell the state's sordid secrets—Julian Assange of WikiLeaks and Daniel Ellsberg—have discovered.

In releasing the Vietnam War's Pentagon Papers, Daniel Ellsberg did both, bringing to light the reasons for the war and revealing the presidential lies that had sustained it. As representative of the lies, Ellsberg, then a defense analyst, describes a return flight from Saigon in 1966 after an assessment of progress in the war, with Secretary of Defense Robert Strange McNamara. Only moments after telling Ellsberg and others aboard the flight that the situation in Vietnam was "much worse than the year before," McNamara deplaned to hold a press conference on the tarmac at Andrews Air Force Base, announcing, "We're showing great progress in every dimension of our effort."

When Ellsberg released the Pentagon Papers a few years later, revealing that the government had been systematically lying to the American people about the reasons for the war, its conduct, and its likely casualties and outcome, the act earned him the title "the most dangerous man in America" by Henry Kissinger. It also had him targeted for drugging by a covert operations team from the Nixon White House and likely singled out for assassination as well.

While the documents involved predated the Republican Nixon's presidency and served more to discredit and embarrass Democrat Lyndon Johnson for his wartime deceptions, upon the Pentagon Papers' release, Donald Rumsfeld, notorious for his role in George Bush's elective Iraq war but at the time a Nixon cabinet member, zeroed right in on the transcendent importance of the Pentagon Papers affair to the state. He shared this with Nixon aide H. R. Haldeman, who thought the observation important enough to pass directly to Nixon. Haldeman is heard on the Nixon White House tapes sharing Rumsfeld's observation with the president that for the average American, the message is "you can't trust the government; you can't believe what they say; and you can't rely on their judgment. And the implicit infallibility of presidents, which has been an accepted thing in America, is badly hurt by this . . ."

Presidential infallibility. It is in this numinous environment of the unconscious conjoining of God and state that reason falls away and violence threatens. But it is not those responsible for the calculated lies of the state who are threatened. In fact, seventeen months after the release of the Pentagon documents, Nixon won one of the largest landslides in presidential election history against an explicitly antiwar candidate. Violence threatens those who challenge the sacred state and its exalted liars. So Nixon's initial indifference to the release of the Pentagon Papers was transformed. The archetype of the ruler that possessed Nixon ("Well, when the president does it that means that it is not illegal") had been sparked. Just weeks after the secret documents were published, Nixon formed the "White House plumbers," a covert group whose first illegal operation was to break into the office of Daniel Ellsberg's psychiatrist in search of information to discredit Ellsberg. But Nixon's growing obsession proved his undoing as the "plumbers" and their activities morphed into the Watergate break-in, which led to Nixon's eventual resignation.

When the state has taken the place of God, says Carl G. Jung, "socialist dictatorships are religions, and State slavery is a form of worship." Each of our literary precedents illustrates this observation. Consider the current forms the archetypes of these three dystopias take in the world today to judge how they impact our freedom and what the consequences are for our prosperity.

The Grand Inquisitor

THE LITERARY ARCHETYPE

Despotic rule that rests primarily on the provision of bread.

The Grand Inquisitor says, "In the end they will lay their freedom at our feet, and say to us, 'Make us your slaves, but feed us.'"

THE MODERN MANIFESTATION

As a literary device, the provision of bread refers to more than just food. It is about dependence on the state for subsistence. But the examination of food programs alone reveals something of the magnitude and growth of state dependency. In 2011, one in seven Americans, 45.75 million people, were dependent on the federal food stamp program. That's up from 17 million in 2000. In some states twenty percent or more of the population are on food stamps; in May 2011, thirty-six percent of Alabama's population were living on food stamps. The federal food stamp program is just one of a veritable alphabet-soup kitchen of dozens of federal food programs operated by a handful of agencies, among them:

- CN, the USDA's Schools/Child Nutrition Commodity Program, which includes the National School Lunch Program (NSLP), Child and Adult Care Food Program (CACFP), and the Summer Food Service Program (SFSP).
- WIC, or Women, Infants, and Children, provides federal grants for supplemental foods and nutrition education for pregnant, breast-feeding, and non-breast-feeding postpartum women, and to infants and children.
- SBP, the School Breakfast Program, provides cash assistance to states to operate breakfast programs in schools and other institutions.
- FFVP is the Fresh Fruit and Vegetable Program, providing children with a variety of free fruits and vegetables.
- SMP, the Special Milk Program, reimburses schools for the milk served in schools and other institutions.
- CSFP, the Commodity Supplemental Food Program, provides commodity foods to pregnant and breast-feeding women, new mothers, children, and the elderly.
- FDPIR, the Food Distribution Program on Indian Reservations, provides food to low-income households, including the elderly living on Indian reservations and to Native American families residing in designated areas near reservations.
- NSIP, the Nutrition Services Incentive Program, formerly the Nutrition Program for the Elderly (NPE), is administered by the U.S. Department of Health and Human Services (DHHS) Administration on Aging, but receives USDA foods from the Food and Nutrition Service.
- DODFFVP, the Department of Defense Fresh Fruit and Vegetable Project, through the Defense Supply Office (DSO) provides schools with produce under contract through the Department of Agriculture.

These food subsidy programs exceeded $79 billion in FY2009 and they are growing. The food stamp program itself cost $17.1 billion in 2000. By 2009 it was up to $56 billion. The school lunch program grew from $9 billion in 2000 to $16 billion in 2009. The WIC program grew from $4 billion to $7 billion over the same period.

But there is more to the story than just the state's provision of food at the consumer level. It seeks to control production as well. There is a snarled spaghetti dinner of federal programs at the farm and agribusiness levels that contribute to the fast-growing nationalization of food production in America. This tangled complex of programs includes direct payments, countercyclical payments, revenue assurance payments and marketing loans, disaster payments, federal crop insurance programs, and the Commodity Credit Corporation (CCC). The CCC was created in 1933 to artificially increase agricultural prices. It makes annual farm subsidy payments of almost $13 billion. Taxes and tariffs raise food prices to artificial levels at the expense of the people; those needlessly high prices are then used as a rationale for the parade of programs that subsidize the purchase of "unaffordable" food. And thus are the taxpayers squeezed from both sides. It is in spirit exactly like the Grand Inquisitor's ironic admission that his rules rest on taking the bread made by the people's own hands and then giving it back to them.

Brave New World

THE LITERARY ARCHETYPE

A global, totalitarian state in which control depends on the relentless conditioning and drugging of its citizens.

The Resident World Controller says, "It would upset the whole social order if men started doing things on their own."

THE MODERN MANIFESTATION

The mindless state sloganeering in modern American life is almost as inescapable as it is in Huxley's novel: "See something, say something." "You're either with us or against us." "They hate us for our freedom." Even more powerful and insidious are the simple names that mask the true nature of various government programs: entitlements, Social Security, stimulus spending, transfer payments, fair trade, war on drugs, war on poverty, war on terror. Titles like "Department of Education" or "Department of Energy" are more effective at deflecting serious questions about what those bodies do than the bureaucracies are on any metric of educational achievement or energy provision. And really, "Department of Defense" is an odd name for an institution that used the cold war as a pretext for the deployment of American forces around the globe, spending trillions of dollars in the process, while providing absolutely no defense against the most devastating military threat conceivable: thousands of Soviet missiles pointed our way and armed with thousands of nuclear warheads.

But as with *Brave New World*'s State Conditioning Centers and College of Emotional Engineering, the real work of controlling the masses by conditioning consists of more than sloganeering and names that short-circuit serious reflection. Written before the promise of television was realized, techniques of mass control in *Brave New World* consisted of sustained audio indoctrination and whispered "sleep teaching." But the subconscious is more readily accessed by means of imagery; today this access is exploited at an ever-accelerating pace.

Nowhere is this means used more vividly than in the modern martial state. In his book *The Psychology of War*, Lawrence LeShan, a former army psychologist, distinguishes the "mythic" perception of war from its "sensory" reality. It is especially in the drive to war that the state makes good use of these mythic images and representations. Chests swell with pride and hearts are set pounding by the waving of flags and bright displays of bunting, sharp uniforms adorned with shiny medallions, and the synchronized parades of soldiers marching to the stirring music of brass bands. Fearsome armaments pass reviewing stands on which politicians stand with veterans of wars gone by and generals draped in decorations, awaiting the deafening flyover of formations of fighter jets. Playing the part of state media, television networks strive to outdo one another in the red, white, and blue of their newscasts. A flood of star-spangled graphics pours out of every screen day after day, while presidential aides scramble to make sure that his every backdrop and stage is festooned with flags, flags, and more flags. This is all designed to evoke the myth and glory of the coming war and the certainty of victory.

The sensory reality of war, of course, is something quite different. It is the screams of the injured and dying, the weeping of parents clutching a child's lifeless form, the deafening sound of explosions and showers of debris, and the sight of human limbs spread across the battlefield. It is refugees by the millions, made homeless by weapons raining down from invisible sources in the clouds, the warmth of splattered blood, and the smell of burning flesh. It is the atrocities committed on both sides. It is the seething pain of the wounded and the fear of those soon to be wounded. Because these actualities threaten to shatter mythic illusions, the state's conditioners and manipulators must take pains to control images that reflect war's sensory reality. Battlefield photographs of dead American bodies in Iraq were treated like contraband, while even the release of photos of the flag-draped coffins of the fallen was fought as vigorously as the release of photos of the blatantly sadistic behavior inflicted on prisoners at Abu Ghraib or the trophy mutilations in Afghanistan.

If a nation of people can be stampeded like cattle into unnecessary wars, if the cream of a country's youth can be marched willingly to early graves (there is a reason the Pentagon spends $500 million a year on brass bands), other less demanding forms of social conditioning including habits of conformity, obedience to authority, and fear of disobedience are far more readily achievable. The avenues of access, beginning in childhood, are broad. According to one 2010 report, children ages eight to eighteen are exposed to four hours of television viewing a day, while ninety percent of students from kindergarten through twelfth grade are educated in government schools.

But it is in describing the widespread use of drugs for social control that Huxley was most prophetic. Today the power of imagery is skillfully put to use promoting psychopharmacology: tranquil morning meadows are disturbed only by the flutter of butterflies; composed parents sharing measured laughter romp along beautiful beaches at midday with their dogs and children; attractive couples lift deep glasses of rich red wine and speak in loving tones as they share serene sunsets. It's just another halcyon day of direct-to-consumer drug advertising spending, which totaled $4.7 billion in 2008, mostly on television. Mood alteration is now the target of medication in America in a manner that can only be described as promiscuous, by an array of drugs broadly associated with emotional numbing, lack of motivation, passivity, complacency, indifference, detachment, self-harm, widespread thoughts of suicide, and actual suicides among many users of these medications. Since one study found that the typical American television viewer would see sixteen hours a year of consumer drug commercials, it should not come as a surprise to learn that usage of these drugs has escalated. In 1996 less than $1 billion was spent on consumer ads; by 2005 promotional spending had grown more than fourfold. Over the same period, 1996–2005, the number of Americans on antidepressants, the most widely prescribed class of medications, practically doubled, rising to 27 million, while almost 24 million were using antipsychotic drugs. Altogether by 2008, 164 million antidepressant prescriptions were filled in America, while a study published in the *Journal of Clinical Psychology* in 2010 reported that a quarter of people taking antidepressants had not been diagnosed with any of the conditions, such as major depression and anxiety disorders, that the drugs are nominally intended to treat.

Despite little understanding of the long-term consequences of these pharmaceuticals on human growth and consciousness, medicating with psychoactive substances is not confined to adults. In January 2011, Donald Barlett and James Steele pointed out in *Vanity Fair* that the use of antipsychotic medications on children between the ages of just two and five more than doubled between 1999 and 2007.

One study found that American children, a quarter of whom are taking prescribed medications of one sort or another—some on two or more drugs at a time—were prescribed antidepressants and stimulants like Ritalin at three times the rate of children in Europe. Even so, widespread mood-altering medication is common now to all of Western civilization; in 2009, 33 million antidepressant prescriptions were filled in Great Britain.

A moment's overview of the state's drug programs reveals something that could itself have been created by the drug-addled. The Associated Press calculates the government has spent a trillion dollars in its failed war on illegal drugs. But Barlett and Steele estimate the number of American deaths from "safe" prescription drugs at 200,000 a year, a number that dwarfs the annual death rate from cocaine, heroin, and other illegal street drugs. Meanwhile, just as all state subsidies promote the overutilization of resources, it is inescapable that government programs like Medicare and Medicaid would provide for the overutilization of pharmaceuticals. This extends to the mushrooming use of psychoactive drugs, even among young children. When the Bush prescription drug subsidy, Medicare Part D, took effect in 2006, prescription drug spending suddenly jumped eight and a half percent; of the total $216.7 billion spent that year, more than a third was paid for by government: Medicare, Medicaid, the Defense Department, the Department of Veterans Affairs, and state and local programs. In fact, at the time the Bush program was enacted, it was expected that the plan would begin with 11 million participants. By April 2010, 27.6 million people were enrolled in the plan.

It is in the presence of the state that the practice of psychopharmacology spikes. Many critics, among them psychiatrist Dr. Peter Breggin, author of *Medication Madness: The Role of Psychiatric Drugs in Cases of Violence, Suicide, and Crime*, charge that the pressure to medicate children originates with government schools and social agencies that have threatened school enrollment and even parental rights, and that teachers and social workers are sometimes propagandized about the merits of psychoactive drugs in workshops put on by the professional advocates of those drugs. One multistate study found that children in foster care were prescribed antipsychotics at a rate nearly nine times that of other children on Medicaid; meanwhile the use of psychoactive drugs in the active-duty military has increased by seventy-six percent since the start of the war in Afghanistan. Since 2001 spending on psychiatric drugs in the services has more than doubled, to $280 million in 2010.

But there is much more to be feared than aggressive and promiscuous medication in the nationalization of drug policy and the state's interest in exploiting drugs. Consider:

A 2004 presidential commission called for the mandatory state mental health screening of every child in America. This forced screening would include even pre-school-aged children. Critics point out that such screening is highly subjective, can be constructed with an eye to conformance to arbitrary social norms, and threatens those who don't subscribe to political or religious orthodoxies. The New Freedom Commission on Mental Health was a George Bush initiative. The doctor portrayed by Robin Williams in the popular motion picture *Patch Adams* was among the measure's opponents. Adams even volunteered to screen Bush, saying, "He needs a lot of help. I'll see him for free."

In 2009 an article in the *British Journal of Psychiatry* began a conversation in American medical circles about the introduction of low doses of lithium, used in the treatment of bipolar disorder and other psychiatric conditions, into government drinking water supplies. Writing in the *Huffington Post*, "bioethicist" Jacob M. Appel suggested that cholesterol-lowering statins and thiamine, used to treat dementia in alcoholics, might be future candidates for addition to the public water supply. Appel insisted we should not allow abstract arguments about our "freedom" to drink unadulterated water to enter the picture, and made an astonishing claim for mass medication of the public: "One person's right to drink lithium-free water is no greater than another's right to drink lithium-enhanced water."

The nationalization of drugs and health care represents a gold mine of opportunity for profiteers who can be expected to lobby and spend extravagantly to influence federal policy.

In 2009 Secretary of Homeland Security Janet Napolitano declared a "public health emergency" over the swine flu; soon the World Health Organization jumped on the bandwagon to declare a "global pandemic," although in order to do so it had to change its own internal definition of "pandemic." President Obama's Council of Advisers on Science and Technology suggested that the swine flu could strike up to fifty percent of the population, that 1.8 million Americans could be hospitalized, and that 90,000 could die from it. The advisers called for Obama to rush through a vaccination program for 40 million people. As the hysteria mounted and the bandwagon rolled, the Centers for Disease Control in Atlanta began hosting swine flu forums around the country, and even paying people $50 to attend. It even went so far as to sell cute, pink, piggy-looking swine flu stuffed toys. As it turned out, the swine flu was actually less severe than ordinary seasonal flu and responsible for only a tiny fraction of the deaths attributed to seasonal influenzas. The World Health Organization was accused of widely overplaying the prospect of a pandemic, and charges and countercharges flew, particularly in Europe, that the threat had been overblown because of the influence of major drug manufacturers looking for a booster shot in the $20 billion global vaccine market.

In the 1976 swine flu fiasco, 46 million Americans were persuaded by the Ford administration to be vaccinated, an initiative more about politics—Ford was up for election and the first vaccines were given a month before the polls opened—than good medicine. Indeed, only one person died from swine flu that year, while 500 cases of Guillain-Barre syndrome, a paralyzing neurological disorder now known to have been associated with the vaccine, were found along with twenty-five deaths from the condition. Of course billions of dollars in lawsuits ensued. The irony in libertarian eyes is that when the state acts as dispenser-in-chief of medication, the chain of responsibility is perversely upended. Manufacturers of untested and unsafe medicines, such as the 1976 vaccines, are better positioned than Gerald Ford or Janet Napolitano to assess the risks of their products. This is something they do daily or risk their solvency. Yet they are generally relieved of that responsibility and indemnified by the government for the harms they may cause. In a pattern that has become tiresomely familiar, the major companies are guaranteed their profits, while the losses—in this case their liabilities—are shifted onto the backs of the taxpayers. Equally troubling are repeated government attempts to criminalize those unwilling to participate in state medical practices, such as mandated vaccinations. In the 2009 swine flu scare, legislation was introduced in Massachusetts not only limiting the liability of those involved in propagating wrongheaded government medicine, but also threatening heavy fines and imprisonment for those who refused to be vaccinated. Of course, according to the rationale of the state mandate, those who refuse to be vaccinated are placing only themselves at risk and represent no threat to those who choose to be immunized, since they are by definition immune. So individuals exercising self-determination but harming no one else are criminalized, while the purveyors of real risk and harmful medications proceed without risk to their profit or fear of loss. Like a contrived casus belli or the outbreak of war, the proclamation of "public health emergencies" and "global pandemics" represents the health of the state, allowing it to assume powers and command resources without question. In such cases, dissent is always dangerous. But far more dangerous is the universal medicating of a nation.

And finally there is the prospect of tactical psychopharmacology. Because autocrats in places like Beijing, Moscow, and Cairo know there is always a risk to themselves in asking the military to mow down demonstrators—for fear soldiers may think twice before opening fire or that opportunistic colonels might spot a historical moment for self-promotion—they have no doubt longed for a nonlethal means of disabling protestors in places like Tiananmen Square, Red Square, and Tahrir Square.

The use of drugs as weapons entails significant life-threatening risk to those not targeted. Sedative gases were used by Russian forces in a Moscow theater in 2002, resulting in the deaths of 39 Chechen terrorists and 129 or more hostages. The U.S. government has been experimenting with Fentanyl, the knockout drug believed used in the Moscow incident, for crowd control in both military and nonmilitary applications. There is nothing new about the state's interest in the use of so-called calmatives and other tactical psychoactives. Until the 1980s, according to the British newspaper *The Guardian*, "the US maintained stockpiles of a chemical incapacitant known as BZ or Agent Buzz. BZ is a psychoactive chemical causing stupor, confusion and hallucinations lasting for more than 24 hours." Although the subject is shrouded in secrecy, perhaps because it may violate the U.S. Chemical Weapons Convention, research envisions chemicals that work on the central nervous system that can be deployed against "agitated populations" by administration through water supplies, aerosol spray propagation, and even drug-filled rubber bullets. One research report even asked the pharmaceutical industry to reconsider as possible weapons of population control thousands of drugs shelved because of unwanted side effects in medical applications. Such unattractive side effects are of little concern in a brave new world that seeks to use all the latest techniques of drugging and conditioning to control people as if they were property.

1984

THE LITERARY ARCHETYPE

The all-powerful, one-party police state under the nominal leadership of Big Brother, driven by surveillance, spying, secret prisons, censorship, and torture and accompanied by endless warfare. Winston, the protagonist, comes upon a book, *The Theory and Practice of Oligarchical Collectivism*, written by inner-party members. This book within a book candidly describes the organizational principles of their totalitarian state:

> It systematically undermines the solidarity of the family, and it calls its leader by a name which is a direct appeal to the sentiment of family loyalty. Even the names of the four Ministries by which we are governed exhibit a sort of impudence in their deliberate reversal of the facts. The Ministry of Peace concerns itself with war, the Ministry of Truth with lies, the Ministry of Love with torture, and the Ministry of Plenty with starvation. These contradictions are not accidental, nor do they result from ordinary hypocrisy: they are deliberate exercises in "doublethink."

THE MODERN MANIFESTATION

Although highly inconvenient for champions of the national security state, it is hard to make the case that the 9/11 attacks took place because of a deficit of meaningful intelligence. Concerned that someone would be found accountable for the failure to detect and stop the attacks, the Bush administration doggedly fought the formation of a 9/11 investigating commission, arguing that it would be a distraction from the "war on terror." Why, as a corollary, a war on Iraq would not be a distraction from the pursuit of Osama bin Laden it did not explain. But as it turned out the governing classes had nothing to fear from a commission comprised of former officeholders and federal officials. And in the end the bungled 9/11 Commission report tried its best to make the calamity a case of intelligence failure. (Its cochairmen later wrote that the commission was "set up to fail," and both they and staff members maintained the Bush Pentagon and its Transportation Department had "misled" them, and they even debated making criminal referrals in the matter.)

But the intelligence was clearly adequate to the event. There was the CIA briefing that President Bush received on August 6, 2001, just thirty-six days before the attacks, entitled "Bin Ladin Determined to Strike in US." The report cited FBI information indicating "patterns of suspicious activity in this country consistent with preparations for hijackings . . ." A month earlier, in July, an FBI agent in Phoenix sent a memo to FBI headquarters warning of "a coordinated effort" by bin Laden to send students to aviation schools in the United States. There was Zacarias Moussaoui as well, arrested in mid-August in Minnesota, where he had paid cash to train in a 747 flight simulator. The FBI agent who interrogated him was convinced he was plotting to hijack an aircraft and alerted his supervisors some seventy times before the 9/11 attacks. Despite the contention of President Bush and National Security Advisor Condoleezza Rice that no one could have envisioned flying airplanes into buildings or using airplanes as missiles, the evidence is to the contrary. Precisely that prospect had been envisioned for the G8 summit held that summer in Genoa, Italy—and both Bush and Rice had to know it. Warnings that terrorists might attempt to target Bush and others at the July meeting were taken so seriously that airspace around the summit site was shut down, fighter jets were kept aloft, and antiaircraft missile batteries were installed. So extraordinary were the precautions that Bush took the unusual step of overnighting during the summit on an American aircraft carrier, the USS *Enterprise*. That account reveals the common and disturbing predilection of government figures to exercise a special vigilance over their own well-being that is not extended to their subjects. The ABM Missile Treaty of 1972 is illustrative. The United States and the Soviet Union both agreed to leave the American and Russian people defenseless against the threat of nuclear attack by the other—the aptly named MAD doctrine, or Mutually Assured Destruction—in which each side held its own people hostage against the intentions of the other. But the treaty carved out a special exception, allowing each side to defend its national capital with strategic defensive armaments, in this case ground-based missile defenses, while the rest of the country would go defenseless.

Egyptian president Hosni Mubarak was among those who provided warnings about the threats from the air that resulted in the special precautions afforded Bush in the summer of 2001. Mubarak specifically claimed that Al Qaeda suicide pilots intended to assassinate Bush at the Genoa summit. His was but one of a multitude of 2001 alerts that came from foreign governments. Serial warnings about an imminent Osama bin Laden–directed attack on the United States were issued by Italy, France, Germany, Russia, the United Kingdom, Israel, Afghanistan, and Jordan in the days leading up to 9/11, warnings that did not receive the serious attention accorded the summit warning. Something seems inverted in the affairs of state. Was the state erected and given the power to establish rules and commandeer resources with the primary purpose of preserving and perpetuating itself? Are the people to be put at risk by foreign meddling—the creation of enemies in places most of them can't find on a map—and their security jeopardized by black operations they can't even begin to suspect, all by a state entity that subordinates the security and financial well-being of the innocent to its own protection and preservation?

Faulting intelligence for the failures of 9/11 while excusing policy makers and exonerating officials in positions of responsibility supercharged the growth of the U.S. national security state. Chalmers Johnson, author of the prescient *Blowback: The Cost and Consequences of American Empire*, the 2000 book in which he tried to warn Americans of the consequences of foreign meddling ("I had become convinced by then that some secret US government operations and acts in distant lands would come back to haunt us"), later wrote of the 9/11 Commission that in providing cover for the blunders of the political classes, inadequate intelligence would take the fall. "The fix was in," wrote Johnson in *Nemesis: The Last Days of the American Republic*. "The commission was constrained to concentrate on 'intelligence failures' instead of the failure of policy makers to heed the intelligence that came their way." But even a finding of intelligence failure did not mean any heads would roll for "the worst attack on American soil in history." Indeed, more than a year after the attack the chiefs of the three prominent intelligence bodies, the CIA, the FBI, and the NSA, told a joint House–Senate panel looking into their performance that no one in any of the agencies had been fired or punished, while President Bush actually awarded CIA head George Tenet the Presidential Medal of Freedom and named National Security Adviser Condoleezza Rice secretary of state.

As is Washington's way, intelligence errors—like failures in education policies, fiscal management, and virtually every other federal activity—must be answered with bigger bureaucracies and even bigger budgets. No good crisis is allowed to go to waste. And so the U.S. intelligence budget, estimated at $30 billion at the time of 9/11, had mushroomed by fiscal year 2010 to $80 billion. The other predictable consequence of 9/11 was the curtailment of American civil liberties. Within weeks, and virtually without debate, Congress passed and the president signed the USA PATRIOT Act. The name was an acronym for "Uniting and Strengthening America by Providing Appropriate Tools Required to Intercept and Obstruct Terrorism." (Perhaps in a proper sense of accountability for the tragedy somebody should have suggested instead a USA FREEDOM Act: "Firing Responsible Executives and Elected Dolts for Obvious Malfeasance.") The 342-page PATRIOT Act provided for increased state surveillance, investigation, detention, and other police powers.

The *Washington Post* spent two years investigating the metastasizing of the national security state after 9/11. The 2010 series of articles, Top Secret America, details a government surveillance, data-mining, and intelligence-gathering undertaking of incredible proportions. The vastness of the enterprise is apparent in its infrastructure, which, the *Post* reports, includes:

- 1,271 government organizations and 1,931 private companies in 10,000 locations; 854,000 people hold top secret clearances, while 265,000 contractors are involved in top secret work.
- Twenty-four new military and intelligence agencies created at the end of 2001, including the Department of Homeland Security. Thirty-seven more such organizations were created in 2002; thirty-six more in 2003; twenty-six in 2004; thirty-one in 2005; thirty-two in 2006; and twenty or more each in 2007, 2008, and 2009. In all, the *Post* reports, the 9/11 event has driven the formation or reorganization of at least 263 organizations.
- The expansion of the CIA into two additional buildings, adding to its office space by a third; the growth of the Defense Intelligence Agency from 7,500 people in 2002 to 16,500 employees today; 35 FBI Joint Terrorism Task Forces have grown to 106.

- Thirty-three building complexes for intelligence activities in the Washington metro area built since 9/11 or under construction, altogether about 17 million square feet. Liberty Crossing, the joint headquarters of the new director of National Intelligence and the National Counterterrorism Center, is part of the building spree, a complex housing 1,700 federal employees and an additional 1,200 private contractors.
- Continued expansion outside of Washington as well, including a $1.7 billion National Security Agency data-processing center near Salt Lake City and a new 270,000-square-foot U.S. Central Command intelligence office in Tampa.
- The crown jewel of all this expansion: the new headquarters for the Department of Homeland Security, a department that didn't exist until 2002 and now has 230,000 employees. To be permanently located on the grounds of a former mental institution five miles southeast of the White House, the $3.4 billion headquarters will be the largest government complex since the Pentagon.

"Command centers, internal television networks, video walls, armored SUVs and personal security guards have become the bling of national security," says the *Post*. What are the activities that occupy all these new agencies, buildings, and bureaucracies? An incomprehensible amount of information flows through these bureaucracies. Every day the NSA collects and stores 1.7 billion phone calls, emails, and other communications. Analysts publish 50,000 intelligence reports a year, "a volume so large," the *Post* says, "that many are routinely ignored." The DHS can and does open mail coming into the U.S. from outside the country, including personal correspondence. The department won't say what criteria it uses to select mail for opening.

Government surveillance activities extend to ultra-high-tech face recognition technology; biometric data collection and database systems; camera surveillance enhanced with software designed to detect "suspicious" behavior; surreptitious access to personal cell phones for eavesdropping and tracking purposes; research into ways to harvest personal information and create databases from social networks like MySpace and Facebook; expansion of the domestic use of secret overhead imagery captured by reconnaissance satellites; and developing the domestic use of drones (unmanned aerial vehicles) for general population surveillance.

Big Brother is watching you.

The modern manifestations of these three archetypal examples from *The Brothers Karamazov, Brave New World,* and *1984* represent a full spectrum of dehumanization: the cultivation and growth of physical dependency upon the state; the suppression of independent thought and subordination of all consciousness to the state; and the fear-driven extinction of individual will, initiative, and aspiration. The state insists on the command of body, mind, and spirit.

The prosperity we seek cannot flourish when the individual is reduced to nothing more than a function of the state. Prosperity only flowers in the rich garden of freedom; it withers and dies in the aridity of totalist government and the barren soil of the police state. When humans are used as beasts of burden, creativity cannot escape fatigue and exhaustion. When minds are clouded by drugs and thought is limited by conditioning, innovation and insight are not possible. When human beings are reduced to soulless automatons by the state, genius and inspiration have no home.

Nobody can make a compelling case that mankind is no longer susceptible to state barbarity of the sort still fresh in the memories of so many of the living. Can one be so wooly-minded as to believe that today's wielders of power are unsusceptible to the same human temptations and resistant to the political expediencies that have led to the destruction of so many innocents?

In moments of crisis, especially in the case of economic disruption such as we face—high inflation, the collapse of the monetary system, the destruction of the capital markets—we are most susceptible to the command of authoritarians. The irony is that the authoritarian threat is actually heightened in advanced nations like the United States. Technological development has created police-state resources that would make Hitler, Stalin, and Mao envious and that even visionaries like Dostoyevsky, Huxley, and Orwell could not have foreseen.

SECTION III
DEAD AHEAD

CHAPTER EIGHT

The Dollar Endgame

The whole grim apparatus of oppression and coercion—police-men, customs guards, penal courts, prisons, in some countries even executioners—had to be put into action in order to de-stroy the gold standard. Solemn pledges were broken, retroac-tive laws were promulgated, provisions of constitutions and bills of rights were openly defied.

—Ludwig von Mises

The Dance of Destruction

There they are, clasping one another, a codependent couple locked in a dance of destruction. The music changes, moving now faster, now more slowly, but the dance has been danced before and the outcome is certain. As they collapse together in a heap, it will be said of each—the failing U.S. monetary system and the global American military empire—that each brought the other down.

Clearly the monetary system was corrupted in the service of war. It was on the heels of the most costly years of the Vietnam War that Nixon ended the dol-lar's last link to the gold standard, while the Federal Reserve's fiat dollar has enabled the empire ever since. By the same token, the expansion of the empire has hastened the exhaustion of the monetary system. And what the people should have done for themselves by ending the empire will now be done for them by the discredited money of an economy built on military Keynesianism.

Like the dance of Shiva that first destroys the weary world before it can be created anew, the renewal of Americans' prosperity awaits the last steps of these two enablers of today's economic crisis. We'll examine the empire and prosperity in the next chapter, but first a look at the destruction of the dollar.

For generations, the governing classes have taught the American people that sound monetary policy consists of money unbacked by anything and redeemable in nothing but itself; money that is created out of thin air by the banking cartel.

Do you suppose that if you had twice as much money you could buy twice as many things and live twice as well? That you could dress twice as nicely, dine in places twice as pricey, drive a car that is twice as expensive, and even save twice as much? What if everybody had twice as much money? Could everybody buy twice as many things and live twice as well? The act of providing everybody twice as much money—increasing the money supply or creating another credit bubble—doesn't somehow double the amount of available goods and services. Instead, prices for the things that would enable you to live better would effectively double. The increase in the supply of money and credit is inflation. It is what the Federal Reserve System does.

But if it is a zero-sum game—if doubling or tripling the money supply causes prices to double or triple—why does the Fed do it? Why bother?

What if the amount of money everybody has doesn't increase uniformly, doubling or tripling for everybody at the same rate, increasing prices for everybody at roughly the same time? What if a dramatic increase in the money supply winds up first in the hands of a favored few, say the major banking institutions or Wall Street powerhouses, so that they suddenly have much more money or credit from the Fed available to them? Wouldn't they be able to spend it before the general price level throughout the entire economy caught up to the new money creation? Wouldn't they be able to invest in financial assets before the increase in money and credit was widely dispersed and reflected in higher asset prices? For the rest of the people there may be pay raises and even cost of living increases linked to woefully understated price indexes. But those hikes only take place *after* prices have already risen to new highs. For the favored few, it's not a zero-sum game at all. Able to buy more things or financial assets than before, they do so at the original lower prices. They are better off indeed.

But as we know, wealth consists of real things: goods like food and clothing, houses and cars, books and buildings, factories and farms and ranches, art and digital devices, skis, tools, and toys, and the raw material and factors of production necessary to make the things people seek. So if the amount of real things is little changed, yet a favored few get a windfall of more goods and services, thanks to the increased money supply, somebody must get less.

Who?

The Federal Reserve activity of creating money out of thin air is carried out at the expense of people who save money. Anybody who holds U.S. dollars gets less. That includes bank depositors, children with piggy banks, bond buyers, fixed-income investors, retirees with pension plans, widows with savings, and even people who just carry a few bucks around in their pockets. A penny saved is a penny wasted, as all the virtues of thrift and capital formation that have made our prosperity possible are subverted for the enrichment of a favored class. No new wealth or, for that matter, real money is created by this scheme. Instead the value of money already in existence is diluted to the extent the money supply is increased. The favored few are thus enriched to the extent that everyone else is made worse off.

Historically, monetary systems have evolved out of the trading practices of people. Primitive and cumbersome barter gave way to the natural development of money of universal appeal, like gold and silver, which provided for more efficient trading and enhanced the division of labor and, along with it, our prosperity. I've described this more fully in *The Dollar Meltdown*, but a key characteristic of money that develops in a free economy, commodity money like gold and silver—or even barrels of oil or bushels of wheat—is that it cannot suddenly be increased by fiat or by other activity of the state. Resenting this discipline, the state is always eager to give itself a monopoly over money and sever any relationship to gold, preferring the printing of money or its creation digitally by bookkeeping entry.

Perhaps you've noticed the frenzy of Federal Reserve money creation since the mortgage meltdown. On a chart it's a classic hockey-stick graph—a chart formation that suddenly turns straight up, representing an explosive increase. The Fed's Adjusted Monetary Base suddenly tripled, from about $850 billion in 2008 to more than $2.7 trillion by the summer of 2011. If you are concerned about the higher prices you are paying for most things—groceries and gas and government, medical care and medicine, education, insurance, and clothing— now you know why. But even today's higher prices have not yet begun to reflect the explosive growth in the Fed's monopoly money.

Without fully understanding all the mechanisms of the wealth transfers discussed here, the American people were furious with what they did see of bailouts and stimulus giveaways. Determined not to let it happen again, people across the country began linking arms in activism and tea parties. In November 2010 they changed Congress. Dozens of bailout supporters from the House and the Senate were turned out of office. So you'd guess that, the people having spoken, it would have pretty much put a lid on bailouts and wealth transfers, right?

Wrong.

With timing either stunningly inept or provocatively cavalier, on the very day after the election the Federal Reserve announced a massive new money-creating, wealth-transferring operation euphemistically called Quantitative Easing II (QEII).

In an operation larger than either Bush's $700 billion bailout or Obama's $787 billion stimulus bill, the Federal Reserve Open Market Committee decided with new purchases and reinvestment to buy up to $900 billion in "longer-term" U.S. Treasury bonds. That it was a policy aimed at inflating stock prices was widely understood on Wall Street. As prominent market commentator Art Cashin of UBS Financial Services wrote, its apparent purpose was "to lift the stock market and promote a wealth effect." In his defense of the move, Ben Bernanke admitted as much, saying stock prices got a boost last time and "higher stock prices will boost consumer wealth."

It is worth noting that the total $900 billion QEII operation represented the purchase of U.S. treasuries by the Fed in an amount roughly equal to the treasuries owned by the central banks of foreign nations like Japan or China. When Japan and China buy U.S. treasuries, they do so with real money that they earned from actually making and selling real things at the expense of real materials and at the cost of real labor. But when the Fed buys U.S. treasuries, it does so with money it created out of nothing. The process is known as "debt monetization"—turning debt into money.

As the Fed adds $900 billion in treasuries to the asset side of its balance sheet, it does so by creating money that did not exist that morning. In buying those treasuries, it "pays" for them by adding to the liabilities side of its balance sheet in the same amount; it simply makes a bookkeeping entry that represents the creation of additional reserves in the banking system to the same extent. These newly created reserves show up as additional deposits that commercial banks hold with the Fed, in this case additional deposits of as much as $900 billion.

While we use the term "money printing" as a euphemism for these activities by the Fed, creating new money by digital bookkeeping entry is a process vastly more efficient than just printing cash and shoving it out helicopter doors. Because of the fractional reserve nature of the U.S. banking system, banks are empowered to lend out multiples of their reserves. When bank lending gets going in earnest, these new enlarged bank reserves created by the Fed become the basis for the expansion of money and credit many times over. I have likened this to a car at the racetrack. Revving its engines at the starting line, nothing happens—until the clutch is popped. Then it takes off in a cloud of smoke and burning rubber. Similarly, these bank reserves are a powerful engine of monetary expansion and dollar destruction that will take off in earnest with renewed commercial bank lending.

Spending Our Way to Prosperity

When you see a government make-work project where six guys are leaning on shovels and one guy is digging, you have John Maynard Keynes to thank. When the economists around Republican and Democrat presidents start muttering about "aggregate demand," grab your wallets and clutch your purses, for the ghost of Lord Keynes is afoot. They want the state to spend money it doesn't have to give to powerful interests or to key constituencies. Or in the popular variation, they wish to either artificially contrive interest rates for favored borrowers or to drive the stock market higher or to subsidize banks. In any variation, in the end, you will pay.

In these activities, from stimulus spending and government make-work projects to interest rate and monetary manipulation, the fiscal authorities (Congress and the executive branch) as well as the monetary authorities (the Federal Reserve) are applying the operational principle drawn from Keynes that was discussed earlier: that unemployment and recessions can be cured by deficit spending, creating demand in the economy; that government can prime the pump of the economy by the spending of money it doesn't have or by driving down interest rates without regard to the availability of capital.

Having mentioned Keynes, Keynesian economists, and the Keynesian devotion to deficit spending as a panacea for our economic ills, perhaps it's time to let you hear from the master in his own words. In the high unemployment conditions of 1936, Keynes published *The General Theory of Employment, Interest and Money*. Among his "better than nothing" suggestions to stimulate the economy and employment was this piece of Keynes's essential monetary madness:

> If the Treasury were to fill old bottles with banknotes, bury them at suitable depths in disused coalmines which are then filled up to the surface with town rubbish, and leave it to private enterprise on well-tried principles of laissez-faire to dig the notes up again (the right to do so being obtained, of course, by tendering for leases of the note-bearing territory), there need be no more unemployment and, with the help of the repercussions, the real income of the community, and its capital wealth also, would probably become a good deal greater than it actually is.

Keynes is suggesting that the authorities could stuff cash into empty bottles, bury them in abandoned mines, and turn the site into the town trash dump. Once word leaks out that there is money buried deep down in the dump, the rush of consequent economic activity, such as people buying shovels, food, and shelter, would end unemployment and raise incomes and prosperity. In this you see the outline of today's Keynes-inspired stimulus programs in which the government spends—even money it doesn't have—in the hopes of increasing "aggregate demand," or demand for goods and services in the economy. Much goes unsaid here. The activity of burying the bottles and digging them back out is a case of such wasted effort as to leave one speechless. It is effort that could have been employed productively, even as the money spent on leasing claim sites in the dump and buying shovels to dig through the refuse is money not available for real wealth-producing activity. Meanwhile the labor and all the other resources employed are resources that are not available for more valuable purposes. Furthermore, the cash that was buried came from somewhere to begin with, so those from whom it is taken (or who suffered the inflation if new banknotes were simply printed) are made poorer by the scheme, while the capital taken from them cannot now be productively deployed. And perhaps most galling of all is the expenditure of good money on the statists who dream up and the armies of bureaucrats who oversee such fathomless imbecility.

It is in the grip of this Keynesian notion, even as we are told we are securing our prosperity, that the nation's debts have gone stratospheric. Oblivious to the reality of fiscal reckoning, which, like earth's gravity, keeps us all grounded, the Washington team continues to offer up new imperial adventures abroad and grandiose programs at home. They've gone for escape velocity.

While it is clear that generations of this Keynesian therapy have left us debilitated, it is also clear that politicians do not think seriously about the economics involved. As economist Don Boudreaux has observed, to expect people in Washington to be involved in serious discussions of economics is like expecting people at a Star Trek convention to be involved in serious discussions of astrophysics. People like Ben Bernanke, former chairman of the Princeton economics department, appear to respond to Keynesianism as though transfixed by an intellectual shiny object, academic cut glass mounted like a diamond of wisdom. But it is not the sparkling economic gewgaw of Keynesianism that appeals to the politicians; they simply find Keynes to be a convenience. He provided an academic pretext for what they wanted to do anyway: spend money, reward supporters, generate contributions, and buy elections. In 1971 even President Nixon, knowing it would mean having to burn a lot of old speeches against deficit spending, announced himself "now a Keynesian in economics." Howard K. Smith, a prominent network news anchor at the time, observed that it was as though Mohammed had said that, all things considered, the Crusaders weren't so bad! Since then the twin Washington parties, Republicans and Democrats, have been the Tweedledums and Tweedledumbers of deficit spending.

While Keynesianism provides the fig leaf of cover for the naked wealth-transfer schemes of the Republicans and Democrats—bailouts, jobs programs, stimulus bills, money giveaways such as cash for clunkers and other so-called employment spending measures—there is another calculus at work. The giveaways depend on the recipient industries and groups—whether automakers bailed out with billions, a failing but politically well-connected solar technology company awarded a half billion dollars in taxpayer loan guarantees, or recipients of government contracts for supposed "shovel-ready" infrastructure projects—being concentrated and therefore highly visible to the media and in the political debate. Because the rewards they receive from the programs are substantial, their incentive to drive the program to enactment is great. They are willing to pay the price involved—the cost of lobbyists, campaign contributions, and advertising—to secure their windfalls. But those who pay the final bill are not concentrated; they are spread throughout the economy. Their story is not reported in the news. And while the cumulative cost of such programs is great, for an individual the expense of mounting a fight against each new program is often more than the tax burden involved. So the giveaways are often enacted without much of a battle.

Despite the self-evident wastefulness of these policy prescriptions, quack doctors extol the virtue of such economic leeching. If the productivity of the people and what remains of a free economy should still remain resilient enough to overcome this bloodletting, the quacks then proclaim the success of their therapy. If the United States is to be finally drained of its economic vitality in this fashion, it is an irony worth noting that George Washington is believed to have finally succumbed to the practice of leeching and bloodletting, expiring at the age of sixty-seven from the loss of five pints of blood.

The Dollar Bubble

The red glare of America's skyrocketing debt has not gone unnoticed by the rest of the world. By any other name—deficit accommodating, liquidity operations, TARPing, quantitative easing, debt monetization—the rest of the world is printing money, too: Japan, China, the UK, the European Union, and even Switzerland. These actions defraud the current holders of those currencies just as in the last hundred years the Federal Reserve has destroyed ninety-seven percent of the dollar's purchasing power at the expense of the American people and other dollar holders. But because the U.S. dollar is the reserve currency of the world, when the dollar is debauched in this way, it has special consequences.

Americans have had a pretty good, if undeserved, deal since the end of World War II. First the dollar exchange standard buttressed the value of the U.S. dollar as other nations began to hold their reserves in dollars and issue their own currencies against them—as they once had issued their currencies as a claim check for precious metals. The idea was that they could tie their currencies to the dollar and hold these dollars without fear because the dollar would forever be exchangeable for gold held in the depositories of the United States.

It couldn't last, and it didn't. Republicans and Democrats were no more to be trusted with your money then than they are now. After all, back then as in our time, they had big welfare and warfare ambitions. There was the Great Society and the Vietnam War, too. Because they had the Federal Reserve to print money for them, they were off to the races. As if writing bad checks, the state began issuing more dollars than it could possibly redeem. The rest of the world saw the money printing under the dollar/gold exchange standard and raced for the exits. On just one day in March 1968 dollar holders lined up to cash in their paper money and took 400 tons of gold off America's hands. By 1970 the U.S. had only enough gold to cover twenty-two percent of the dollars held by foreign central banks. Like a run on the bank, the demand to exchange dollars for gold was beyond containment, so in 1971 Nixon closed the gold window and abandoned any pretense of the dollar's redeemability in gold.

What has acted as a restraint on the issuance of more dollars since then? Nothing. As long as the rest of the world was willing to continue holding dollar reserves, demand for the dollar would bid its price higher than it would be otherwise. As long as oil producers were willing to sell their depleting commodity for a depreciating, irredeemable currency—OPEC oil, like most global trade, is priced in dollars—Americans were the beneficiaries of this added dollar demand. If the world would just continue to go along, the Federal Reserve could accommodate spendthrift U.S. politicians and create new dollars at virtually no cost.

Today the rest of the world sees the state's uncontrolled spending, its endless borrowing, and the Fed's debt monetization/money printing operations like QEII for what they are. While foreign states don't mind victimizing their own people with inflation, they don't want to be victimized by ours, so they are looking for the exit. The dollar reserve standard is coming to an end.

The replacement of the dollar as the principal international currency is on the lips of central bankers and heads of state around the world, from China and Russia to the other BRIC nations Brazil and India. In the summer of 2011 the antidollar rhetoric heated up. Russian prime minister Vladimir Putin said the dollar role was allowing the U.S. to live "like parasites off the global economy," while the head of China's top financial rating agency said the dollar is being "gradually discarded by the world." Gulf states and other oil producers wonder why they should continue selling oil, recovered at great cost, for dollars produced at only the cost of paper and ink—or even just created digitally. Countries as diverse as Mexico, India, and Thailand are joining China and Russia in adding hundreds of tons of gold to their reserves, a vote of no confidence in the dollar.

As the dollar reserve standard continues to decay, it will make Americans poorer. As the global demand for the dollar weakens, its purchasing power will decline. Oil, electronics, automobiles, food, and consumer goods purchased from overseas will cost more. Interest rates will have to move higher to entice once captive buyers to keep funding U.S. debt. Higher interest rates will affect everything else in the domestic economy, from credit card rates to automobile and real estate loans.

The popping of the dollar bubble and falling living standards will be the fault of the Republicans and Democrats who blew up the bubble in the first place with generations of their fiscal and monetary malfeasance. Of course they will try to find someone else to blame. When the U.S. was caught in 1971 issuing the rest of the world receipts for gold it didn't have, Nixon went on TV to announce the end of dollar/gold convertibility ("temporarily" he said; that was more than forty years ago). It was all the fault of "international money speculators," claimed Nixon. They were "waging an all-out war on the American dollar." It's an old refrain. Fifteen years earlier Harold Wilson, the British Labour Party figure (and eventual prime minister), conjured up sinister and subterranean forces at work when he blamed "the gnomes of Zurich" for the woes of the British pound.

The declining U.S. credit rating is also letting air out of the dollar bubble. Bond rating agencies like Moody's and Standard & Poor's repeatedly warned of a possible downgrade of the U.S. Treasury's AAA bond rating. Many people in the markets think that by the time the rating agencies figure it out, it's too late. It was a risk that was long apparent to many. When Treasury secretary Timothy Geithner told students at Beijing University in 2009 that Chinese dollar holdings were "very safe," his assurance drew loud laughter.

When Congress voted to raise the national debt ceiling to $14.3 trillion in

February 2010, Moody's put the Treasury on a negative watch list. Geithner responded with a hasty appearance the following Sunday morning on ABC's *This Week* to insist there was no risk of the U.S. losing its AAA bond rating. "Absolutely not," he vowed. "And that will never happen to this country."

Nobody in Washington laughed. They should have. When the debt ceiling was hiked again eighteen months later, in August 2011, Standard & Poor's cut the U.S. debt rating. U.S. bonds were rated less than AAA quality for the first time in seventy years. It appears that Chinese students know more about the dollar's trajectory than Americans do.

It's Not My Debt

The pictures started appearing on billboards created by activists, on placards at Tea Party rallies, and in videos and on bumper stickers: images of infants, toddlers, and little schoolchildren, all saying "It's not my debt!" Elsewhere, in response to entitlement reform proposals, protestors carried signs reading, "Hands off my Medicare." (Signs have actually been spotted reading, "Keep the government out of my Medicare." Such confusion is widespread. A national poll in 2009 found that thirty-nine percent of voters surveyed think government should stay out of Medicare.)

These are the warning signs of intergenerational warfare. There were seventeen workers for every retiree as the baby boom generation was being born. Now, as the boomers move into retirement, there are only three workers for every retiree. Soon there will be two workers to support each retiree. They will not gladly carry that burden, especially in "the new normal"—an era of diminished prospects.

Surely one must question the morality of people who would approve paying for present consumption by burdening little children and those yet to be born with a lifetime of debt. But Americans have approved it anyway. Since LBJ's Great Society got under way in 1965, "entitlements"—legislated spending on benefits—have increased eleven times over while real GDP has increased only three times.

Either the state goes bankrupt, or it takes everything the people earn and *they* go bankrupt. Which will the people choose? Will people in large numbers willingly become destitute because an earlier generation voted itself benefits and sent the bill to them? Will they drop out, join the underground economy, become tax scofflaws, leave the country, or just not work? Or they will vote their own economic self-interest and stop the benefits?

Deficits Don't Matter

"Reagan proved deficits don't matter." So Vice President Dick Cheney famously claimed. (Reagan budget director David Stockman: "Reagan proved no such thing.") It is obvious that deficits didn't matter to the Bush administration; the deficits grew relentlessly every year for eight years. And while they didn't matter to Bush and Cheney, who have now garnered their rewards (millions in federal retirement payouts, inflation-adjusted of course, and millions more in speaking fees), for those burdened with the towering debt left behind, deficits matter very much indeed.

When Bush came into office the federal debt ceiling was less than $6 trillion; it was $11.315 trillion when he went out the door. Bush presided over seven increases in the debt ceiling in eight years, while there were more than five increases in just the first thirty-two months of Obama's presidency. The presumptive lid of at least $16.4 trillion works out to $211,000 of debt for a family of four. But that's just the visible debt and only tells a small part of the story. The real debt also includes benefits like Social Security and Medicare. The people to whom this debt is owed view it as a real obligation of the state, no less than a government bond. And why not? It represents benefits promised to them by the state and upon which they have become dependent. With some justification, they believe they are entitled to these benefits, having paid Social Security and Medicare taxes for a lifetime under the pretense of reliable future benefits. Lost on most people, or at least those trusting of state propaganda, is the fact that they have been victimized by an actuarial Ponzi scheme. While the debate about raising the ceiling on the visible debt is very public, these hidden debts of the state are much larger, estimated to be as much as $120 trillion. A family of four's share of this hidden debt is more than $1.5 million. When the state tries to pay these obligations it will look to you for the money. Where will you get your share?

Even the staggering dimension of these figures may not tell the whole story. Boston University economist Laurence Kotlikoff doesn't mince words. He says the state "is engaging in Enron accounting." Kotlikoff is a research

associate at the U.S. National Bureau of Economic Research and a former senior economist with Reagan's Council of Economic Advisers. The net present
value of the debt, says Kotlikoff, accounting for all the projected future costs
minus all the future revenue, is really $211 trillion. Covering this shortfall
would demand an additional twelve percent of GDP—forever.

"Let's get real," Kotlikoff says. "The U.S. is bankrupt."

Does it need restating that the money people have paid into Social Security
for a lifetime is gone? The state has already spent that money and in its place
left an IOU. So when the Treasury Department reports from time to time on
the condition of the trust fund, it must be understood to be the representation
of a Ponzi schemer. When it reports that Social Security won't run out of
money until 2036, it pointedly doesn't say that that calculation is made by
counting imaginary money, because the money paid in has already been spent.
To say that Social Security is a Ponzi scheme of criminal (and colossal) proportions is not rhetorical excess. To judge the fraudulent nature of the affair one
need only ask what kind of charges would an individual face who promoted
such a scheme. Suppose an insurance executive decided to withhold payments
on a policy due you at age sixty-five and not pay until you turn sixty-seven.
Suppose the executive decided you had enough money of your own already and
therefore he wasn't going to pay your benefits, or imagine he simply unilaterally reduced the amount of payments promised you in an annuity. Suppose he
were dependent on selling new policies today to pay you for claims due tomorrow. The state does these things on such a massive scale it makes Bernie Madoff
look like a mere street-corner hustler. And while a Ponzi schemer only vic-
timizes those who participate willingly, Social Security's victims are forced to
participate under threat of law.

We are at an impasse. Can America's hidden debts be met with personal and corporate tax hikes? Not long ago the president of the Dallas Federal
Reserve reported that that would require a permanent sixty-eight percent increase in income tax receipts, a move that would collapse the already stumbling economy. What about meeting entitlements with spending cuts? That
would require eliminating virtually everything else the state does, cutting dis-
cretionary spending by ninety-seven percent. Since he made those estimates,
the visible debt has increased by more than fifty percent, the hidden debt has
increased by at least $16 trillion, and real GDP has declined. In any event both
approaches—massive income tax hikes or equally large spending cuts—are

abominations to the governing classes. But just because we are at a political standstill does not mean everything comes to a stop. Only now, economic events are in the driver's seat.

There is no reasonable prospect of the federal debt ever being paid. Nor can anyone possibly believe that today's government bonds can be paid except by issuing new bonds tomorrow. The representation that Social Security is solvent until 2036 is incomplete; full disclosure of the kind private financial institutions are required to make would demand revealing that paying these obligations is dependent on the state being able to borrow more money to do so. But the state's credit rating is already falling, and its creditors are growing increasingly apprehensive. As the world dollar standard breaks down, as Treasury debt ratings deteriorate, creditors will demand higher interest rates. Suppose the cost of financing the state's visible debt of $16 trillion were to rise by just three percent, with ten-year treasuries yielding in the range of five to five and a half percent instead of recent lows of two to two and a half percent. Those rates are not extreme and should not be unexpected since they are rates seen repeatedly in the last decade. Even so, it would add almost another half trillion dollars to the annual cost of servicing the federal debt. As interest rates rise, the federal debt chart goes parabolic, and heated Washington deficit debates about cutting $2 trillion over ten years are grossly inadequate to the challenge.

U.S. fiscal and monetary authorities have no contingency whatsoever to replace foreign holders of our debt as those holders begin to show aversion to its risk. Indeed, only the printing of money by the Fed remains to cover the state's massive borrowing and deficit spending. Deficits don't matter, Dick?

To make the reality of the situation clear, in order to keep the federal debt funded the Federal Reserve has now had to surpass China and Japan as the largest holder of U.S. debt. Between July 2010 and July 2011, the Fed increased its holding of U.S. treasuries from $777 billion dollars to $1.632 trillion. That's a staggering 110 percent increase in just one year. This compares to China with $1.16 trillion in U.S. treasuries, and Japan, which holds $912 billion.

To repeat: When China, Japan, or other countries buy U.S. treasuries, they do so with real money they earned from actually making and selling real things at the expense of real materials and at the cost of real labor. But when the Fed buys U.S. treasuries, it does so with money it created out of nothing that morning.

Managing Default

If debts cannot be paid, they will not be paid. The state will repudiate some of its debts and default on others. By repudiating debt, the state disavows its obligations, refusing to pay them on the grounds that the debts are not legitimate and are not owed. One instructive precedent of such repudiation also provides an example of the Federal Reserve's role in making possible war that people might otherwise be unwilling to support if required to pay its cost directly in taxation. Almost a century ago the newly created Fed helped conceal the costs of World War I through monetary inflation that devalued the dollar, practically doubling prices throughout the economy. Under the circumstances, and to protect themselves from future monetary debasement, buyers of U.S. Treasury debt during the period insisted that the bonds be payable in gold. The last of these gold Liberty Bonds from the First World War era were called in for redemption in 1934 during Franklin Roosevelt's administration. Despite the bonds' clear language upon which the buyers had relied—"The principal and interest hereof are payable in United States gold coin of the present standard of value"—the state repudiated its promise and bondholders were swindled out of billions of dollars.

In the current debt crisis, repudiation can be expected in transfer payments and entitlement programs that cannot be adequately funded. The hollowness of terms like *trust fund, trustees, security, insurance, contributions,* and *employer contributions* will become apparent as the state disavows the representations upon which people have relied. Means testing of Social Security, the state's refusal to pay benefits to people with a certain level of net worth, is an act of debt repudiation. It is the state's disavowal of what had been its promise. It makes Social Security explicitly a welfare program, and is a concession to the truth that it was never an insurance program to begin with. Cutting benefits and delaying the age of eligibility for Social Security are other forms of debt repudiation. And finally, the people can repudiate the debts of the state as well by refusing to pay taxes.

Default is a straightforward event that spares citizens the hypocrisy that the state's debts were never owed. A default occurs when the state is unable or unwilling to meet its obligations. The legitimacy of a debt is not at issue. Through the ages inflation has been the governing classes' preferred form of defaulting on unsustainable debt. Inflation is debt default by stealth. As the state defaults on a portion of its obligations in this manner, it hopes nobody notices. Indeed, inflation is only effective as long as there are unsuspecting victims willing to hold the currency that is being debauched. Inflation cuts real benefits to all beneficiaries and welfare recipients alike, while allowing payments to be met in nominal terms. The face amount of your Social Security or pension check remains the same; it just doesn't pay for the groceries, fill the gas tank, or pay the rent any longer. Inflation robs retirees, anyone on a fixed income, savers, and bond investors alike. When the unit of accounting is unstable, everyday commerce bears abnormal risk and fair dealing is replaced by widespread exploitation. Inflation creates a war of all against all, while it destroys the element of trust in the social fabric. Because the value of the currency tomorrow cannot be relied upon today, inflation collapses people's time horizons and their willingness to provide for the future. In subverting thrift and capital accumulation, it precludes a return to prosperity.

The appeal of inflation to the governing classes as a form of debt default is twofold:

1. Historically, inflations have allowed them to scapegoat others for their own malfeasance and to retain their hold on positions of authority. A dependent, conditioned, and fearful public as described in Chapter Seven, perplexed by monetary issues and central banking, is susceptible to manipulation and blame shifting.
2. There are clear beneficiaries of inflation, especially favored financial institutions and bankers who get the money first, as described at the beginning of this chapter. A period of inflation provides a crude opportunity for the transfer of wealth to those with inside knowledge of the operation.

An alternative means of addressing the fiscal and monetary crisis, although less likely than prolonged inflation, is a candid and straightforward default. The state acknowledges that it created money that had no enduring value. It made extravagant promises it could not keep. It wasted valuable resources on countless costly follies. Now it cannot pay bills coming due. It stops paying.

Whether Americans must undergo the dislocations and suffering of a sudden abrupt default by the state or one prolonged over some years of currency destruction, it is important to remember that the default was not the cause of itself. The pain and wreckage that follow in its train were implicit in the state's unsupportable borrowing and spending to begin with. The default is a consequence of prolonged reckless behavior that should have provoked a public outcry at the time. Instead, the public is only moved to anger when the damage has been done and their outrage is too late to be of any help.

Let me be more explicit. Someone asked me as I wrote this section if I was in favor of a default. No, I am in favor of fiscal responsibility and have been outspoken about it all of my adult life. But the Republicans and Democrats chose a different path. It is their recklessness that has led to state insolvency. It is because of what they have done in the past that a default is certain now. The governing classes' addiction to debt and their willingness to pile on even more in the face of perilous circumstances was on display during the debate over raising the statutory debt ceiling in the summer of 2011. Responding to a crisis of too much debt with agreements to provide for even more debt makes the case conclusive: a default is inevitable.

The choice before us now has only to do with management of the state's default. Like withdrawal from an addiction, neither tapering off slowly nor going cold turkey is pain free. The gradual approach is an attempt to avoid confronting the reality of insolvency. This can unfold as a start-and-stop process that entails backsliding as reformers abandon their good intentions when the next election approaches. Going cold turkey is a game ender for the governing classes as they bring the temple down upon themselves. Signaling the governing classes' preference for stealth default by means of inflation, former Federal Reserve chairman Alan Greenspan appeared on NBC's *Meet the Press* in August 2011, right after the U.S. debt rating was downgraded from AAA. The probability of a U.S. default was "zero," said Greenspan, who was candid about the alternative. "The United States can pay any debt it has because we can always print money to do that." In either case, the state's bills cannot be paid honestly and Americans are in for an enormous shock.

Wealth is not wished into existence. It does not materialize in response to tears of lamentation. Nor can it be increased by taking it from one citizen to give to another. Because only production creates wealth, the only meaningful question is which course—a sudden default or a default by means of prolonged currency destruction—will allow us to liquidate the mistakes of the past as quickly as possible so that suffering is mitigated and we may return to our former state of prosperity. In *The Dollar Meltdown* I have described the social breakdown that followed default by inflation in both the French Reign of Terror and that of the Weimar Republic of more recent German history. It is sufficient here to point out that the course of a drawn-out default by means of currency destruction led to utter social chaos in both instances, which in turn gave way to autocracy, war, and death: death at the hands of Napoleon in one case and Hitler in the other.

Does a sudden, overt default have any special advantages over the long, slow grind of currency destruction and of commerce being destroyed over time? It does if the goal is a return to prosperity as quickly as possible. The recuperative power of a free economy can be quite astonishing. The German recovery after World War II provides an instructive example.

The Allies' occupation government prolonged Germany's collapsed financial state, enforcing a command economy that included many of the elements of the Nazis' wartime regime, such as state production controls, wage and price controls, and rationing. When those controls were suddenly abolished in 1948 by a daring German economic official, Ludwig Erhard, who was exceeding his authority in doing so, the results were dramatic. Consumer goods and foodstuffs that had been characterized by shortages were now plentiful. Production exploded and unemployment fell as the economy added millions of new jobs. The country was rebuilt with record economic growth in what has become known as the German *Wirtschaftswunder,* or economic miracle.

This auto-dynamic power of an economy free of the hand of the state, and its ability to right itself when capsized, can be seen in the American experience as well. Thomas Woods, the author of *Meltdown: A Free-Market Look at Why the Stock Market Collapsed, the Economy Tanked, and Government Bailouts Will Make Things Worse,* likes to ask why no one ever heard of the Depression of 1920, a downturn in the economy in which unemployment roughly tripled and industrial production fell sharply. Despite the fact that conditions at the time were even worse than they were after the first year of the Great Depression in 1930, the economy recovered quickly. Absent a frenzy of Keynesian-type or other statist countercyclical policies to prolong the malinvestments responsible for the downturn, a correction was allowed to take place and productivity was soon restored.

Can any lesson be learned from the suffering of economic dislocations ahead? If so, it is a bitter one indeed. It is to be hoped that Americans will not be so quick to be sold another bill of goods down the road. A clear accounting of their own enabling of the recklessness in the affair may also inoculate the people from that common malady of making some foreign enemy responsible for our plight. All too often, the scapegoat politicians use to deflect blame from domestic calamities of their own making provides a pretext for war.

But war is not the only threat that may be expected in the face of debt that must be liquidated and a currency in decay. These are explosive conditions that threaten more financial deceit, and even the outright confiscation of wealth and property by a ravenous and destitute state. The upending of property rights and policies that leave the country inhospitable to wealth going forward are to be avoided at all costs. This is not your father's world. If America, besides being reckless and insolvent, presents itself as hostile to property, wealth, and industry, there are now plenty of other continents, countries, and time zones that will welcome what we do not, and prosperity will pass America by.

Prosperity cannot flourish under the weight of the state's visible and hidden debt. And sound money is a prerequisite to a prosperous society. The restoration of our prosperity awaits the liquidation of the debt and the development of sound money. To describe the dollar endgame is not to say that the dollar will no longer exist as a currency. But it is an acknowledgment that its role is changing and its days of being considered a dependable unit of accounting and a store of value are numbered, just as its status as the world's reserve currency is rapidly coming to a close. It will no longer be anyone's favorite currency. As capital abandons the shaky dollar, it will flow into gold and other commodities and currencies, all of which will appreciate against the dollar. As the dollar is substantially debased as a means of defaulting on the state's debts, is there anything that people can do to protect themselves from being victimized by the process? There is.

Sound money is a necessary prerequisite for a return to prosperity. Examples abound of the role of dependable and desirable money in making the thriving, dynamic economies of history possible: Athens of Greece's golden age, the Byzantine Empire, Florence of the Renaissance, the British Empire, and a dynamic young country called the United States. All these prosperous economies were made possible by an honest precious-metals coinage.

Is there something that can be done to ensure that Americans have access to sound money as the dollar is progressively debauched by the monetary and fiscal authorities? Is there some way they can insulate themselves from the dollar endgame to ensure that commerce doesn't grind to a halt in the face of a currency breakdown—a way that allows them to begin to rebuild prosperity anew? There is.

And as usual, freedom is the answer.

Legal-Tender Laws

The monetary crisis is global. The world is awash in fiat currencies, none of them redeemable in anything other than more of the same. Freed from any restraint on their issuance of currency, all the major nations' currencies are inflating. At some point, as has happened again and again throughout time, these currencies will be rejected and the printing presses will grind to a halt. In prior calamities, from Argentina to Zimbabwe, there has been a currency to backstop the one in crisis, one that has been able to serve as a unit of financial accounting and a store of value so that commerce can continue. The U.S. dollar has served this role during the destruction of other currencies, enabling commerce to continue in those countries, even if at a less than optimal level.

In America today there is no backstop currency. Beyond our borders countries are developing dollar alternatives: diversifying central bank reserves away from the dollar, creating new bilateral and unilateral trade agreements to end-run the dollar, and acquiring gold. Why then are people not doing the same thing at breakneck speed within our borders?

Because the state forbids it. Legal-tender laws in the United States prohibit the use of anything but the state's money for all debts, public and private. These laws therefore forbid the use of more stable currencies and heighten the risk that all life-sustaining commerce except for the most primitive barter will come to a standstill in the event of a currency crisis.

Because of legal-tender laws, the courts refuse to enforce contracts denominated in gold in an evenhanded way, settling them in Federal Reserve notes, subverting the intention of the parties when the contract was executed. Why the law should prohibit contracts in gold between consenting adults is not clear.

It is nothing new for states facing a currency crisis to criminalize the use of competing forms of money. Because it recognizes the threat of a superior competitor, the state is especially opposed to the use of gold and silver coins as currency. In addition to the legal-tender laws, it subjects gold and silver to capital gains taxes. Imagine you have a gold coin with a value of $1,000.

If Fed money printing reduces the value of the paper money by half, other things being equal, the price of the goods you purchase will double, as will the price of gold. (Gold may actually move much higher, outpacing other prices as greater numbers of people seek to protect themselves from the currency she-nanigans. But to simplify the illustration, let's assume the gold price doubles.) Your gold coin is now worth $2,000, although it is exchangeable for, or will buy you, the exact same amount of goods as before. Even though its real purchasing power is unchanged, in order to use it the state would expect you to pay capital gains taxes on the increase of $1,000 in its nominal value. It is an exorbitant tax on an illusory gain, resulting in a net loss in purchasing power. It's like the old expression "the hurrieder I go, the behinder I get." (Incidentally, the U.S. government is so hostile to the threat of gold as an alternative to its money that it taxes gold at a special punitive rate.)

This taxation of money by the state and the legal-tender laws are danger-ous indeed. In the event of a dollar crisis these policies will operate like sand in the gears of commerce. The wheels of business activity will cease turning, and America will quickly be relegated to second-class commercial status. These policies must be repealed or as the dollar is devalued by inflation, com-merce will move underground and to the black market as people resist being victimized by the state's money.

It is becoming increasingly clear that gold's monetary role is reemerging. One of Canada's most prominent investment managers, Eric Sprott, says gold has already become the world's reserve currency. Former GOP presidential candidate and *Forbes* magazine publisher Steve Forbes said in 2011 that the U.S. will likely adopt a gold standard in five years. "What seems astonishing today could become conventional wisdom in a short period of time," said Forbes. In calling for a return to monetary gold, Forbes is joining what Con-gressman Ron Paul, Austrian school economists, and libertarians have been saying for years. James Grant of *Grant's Interest Rate Observer* says the gold standard is the only answer to the question, "If not the dollar, then what?"

The evidence for the reemergence of gold is apparent in its remarkable market performance in the new millennium, as it has risen from about $250 in 1999. But the evidence also comes from unexpected quarters. In 2010, Robert Zoellick, the president of the World Bank, called for the reintroduction of gold in the world monetary system and notes that "markets are using gold as an alternative monetary asset today." The University of Texas's endowment, one of the largest such funds, has added a billion dollars' worth of gold bullion to its assets and, more remarkably, has taken physical delivery of the gold. Investors can be reluctant to take delivery of such large amounts of precious metals because of transportation, insurance, storage, and security costs. But the endowment board members, among them Dallas hedge fund manager Kyle Bass, are apparently aware of the risks of shortages and the exchanges' ability to make delivery, and other counterparty risks, to say nothing of the possibility of nationalization by the state.

Meanwhile, legislators in a dozen statehouses across the country, most notably in Utah, taking note of the Constitution's long-forgotten Article 1, Section 10 (*"No State shall . . . make any Thing but gold and silver Coin a Tender in Payment of Debts"*), have begun to take steps to advance the remonetization of gold in their home states.

Repeal of the legal-tender laws does not require anybody to do something they might find objectionable. If economists from Princeton like Ben Bernanke and Paul Krugman and other Keynesians believe, as did Lord Keynes, that gold is "a barbarous relic," they are free to continue using dollars, the Special Drawing Rights of the International Monetary Fund, or any other freshly printed currency they prefer. But they might find other people unwilling to accept more fiat money. Thousands of years of experience says that given a choice, people prefer gold to pieces of printed paper.

But one must ask, before leaving the topic, why legal-tender laws should ever be necessary. If the currency is of self-evident value and not at risk, they aren't needed. People gladly do business in sound forms of money without the state's insistence. If the money is not what it purports to be, legal-tender laws victimize the people by forcing them to accept it. This begs a question we have asked before: Are the laws of the state created to protect the interests of the people or to protect the state? Was the state created to serve the people or were the people created to serve the state?

The Parable of the Three Little Pigs

America's monetary history—and perhaps its future—can be told in the tale of the three little pigs. Except that this version of the story is in reverse and it comes with a warning.

Once upon a time—and for a very long time—Americans lived in a solid gold monetary system. It was so solid it was built like a brick house. And then in 1933 the state decided it wanted all that gold for itself, and it demanded all the gold bricks from the monetary house and threatened the people with jail if they didn't turn over all the gold, brick by brick.

So the people were forced from their brick house and moved into something called the gold exchange system. This monetary system pretended to be built of gold, but it really wasn't—at least for the people who lived in it, it wasn't. It was so flimsy you could say it was built like a house of sticks. It collapsed in 1971.

When the house of sticks collapsed the people were told that they must now move into a monetary house made of straw—the dollar standard. This, they were told by the state, was even better than a house of bricks or sticks. But of course it wasn't. And now the winds of economic reckoning have begun to blow. And as the straws of today's dollar system begin to be scattered to the four winds, the people must look for a new monetary home.

Will they be guided by those responsible for their rude and flimsy dwellings, the statists and Keynesians and politicians and bureaucrats who have driven them from home to home, each one more decrepit than the one that preceded it?

Some of the people have begun suggesting a return to a sound monetary system and moving into something built like a brick house, such as the solid gold one they had before.

The tale must be accompanied by a warning. The monetary and fiscal authorities, sensing the people's unhappiness with their diminishing circumstances and their nostalgia for the permanence of the monetary brick house of gold, are likely to offer them something that purports to be tied to gold, a contrivance represented as somehow pegged to gold. Zoellick, the World Bank president, referred to the use of gold in the monetary system as "an international reference point of market expectations." But if the currency is not redeemable in real gold that you can take anywhere you go and keep anytime you wish, it is not really a gold house at all but only another monetary flimflam by the state. It may be constructed to appear like the brick house made of gold, but it will only be a house of paper, painted to look exactly like bricks of gold.

And remember that a house of paper is even more flimsy than a house of sticks or of straw.

CHAPTER NINE

Twilight of the Empire

Look back over the past, with its changing empires that rose and fell, and you can foresee the future, too.

—**Marcus Aurelius**

The Crumbling Sound

Did the Republicans and Democrats think we were to be spared the fate of empires? The answers is no, they did not think we would be spared that fate. They simply did not think about the matter at all.

It is self-destructive national behavior that has been repeated so many times that rulers and leaders who fail to learn from it must be deemed ignorant or just fools. The Roman Empire, Napoleon's France, the British Empire, the "evil empire" of the Soviet Union, and many others all extended themselves until at last they crumbled into bankruptcy. The precedent is now playing out in the American empire.

Today the United States spends almost as much on armaments as the entire rest of the world combined. Similarly, and not coincidentally, in 2010 the U.S. also issued as much debt as the governments of the rest of the world combined. Three-quarters of a century after VE Day and VJ Day, and long after our former enemies rebuilt themselves, the United States still maintains troops in Germany and Japan.

Our standing armies are maintained by borrowing from abroad. Total war spending can be hard to determine. That number is concealed by supplementary war appropriations that are not even part of the defense budget itself but hidden within the black budget operations of classified projects, obscured as civilian contractors perform military jobs to minimize the count of persons in uniform, and tucked away in the budgets of different departments like State and Energy.

The current wars have exceeded many times over the cost of World War I. The Vietnam War was the longest lasting in American history. Today's Middle East wars have now lasted longer and cost more. By some measures they now rival the cost of World War II, the most expensive and bloodiest war of all. While America bombs and rebuilds roads, bridges, and buildings in the Middle East and tosses around cash like confetti, infrastructure on the home front crumbles.

The war remains a major impediment to America's prosperity in ways seldom considered. A small example: The U.S. military is the world's single largest consumer of oil. It's not simply the massive fuel consumption of ships, aircraft, and military vehicles, either, but the substantial cost of air-conditioning the troops in Iraq and Afghanistan that runs billions of dollars a year. It is energy demand that does not retreat in the face of limited supplies or higher prices. It bids up the cost of every gallon of gasoline Americans buy and contributes to the decapitalization of the people.

It may be that some will prefer to continue hostilities in Iraq, Afghanistan, and Libya, and the usual suspects will beat the drums for wars with Iran and Pakistan. Whatever the case, few Americans realize how deeply the state is involved in foreign military activities. In 2010 the *Washington Post* reported that the U.S. had Special Operations forces deployed in seventy-five countries. But Americans must be told in the clear terms they were denied before the latest adventure in empire began that the elective wars of Bush and Obama are at the expense of their present and future prosperity.

The empire may lash out again in its twilight; it may rage against the dying of the light. But the economics of insolvency will prevail.

The Cost

The 2012 National Defense Authorization Act—the $690 billion Pentagon budget for 2012—may have seemed like quite a bit and quite enough, but it really only reveals part of the cost of the garrison state that America has become. Spread out across departments and tucked into appropriations across Washington, the spending is difficult to track. Chris Hellman, a budget analyst with the National Priorities Project, calculated total national security spending for a report called "The Real US National Securities Budget: The Figure No One Wants You to See." It begins with the appropriations for the Department of Defense, but by the time you add in nuclear weapons–related activities in the Department of Energy budget; the State Department's "Overseas Contingency Operations" related to Iraq and Afghanistan; "homeland security spending" elsewhere in the federal budget, including spending by the Department of Homeland Security, the Department of Health and Human Services, and the Department of Justice; $53 billion for the National Intelligence Program (which isn't the entire intelligence budget because there is another $27 billion already in the Pentagon budget itself); billions more in veterans' hospital, medical, and disability benefits; military aid to foreign countries, counterterrorism operations, and international peacekeeping forces; military retirement and Pentagon employee pension spending; and interest on the Pentagon's considerable share of federal borrowing, the total comes to $1.219 trillion.

Spend $1.219 trillion for a few years in a row and it quickly becomes apparent how the visible federal debt has managed to explode, from $5.7 trillion when Bush was inaugurated in 2001, to $10.6 trillion when Obama took the oath of office in 2009, to $16 trillion today.

Hellman notes that even the $1.219 trillion figure is not complete. "To take one example, how much of NASA's proposed $18.7 billion budget falls under national security spending? We know that the agency works closely with the Pentagon," he writes. "Other 'known unknowns' would include portions of the State Department budget. One assumes that at least some of its diplomatic initiatives promote our security interests."

There are diplomatic initiatives aplenty, but one can't ever be sure what, exactly, the State Department is up to. We know from WikiLeaks disclosures that Secretary of State Hillary Rodham Clinton illegally ordered State Department employees to obtain DNA samples, fingerprints, and iris scans from foreign diplomats at the UN, including those of allies, and to steal credit card and frequent-flier numbers. The same order went out to American embassies around the world. It is not known if the program was for a planned computer hacking operation, preparing for future false flag activities, or just to gather information for good old-fashioned blackmailing. Clinton also tasked the U.S. embassy in Buenos Aires with digging up dirt on Argentine president Cristina Fernández de Kirchner. "Washington analysts are interested in Argentine leadership dynamics, particularly with regards to Cristina Fernández de Kirchner and Nestor Kirchner. . . . How is Cristina Fernández de Kirchner managing her nerves and anxiety?" Clinton's cable asks. "How do Cristina Fernández de Kirchner's emotions affect her decision making and how does she calm down when distressed?" Even in the guarded language of a diplomatic cable, it smells like the sort of information gathering Clinton might have suspected of Linda Tripp. Are these activities part of just another day at the State Department? Or can such spying be added to the imposing national security total?

Even a complete accounting of national security spending in the federal budget doesn't count the price the American people have paid for a global empire. For example, the fear premium added to the price of oil during periods of heightened threat of attacks on oil-producing states, including Iraq and Iran, are not part of any budget. Prolonged war anticipation before the invasion of Iraq and saber rattling about an invasion of Iran by both the Bush and Obama administrations have added as much as $20 to $40 per barrel to global oil prices at times, amounting to a massive transfer of wealth from the American people to Mideast oil sheiks and autocrats in places like Argentina and Russia.

The tentacles of the American empire are everywhere. Sources estimate the presence of U.S. military personnel in 156 countries. In 2009, Chalmers Johnson estimated there were 800 U.S. bases "dotted across the globe in other people's countries." We pay quite handsomely for many of them, notes Johnson:

> Even as Congress and the Obama administration wrangle over the cost of bank bailouts, a new health plan, pollution controls, and other much needed domestic expenditures, no one suggests that closing some of these unpopular, expensive imperial enclaves might be a good way to save some money.

Instead, they are evidently about to become even more expensive. On June 23, we learned that Kyrgyzstan, the former Central Asian Soviet Republic which, back in February 2009, announced that it was going to kick the U.S. military out of Manas Air Base (used since 2001 as a staging area for the Afghan War), has been persuaded to let us stay. But here's the catch: In return for doing us that favor, the annual rent Washington pays for use of the base will more than triple, from $17.4 million to $60 million, with millions more to go into promised improvements in airport facilities and other financial sweeteners.

$1.219 trillion a year is a lot of money sloshing around. The New York Stock Exchange Arca Defense Stock Index was begun in 2001, right after 9/11, with a base value of 500. The index was almost 1800 by summer 2011, a 260 percent gain. The American people aren't doing so well. Your neighbor may have lost his job. Someone in the family may have lost his home. But defense contractors are doing just fine. It's just the military variation of Keynesianism.

The Boneyard

President Eisenhower long ago warned a military-industrial complex would not be denied. A breathtaking and eye-opening display of its exorbitant cold war arms spending is on display at the 309th Aerospace Maintenance and Regeneration Group adjacent to Davis-Monthan Air Force Base in Tucson. The facility stores 4,400 decommissioned military aircraft, which would make it the second-largest air force in the world. The "Boneyard" consists of hundreds of bombers, fighters, air support and transport airplanes, surveillance planes, refueling aircraft, trainers, helicopters, and more—expensive aircraft costing millions of dollars apiece, all parked in the blazing desert sun, neatly lined up wingtip to wingtip, laced together in tight geometrical arrangements to save space. It's 2,600 acres of the peoples' cold war money spent by presidents and congresses, Republican and Democrat alike. Aircraft made obsolete not long after they were put in service, only to be replaced by new, improved generations of the same, a stunning display representing tens of billions of dollars of the people's wealth spent with dozens of big-spending and hard-lobbying contractors.

Military spending as the first claimant on the wealth of the people is not just a characteristic of the cold war era. Even after the collapse of the Soviet Union, congressmen remained lined up for Pentagon pork. Secretary of Defense Dick Cheney, who had served in Congress himself, was candid about its impulses before the Senate Armed Services Committee in 1992, when he testified, "You've directed me to buy the V-22, a program I don't need. You've directed me to buy more M-1s, F-14s and F-16s. . . . Congress has directed me to spend money on all kinds of things that are not related to defense, but mostly related to politics back home in the district."

Even the economic slowdown hasn't changed the Pentagon pork barrel practice Cheney identified back then. The air force has not sought to acquire additional C-17 transport planes since 2007, the year the recession began, when it wanted twelve; Congress upped the ante, buying twenty-two that year, five more in 2008, an additional eight in 2009, and ten more in 2010.

The Bush and Obama administrations have been united in their opposition to wasting billions more on designing and building a second engine for the F-35 fighter, yet Congress has continued funding two separate manufacturers of the engines for the fleet that already has a breathtaking trillion-dollar price tag attached to it.

"In the councils of government," warned Eisenhower, "we must guard against the acquisition of unwarranted influence, whether sought or unsought, by the military-industrial complex."

What? Lies Ahead?

Truth is often said to be the first casualty of war. The deceit often begins even before the soldiers march and the bullets fly. On August 5, 1964, a *Washington Post* headline read "American Planes Hit North Vietnam After 2nd Attack on Our Destroyers; Move Taken to Halt New Aggression."

The Gulf of Tonkin incident the story described consisted of two events. On August 2, as part of a program called Operation Plan (OPLAN) 34A, U.S. Special Forces assisted South Vietnamese forces in an attack on a North Vietnamese radio facility on an island off its coast. The USS *Maddox* was maneuvering in sync with those attacks, part of an ongoing "off the books" campaign of military pressure on the North. The *Maddox* was engaged in a fight by three North Vietnamese PT boats. It took four years for Defense Secretary Robert Strange McNamara to admit to Congress that U.S. ships had been participating in South Vietnamese attacks on the North.

Under the circumstances, the August 2 incident went unnoted. It took a second event, on August 4, for President Johnson to seize the opportunity for war.

Wasting no time, with a presidential election just three months away, Johnson went on national television that same day describing to the American people "a number of hostile vessels attacking two US destroyers with torpedoes." Johnson immediately authorized air strikes on North Vietnam. Two days later, Congress passed the Gulf of Tonkin Resolution, giving Johnson the same sort of broad authority to use conventional military forces in Southeast Asia that George W. Bush would later be given for war in the Mideast.

Here's the way *Time* magazine reported the August 4 North Vietnamese attack:

> Through the darkness, from the West and South, the intruders boldly sped. There were at least six of them, Russian-designed Swatow gunboats armed with 37-mm and 28-mm guns, and P-4's. At 9:52 they opened fire on the destroyers with automatic weapons, and this time from as close as 2,000 yards. The night glowed eerily with the nightmarish glare of air dropped flares and boat's searchlights. Two of the enemy boats went down.

It's a harrowing account, and precise right down to the caliber of the guns and the moment of attack. A fine piece of journalism except that, like the tales of weapons of mass destruction that didn't exist in Iraq, it wasn't true. The second attack on the *Maddox* didn't happen.

Well before Johnson addressed the nation, long before he authorized a retaliatory air strike, the commander of the task force in the Gulf of Tonkin, Captain John Herrick, was advising that the whole event was "doubtful." He quickly cabled his doubts to his superiors: "Freak weather effects on radar," "overeager sonarmen," "No actual visual sightings," "Suggest complete evaluation before any further action taken." "Entire action leaves many doubts . . ."

James Stockdale was a prisoner of war in North Vietnam and after he was freed rose to the rank of navy admiral. But on August 4, 1964, he was a squadron commander in the Gulf of Tonkin flying overhead during the attack that didn't happen. Stockdale was ordered to keep quiet about the ghost attack, but after seven years as a POW, he thought the truth mattered enough to be told.

"[I] had the best seat in the house to watch that event, and our destroyers were just shooting at phantom targets—there were no PT boats there. . . . There was nothing there but black water and American fire power."

A year after the nonevent, President Johnson told his press secretary, Bill Moyers, "For all I know, our Navy was shooting at whales out there."

A National Security Agency report on the Gulf of Tonkin incident that was declassified in 2005 was explicit: "No attack happened that night." The report could have been released two years earlier, according to the *New York Times*, but officials were afraid it would undermine plans for Bush's invasion of Iraq.

How little it matters that Johnson was a Democrat and Bush a Republican. Those with long memories remember the deceit of each war and vow not to get taken in again. But a generation later, we're told that it's different this time.

Surely we should remember Bush the Elder telling a joint session of Congress of the threat to Saudi Arabia during the prelude to the first Gulf War. The Defense Department—under the same officials who promoted *Gulf War II: On to Baghdad*—citing top secret satellite photos, estimated there were as many as 250,000 Iraqi troops and 1,500 tanks in Kuwait poised in the south to roll into Saudi Arabia. It was hard to make the case to the American people that their family members should be sent into battle to reclaim the kingdom for Kuwaiti royalty, some of whom were using the occasion of the invasion to go disco dancing in Switzerland. But if Iraq posed a threat to Saudi oil—that was something else indeed! A reporter at a small Florida newspaper, the *St. Petersburg Times*, persuaded her bosses to spend $3,200 on satellite photos and then put satellite imagery experts to work examining the surveillance photos. No troops, no tanks. No threat. "That was the whole justification for Bush sending troops in there, and it just didn't exist," said Jean Heller, the reporter. "It was a pretty serious fib."

All the propaganda, balderdash, and deceit of George W. Bush's Iraq war is so fresh as to be painful. There were all the big stories, whoppers that came tumbling out in jumbled syntax, a breathless string of run-on sentences: weapons of mass destruction Saddam's ties to Al Qaeda Rumsfeld knows where the WMDs are around Tikrit mushroom clouds "It's a slam dunk" White House Iraq Group cakewalk "it'll pay for itself" Ahmed Chalabi intelligence and facts being fixed around the policy mobile bio weapons trailers Curveball "could launch a biological or chemical attack in 45 minutes" yellow cake from Niger "it could last six days, six weeks, I doubt six months" aluminum tubes actively pursuing nuclear weapons Geneva Conventions don't apply smoking gun "he has in fact actively reconstituted nuclear weapons" greet us as liberators Mission Accomplished.

The Obama administration is not in the same rush. Its cadence is the deliberate complete sentence. Its teleprompters roll at a measured pace. But it is propaganda, balderdash, and deceit nonetheless when Obama says that "winning in Afghanistan" is necessary to protect America; that he abolished torture; that he would have all troops out of Iraq in sixteen months; that NATO, not the U.S., is running that war; that he would close Guantánamo; that he would protect whistleblowers; that he would not abuse secrecy in the courts; that he would hold government officials, if not the telecoms, responsible for breaking the law in tapping our phones; that Gaddafi had promised to slaughter every man, woman, and child in the rebelling cities; that there was a "firefight" leading up to the death of Osama bin Laden; that his administration is on the side of the people in the Arab Spring revolts; that we can afford it.

Meet the blue boss, same as the red boss.

Isolationism

Statists are perplexed by people who wish to mind their own business. They are tagged "isolationists," and worse. In the *National Review* such people are accused of "ostrich-like behavior." For George W. Bush it was "retreating within our borders." One conservative web site wrote, "Isolationism is a hypnotic platform that has seduced the American public." One of the most amusing characterizations was in the London *Sunday Times* where an Andrew Sullivan piece was headlined, "The Isolationist Beast Stirs in America Again."

Defense Secretary Robert M. Gates told West Point cadets in February 2011 that in his opinion, "any future defense secretary who advises the president to again send a big American land army into Asia or into the Middle East or Africa should have his head examined." Was this the early stirring of the isolationist beast? Gates is actually not early at all, but ten years late in his recognition of the folly.

One of the conservative web sites described Congressman Ron Paul as an "opponent of U.S. interventions in Afghanistan, Iraq, and just about every other form of contact with the outside world." Which begs the question of this particular mind-set: why does "every other form of contact with the outside world" have to flow from the barrel of a gun?

Statists who toss the term "isolationist" about provide a textbook example of the psychology of projection. After all, their own insistence on state policies of enforced isolation is without end. It consists of a ceaseless demand to erect embargos, isolating trade sanctions, trade restrictions, "smart sanctions," trade barriers, and blockades around the world. It was in 1996, five years before 9/11, that Leslie Stahl asked Clinton administration secretary of state Madeleine Albright on *60 Minutes* about the U.S.-driven sanctions on Iraq that cost the lives of half a million children. (Osama bin Laden later called it the greatest mass slaughter of children mankind has ever known.) Stahl tried to put the scope of the carnage in perspective: "I mean that's more children than died in Hiroshima." In a quote that was given wide propaganda play in the Arabic world, Albright's reply was, "We think the price is worth it."

Then who is the isolationist beast?

While "isolationism" is a pejorative for minding our own business, "foreign policy" is a euphemism for sending the people's money to autocrats and foreign governments so they can either buy U.S. armaments or serve as a staging area for U.S. military intervention. "Foreign policy" has cost the people dearly in blood and treasure. They are recoiling at the bill.

A 2009 Pew Research survey, "America's Place in the World," headlined the finding: "Isolationist Sentiment Surges to Four-Decade High." The statement "We should not think so much in international terms but concentrate more on our own national problems and building up our strength and prosperity here at home" found agreement with seventy-six percent of respondents.

One might well ask why attitudes are only now shifting. It is for the same reason that wars are no longer declared: the cost of wars has been obscured by the Federal Reserve and its manipulation of monetary and credit conditions. For so long the people have believed that inflation and currency conditions are natural phenomena, like the change of the seasons or the alternation of rain and shine. But as people discover the linkage between the costs of the welfare/warfare state and their own distressed circumstances, the number of "isolationists" will grow.

It is the twilight of the empire.

The Everyday Isolationist

The accusation of isolationism is meant to sting. "Isolationist" is supposed to denote a hayseed, a Sleepy Hollow flat-earther, who, unlike his sophisticated betters, wants to keep everybody down on the farm. But it is so misapplied as to make the correlation ludicrous. While every reader will have different experiences, to illustrate the absurdity of the charge, I offer up the example of my own account, one day in the life of an "isolationist":

- I had a cup of coffee this morning—Sumatran coffee—grown in Indonesia, which I bought at Starbucks, an American company. Starbucks opened its first foreign market, Japan, in 1996, and now makes a lot of money from more than 6,000 foreign locations.
- With my coffee I had a blueberry muffin my wife made with fresh, plump blueberries she got at Safeway. Delicious. They came from Chile because they don't grow so well north of the equator this time of year. Of course, people in the Southern Hemisphere get fresh fruit from America when theirs is out of season.
- I caught a few minutes of the morning news—with a couple of stories from foreign correspondents—on my Samsung HD TV. It's a South Korean company, but things work both ways. A South Korean company purchased the rights to publish my last book in that country, where it just hit the bestseller lists. I'm waiting to see how it sells in China, too.
- Then I checked the stock of an American mining company with vast operations out of the country.
- My wife bought a gift certificate from the famous London department store Harrod's for my son and his wife to use when they are there on vacation in a couple of months. He first traveled overseas when he was in high school and now it seems all his vacations have some foreign destination.
- Exchanged email with an Australian documentary filmmaker who will be in town in a few weeks. I invited him to come by the house and spend some time.
- Listened in my Jeep Grand Cherokee (American) automobile to a CD of an American performer I like that I had to buy from Japan, where he is popular and his recordings are still available.

- Filled my gas tank. There's no telling where the petroleum came from. We import about half our crude oil. Most of that comes from Canada, which provides almost twice what we get from second-place Saudi Arabia, while Mexico is third. But things even out. Canadians spend a great deal of money visiting my state in the winter, and my wife, a real estate agent, has several Canadian clients.

- Earlier today my wife and I agreed we'd like to make India our next travel destination. Tonight she and I will share a bottle of red over dinner. It may be American, but among my favorites are Italian. Afterward, if I've finished writing, I will start a book I've been looking forward to reading. It's by an American author who lives in London, from a publisher in Scotland.

Some isolationist! But prevailing opinion in interventionist quarters notwithstanding, not "every other form of contact with the outside world" has to involve high-altitude bombardment.

The Enduring Empire

Imagine these startling headlines with the nation at war in the Pacific six months after December 7, 1941:

NO SIGNS OF JAPANESE INVOLVEMENT IN PEARL HARBOR ATTACK!

FAULTY INTELLIGENCE CITED!

WOLFOWITZ: "MISTAKES WERE MADE"

Or how about an equally disconcerting World War II headline from the European theater:

GERMAN ARMY NOT FOUND IN FRANCE, POLAND, ADMITS PRESIDENT

RUMSFELD: "OOPS!" POWELL SILENT

"BRING 'EM ON," SAYS DEFIANT FDR

So began an article I wrote for *The American Conservative* magazine in 2003, the first year of the Iraq war. In the absence of weapons of mass destruction and the collapse of the ever-shifting rationale for the Iraq war, if those responsible for the calamity were not to be held accountable, could at least the war be allowed to come to a quick end? Would World War II have been allowed to claim all of its 418,000 American lives if those headlines reflected reality?

But the Iraq war was not allowed to end, and Americans continued to die there long after the war's pretext had crashed. Americans still die in Afghanistan even though Osama bin Laden, the proximate cause of our presence there, no longer exists. This is the way of the American empire. Consider:

Both of my sons' grandfathers, one deceased, the other elderly, served in World War II as young men. Ever since 1945, those servicemen and even their parents shouldered the tax burden year in and year out of maintaining victorious American forces on duty in both Germany and Japan. Their children and grandchildren have been saddled with those costs their entire lives as well.

It has required a lifetime of paying to maintain U.S. troops in South Korea, too, although a demilitarized zone was established and the armistice signed in 1953. While American troop strength there is only about four percent the size of South Korea's army, it is a presence large enough to serve as a trip wire, ensuring American involvement in any future conflict.

What often goes unsaid is that the presence of the U.S. empire and its war guarantees in regional conflicts changes the posture of the states involved: the American ally may become less conciliatory in every regard and perhaps even more belligerent, while its opponent is quite apt to feel, if not besieged, at least threatened by the presence of the potential force arrayed against it. In the case of Korea, it is impossible to look at the behavior profiles of the "Dear Leaders" of North Korea and not understand that the presence of the world's "sole superpower" on their border jacks up their already considerable paranoia.

Some acknowledgment has to be made of China's interest in peace in the area. While China was an ally of the North in the Korean War, times have changed and South Korea and China are now major trading partners. China, utterly dependent on exports to drive growth, sells an amount of goods to South Korea each year equal to twice the entire GDP of North Korea.

At the same time, and whatever the threat, one has to wonder why South Korea can spend a percentage of its GDP to protect itself that is less than that which Americans, shouldering the burden of South Korea's defense, must spend on warfare.

With troops still in Germany, Japan, and Korea generations after the end of the wars, the pattern of empire is unmistakable. It is clear that it is only losing the war that has saved Americans from having to pay for decades to garrison troops in Vietnam.

On November 9, 1989, the Berlin Wall fell. Two years later, July 1, 1991, Václav Havel, the playwright who became president of Czechoslovakia, formally ended the Warsaw Pact, the Soviet Union's military alliance. With the independence of the USSR's republics on December 25, 1991, the Soviet Union collapsed. Even the most strident of American interventionists—the governing classes whose Republican and Democrat foreign policy consensus had subsidized international socialism out of America's left pocket while it subsidized global militarization out of America's right—had to admit the cold war was over. So NATO, the North Atlantic Treaty Organization, founded to counter a Soviet threat that was now lifted from Europe, and having outlived its purpose . . . expanded! As empires do, the U.S. drove the expansion of NATO right up to the doorstep of Russia, with even Ukraine and Georgia on hold for now but having been assured membership. Russia, feeling slowly encircled, is provoked. Meanwhile NATO is yet another trip wire, a guarantee that the Americans will be dragged into any future conflicts in Europe—and beyond. NATO was most recently used in 2011 for military action in Libya—which is nowhere near the North Atlantic.

For NATO, it is mission creep. For the United States, it's empire creep.

Since World War II—the last time Congress declared war as specified by the Constitution—the state has had a cold war that cost trillions and fought undeclared wars in Korea, Vietnam, Iraq, Afghanistan, and Iraq again. Without a declaration of war it has sent troops to fight in Lebanon, the Dominican Republic, Grenada, and Lebanon again; bombed Libya, invaded Panama, sent troops into Somalia and Haiti; bombed Yugoslavia, sent troops into the Philippines, and fired missiles at Libya again.

And yet for it all—perpetual war for perpetual peace—Americans are more insecure than ever. They spend $1.219 trillion on the national security state and watch uneasily as their patrimony is traded for a mess of police-state pottage.

Informed libertarians, those who see both the dollar/debt train wreck in motion and the failure of global interventionism, cannot miss the quickening pace at which the American empire is being undone. But Republicans and Democrats, chest thumpers and vote buyers alike, those who created the fiscal calamity we face today, are still in charge and capable of doing more of what they have already done: they are capable of more needless foreign interventionism without regard to its cost. Although Americans are increasingly eager to see their prosperity restored, some of the governing classes seem to want to go empire another round.

Even in its twilight, the empire may not go quietly into the night.

CHAPTER TEN

Last Thoughts

Whoever wishes peace among peoples must fight statism.

—Ludwig von Mises

A Tale of Two Futures

"Shut up," Jack screamed at the crows, waving his arms wildly. "Shut up, shut up!"

Only he really didn't utter a sound. And he didn't dare flail about, either. But gawd, he hated crows. And he hated hearing their grating *caw, caw* twice a week from the vacant lot next to the commissary.

One really didn't dare cause a disturbance in line, Jack knew. He felt uncomfortable even talking to people, much less screaming at crows. You really can't risk being labeled a "disrupter," especially when you've got a family and kids. Ever since the "commissary incidents" two years ago, there were T.O.s— Tranquility Officers—everywhere. Even if you couldn't see them, you knew they were watching. So Jack bottled it up and just closed his eyes tightly for a second. When he opened them he shot a look of hate across the lot where the crows were perched, watching from a bare tree above icy patches in an empty lot. Maybe he could come back on the weekend. Maybe it would be sunny. Jack sure hoped so. And maybe the crows wouldn't be there to remind him of the endless gray winter. But then again, maybe they would. Besides, he thought, he'd already been waiting half an hour and he was almost at the corner and from there it would only be another twenty minutes. Jack pulled his coat a little tighter and kept quiet.

The thought would occasionally occur to Jack, while he waited in life's endless succession of lines, that maybe it wasn't really the crows he hated with all his might. Maybe they were just a convenient focal point, caught in the cross fire of his desolation and deprivation. Maybe it was really the "groat," the government rolled-oat bread he hated. No, there was no maybe about that part. Cold, tough, stale, and flavorless, two big loaves twice a week. Jack knew he hated groat. From time to time he wondered why they couldn't have real bread made out of flour, like people used to eat when he was a kid.

But that's why there was a Food Czar, Jack knew—to figure that stuff out. He remembered watching the first Food Czar almost twelve years ago explain that sending wheat to rich Asian countries was only for the duration of the crisis, and that it was the patriotic thing to do during these times. Well, Jack thought, he was as patriotic as the next guy, even if he had joined in the general discontent a few years ago when it seemed like things just kept getting worse. But he wasn't a "disrupter" or anything like that, although he had a few nervous nights wondering if he had complained too loudly to anybody. But that was before the new Food Czar. The new czar had been a general in the ongoing war and he looked like the kind of guy who could really get stuff done. After all, it hadn't taken him any time at all to come up with the Recovery and Economy in Agriculture Plan, REAP, that set aside an additional 20 million acres for oat production. And he'd promised that REAP would really shorten the lines. Jack sure hoped so.

Besides, there was a presidential election coming up and all the candidates were saying that if the Food Czar didn't produce results next year, heads would roll and they'd get somebody in there that could really take charge. Jack sure hoped so. He was going to start paying more attention to the campaign.

By now Jack had reached the corner. He dug his hand into his pocket and felt for his plastic ration card.

"Gawd almighty," Jack thought. "I hate crows."

John checked his text messages as he got close to his neighborhood. There was one from his wife. "PICK UP BREAD." Seemed like there was always something, he thought.

In the store, John grabbed a cart, just in case, and headed for the bakery department. He knew his wife was going to be tied up this afternoon, but why couldn't she just leave a voice message like most people? he thought with a bit of impatience. Always text messages. Wouldn't it have been just as easy to call? At least then she could have mentioned what kind of bread, or what it was for. Was it that awful white bread the kids like for sandwiches, he wondered, or that tasty sprouted whole wheat that he liked? No, it couldn't be that, since nobody else in the family would eat it. As he strolled through the bakery section he caught a whiff of the fresh sourdough just then coming out of the oven. Irresistible! John knew he couldn't be trusted shopping on his way home at suppertime; he was the perfect impulse buyer. But he grabbed a loaf anyway.

It was at that moment that he spied the long, skinny loaves of French bread and remembered—French bread! Of course. She was making that shrimp pasta they'd seen on the Food Channel last week. It sure had looked wonderful on TV, and she was going to try it tonight! And they'd served it with French bread, so John grabbed a loaf, rolled through the wine aisle, picked a couple of bottles of a favorite, and headed to the checkout.

While he waited for his turn in the express lane, John noted that the lady two shoppers ahead must have had at least twenty items. Didn't she see the sign that said fifteen items or less? he wondered. He wanted to get home and try a slice of the sourdough while it was still hot enough to melt butter. But while he waited, John busied himself reading the tabloid headlines on the rack in front of him. There was that one really good-looking actress he liked, caught up in some weird love triangle. Another featured a psychic's predictions and a headline about a woman who had given birth to an eight-pound Chihuahua. That would be good. Another had something about a presidential race. Some people will read anything, John laughed to himself—especially the old people. They still followed that stuff, out of habit. Ever since the Great Default and the "Leave Us Alone" movement, those campaigns had been about as important as choosing the town librarian.

No sooner had he finished the thought than it was his turn. Took 'em long enough, he noted silently as he felt the sourdough loaf to assure himself it was still nice and warm. He chuckled to himself about the Chihuahua mother story as the cashier finished scanning his purchases, and tapped the gold card payment app on his phone. The payment instantly recorded on her register. "Thank you for shopping with us," she said with a smile.

John nodded his thanks. With his phone in one hand, he grabbed the groceries with the other, and as he headed for the parking lot he glanced at the receipt on his phone. The deduction was .4672 grams of gold from his account. Not bad, he thought to himself, wondering if it was just his imagination or if the same amount of groceries wouldn't have cost him closer to three-quarters of a gram not too many years ago.

Smelling this fresh sourdough is going to make me famished by the time I get home, John thought, moving a little more quickly.

The Social Question

The human race is very young. It has been across only a few generations and over not so many years that there has been a sense of quickening or acceleration in the human condition. Indeed, as others have pointed out, the conditions of life 2,500 years ago would have been much more familiar to people who lived 250 years ago than would today's conditions. The acceleration of life improvement has been extraordinary: anesthesia, widespread literacy, antiseptic childbirth, an almost universal condemnation of the barbarisms of torture and slavery, and adequate dentistry. These blessings and others too numerous to count are taken for granted by those of us who share them, but they would have been regarded with incalculable awe by those who lived without them. Challenges remain, among them the problem of the poor in our midst. And while it is a problem, it is a relative problem, for it is human freedom, and not force, that has assured that the limitations experienced by the poor in much of the world are no longer those of being fed, clothed, and housed.

Western civilization, at least in its mature (and perhaps fatigued) manifestation, appears to have a psychological blind spot in this regard, failing to note freedom's stunning accomplishments, ever seeking instead solutions from the state. This peculiarity is evident in our language, revealing the eagerness with which its societies believe that problems must be met by force and must be overcome by power. A culture exhausted of its creativity confronts every challenge on a war footing. There is the war on drugs, the war on cancer, and the war on obesity, as well as the wars on hunger, racism, and terror. And, of course, the war on poverty. Participants in these wars are engaged in "battles," employ "tactics" in their "assaults," and bring "weapons" to the "fight." War is declared on diseases, which are "attacked" and "fought off," while the search goes on for "better weapons," "heavy artillery," and "magic bullets." These are of course the means of the state which, as the monopoly wielder of force, relies on the war model of life for its own aggrandizement. Or as Randolph Bourne put it, "War is the health of the state."

There is a better way than the state's wars. Our special concern is the advancement of freedom as a primary condition that makes prosperity possible. The enhancement of prosperity has proven to be an approach that is far superior to the state's wars on poverty. It is surprising that this should be a surprise since this is the functioning of a general principle that has been alluded to over and over in the wisdom teachings of mankind. It is a principle that should be familiar to Christians in the admonition to "resist not evil." The thought is reinforced in Eastern traditional texts such as the *I Ching*, the ancient Chinese Book of Changes, which teaches that the best way to overcome evil is to make constant progress in the good.

It is indisputable, and must be reiterated as often as necessary, that the single best thing that can befall the poor is to find themselves in an environment of abundance. It is a wonderful thing to reach out to your fellow man. Years ago I did a broadcast fund-raiser for victims of a natural disaster with the legendary sports personality Joe Garagiola. He used a phrase of simple power that day: "We have to keep each other warm." It is a common slander by simpleminded critics that libertarianism is somehow Darwinian. A survival-of-the-fittest disregard for others can be found among some libertarians, just as it can be found among some conservatives and liberals. Solzhenitsyn portrayed as a typical statist type the Soviet official who was full of concern for the collective "people" but had no use for actual human beings. We have to keep each other warm, and it is my personal view that we should deal as we are able with those in difficult circumstances as life presents them to us and reach out to others where we can. Because of the variety of human dispositions, some devote themselves to those in need while others remain indifferent. It may be that more people will be moved on their own or persuaded to help keep others warm once the pretense that the state is taking care of things is swept aside.

But the hearts of the indifferent are not warmed by being ordered about; nor do they become generous in the face of their own want. In any case, this variety in human dispositions should not be smothered by force, which only provokes resentment, nor can it be conditioned away with the tools of the modern state described in Chapter Seven without great harm to the well-being of everyone, including the impoverished.

It is that manifestation of the uniqueness of the human individual so crucial to every success of our young race, exemplified in the division of labor, which recognizes that while Mother Teresa can be revered for feeding the hungry, still someone has to farm before anyone is fed. We can be in awe of those who, like Saint Francis, give everything they have to the poor, yet others have to save so there is capital for the production that has relieved much of mankind of the backbreaking toil that has long been its lot. Creative advances in production, whether efficiencies in farming that have pulled millions back from the brink of starvation or the labor-saving machinery that has saved millions more from living like beasts of burden, are the work of those who have foregone present consumption for improved circumstances in the future. This deferred consumption by people who can never be thanked, the inspired innovations of countless people forgotten in the past, and other creative human endeavors by people unnamed can hardly be said to take second place to the contributions of creative altruists. But it is clearly not coercion, the tool of the state that solves the problem of poverty. In fact it is the exception to the general human experience when meaningful capital somehow escapes plunder by tribal chieftains, kings, churches, and modern superstates. But such capital as has escaped the state is the very soil in which human prosperity has flourished. There is nothing that one can do more effectively for the dispossessed and destitute than to hold the state at bay and see to it that they live in a free and prosperous land. It is in so doing that our efforts have real leverage.

There are contributing, noneconomic factors by which poverty may be perpetuated even in the presence of abundance. Chief among these are limitations of consciousness, seen in those who do not know that they can think and live differently and—if they wish—escape negative circumstances or limitations of family, place, and custom. But conditions of persistent and prejudicial stratification also yield not to power, but thanks to the life-affirming principles of human dignity and freedom: physical freedom, political and economic freedom, intellectual, academic, and religious freedom, and spiritual freedom.

Coercion is not merely a tactic of the state in its war against drugs or poverty but is rather the congenital nature of the state itself. This is seen in a famous aphorism long attributed to George Washington: "Government is not reason, it is not eloquence. It is force. Like fire it is a dangerous servant and a fearful master." The real question for people of goodwill to consider is how social life is to be conditioned now and in the future, and whether coercion can be minimized. The sociologist Pitirim Sorokin sheds light on the question by observing that all human relationships can be grouped into three main classes: coercive, contractual, and familistic.

Coercive relationships are those of master to slave; of murderer or rapist to victim. These are relationships of conflict, necessarily antagonistic, in which the weaker party is made to bow before superior force.

Contractual relationships are voluntary. They are grounded in mutual advantage. It is to be expected that each party to a contractual relationship seeks his own advantage. A free economy reconciles these self-interests.

Familistic relationships are characterized by love, devotion, and sacrifice. They are seen, as the name suggests, in devoted families, in the care parents provide their infants and children provide their elderly parents without regard to personal advantage. There are libertarian theorists who insist that all acts of self-sacrifice are disguised self-seeking. This reduces the noblest acts of altruism to the vanity of the actor in seeking the flattery or approval of others or otherwise feeding his self-image. Anyone who has encountered genuine acts of self-sacrifice will reject this as reductionism. As I write this I have been watching and reading accounts of the most breathtaking heroism and self-sacrificing rescues taking place in the wake of the Japanese tsunami. These are familistic acts of the first order.

It is helpful to think of these social relationships along a linear scale in which coercive relationships are found at one end of the scale and familistic relationships are found at the other. Contractual relationships then will be found in the middle.

SOCIAL RELATIONSHIPS

Coercive	Contractual	Familistic

The familistic ideal of the brotherhood of man has been held by visionaries since Cain slew Abel. Friedrich Schiller, the libertarian German dramatist whose works were banned by both Napoleon and Hitler, championed this ancient dream in his poem "Ode to Joy." Beethoven joined in the triumphant proclamation of the brotherhood of man, setting Schiller's words to music in the powerful choral movement of his Ninth Symphony.

When the Berlin Wall fell in 1989, the event was celebrated on Christmas Day when Leonard Bernstein conducted the symphony in Berlin. In a grand and moving celebration of newly won liberty Bernstein had the soloists and chorus change the word *Freude* ("joy") in the choral movement to *Freiheit,* meaning "freedom." Many suspect that Schiller intended his work to be an ode to freedom to begin with, but Schiller, having been arrested and imprisoned for one of his plays two years earlier, felt it necessary in eighteenth-century Germany under the rule of emperors and dukes to conceal the tribute. In any case the combined inspiration of Schiller and Beethoven was well chosen to mark the advance of freedom that day and it remains a deeply moving tribute to the brotherhood of man.

The sincerity of those who profess a belief in the ideal of universal brotherhood that the poem and symphony celebrate is here put to the test. It is clear that a movement in social relations to the right on the scale represents a movement toward peace and the unification of the family of man. Contractual relations are to be preferred to coercive ones, just as the humane instincts of Good Samaritans are refinements in the direction of familistic relations. But the statists of our time try to appeal to these age-old aspirations of unity by employing the retrograde means of coercion. Force is the sine qua non of the state; in the absence of force the state withers away. Those who are eager that human progress should deliver up the golden age for which Schiller, Beethoven, and so many others of goodwill have yearned must abandon the state and its coercion as a means to that end. You can't get there from here. To subject social relations and economic life to compulsion is to move backward. It is a dynamic counter to mankind's higher aspirations of brotherhood and family and represents a degeneration of human relationships.

In a passage that sums up much of the material in this book—from the contempt shown the Constitution to the state favoritism of bailouts, state planning and crony capitalism to the debasing of the currency—Sorokin warns about the subversion of contractual relations (movement to the left on this scale) and cites the crumbling of the contractual structure at the hands of "criminal racketeers, unscrupulous politicians, and commercial cynics."

It is evident that as long as degenerate contractual relationships or compulsory relations exist, there is no hope of lasting internal or international peace. The very nature of pseudo-contractual and compulsory relations generates incessant brutal conflicts.

Make no mistake: when a social order of contractual relationships, sufficiently subverted, collapses, the gap is filled not by a familistic structure, but by authoritarianism and political dictatorship.

A Tale of Two Revolutions

Eight years after Lord Cornwallis surrendered to General Washington and the French commander Rochambeau at Yorktown and America won its liberty, France launched a revolution of its own. It didn't turn out as well.

A single-minded devotion to the ideal of liberty could be found in every colony in America. In Virginia it was heard in Patrick Henry's passionate 1775 ultimatum, "Give me liberty or give me death." In Boston it was evident in the Sons of Liberty, formed in 1765 at the Liberty Tree, a popular gathering spot. Soon there were Sons of Liberty and Liberty Trees in towns throughout the colonies. Thomas Paine even wrote a poem about the Goddess of Liberty who came bearing the Liberty Tree "from the gardens above."

But while Americans were faithful in their love of liberty, the French took many lovers; and while tragic, their revolution was in some ways like a French farce of secret affairs and confused identities, because the revolution was characterized by many unclear and contradictory ideals and mottos. There was equality, justice, and reason as well as security, unity, and strength, and most pernicious, the *volonté générale*, Rousseau's "general will," to which the individual was required to submit. But the lasting formulation in France was the three-part ideal of *liberté, egalité, fraternité* (liberty, equality, brotherhood) which, by the time of the revolution, had been linked together in France for a hundred years. This was the motto that Robespierre wished to have displayed on the uniforms and flags of France. It was around these three ideals that the revolution wobbled until it toppled over. Liberty, equality, and brotherhood are fine ideals, but they can only coexist when each is in its own sphere. It was confusion about the sphere of each that led to the horrors of *la régime de la terreur,* the Reign of Terror, in France. It was these ideals misapplied to collectivist purpose that allowed Robespierre and the Jacobins to make the guillotine a source of afternoon public entertainment and set rivers of blood flowing in the streets of France.

Brotherhood, *fraternité*, is an ideal of the familistic relationships about which I have written here and recommend as an aspiration for all people of goodwill. We are of course dependent on an endless network of our fellow human beings who are engaged in activities we little comprehend in places we seldom consider for our material advantages. We are also learning from DNA studies how closely related we all are. The wisdom traditions of the ages also tell us that we are not just related genetically but that we are all connected spiritually. Just as we all stand on the same earth and gaze at the same sky, we all spring from the same source and share a common fate. Implicit in all of this is the possibility of living side by side. But brotherhood is cultivated in the human heart, not in the halls of state where legislative votes are bought and sold or in the smoke-filled rooms of conspiring politicians. To make the spiritual or moral ideal of brotherhood the object of the law is to summon up force, which always produces counterforce. Chapter Four described the failure in America's early history of the communal undertaking of the Pilgrims when brotherhood was made the province of the law. Such force deprives liberty of the oxygen it breathes.

Made a political objective of the state, the *fraternité* of the French Revolution was not of the "love thy neighbor" sort; it was of the "if you're not with me you're against me" variety. So savage were the conditions of the revolution that the diplomat Metternich said later in his life that "fraternity as it is practiced in France has led me to the conclusion that if I had a brother I would call him my cousin." It was a brotherhood no one would wish to have.

Like brotherhood, *egalité*—equality—is an ideal to be revered as well. But it, too, has its sphere. Equality belongs to the realm of the law. Clearly the claim of the Declaration of Independence that all men are created equal has to do not with men's and women's individual gifts or qualities but with their right to equal treatment before the law without fear of prejudice or expectation of favor. The brotherhood of man cannot survive unequal treatment before the law. At the same time, when the law is applied unevenly with an eye to class, wealth, social standing, religion, or other criteria, the law can quickly become oppressive and cruel. The application of the law to all persons without prejudice acts as a moderating force on the law itself.

Human beings are manifestly not equal in terms of intellect, wisdom, creativity, love, or other human qualities. The misapplication of the ideal of equality to something other than their standing before the law is an open door to the coercive means that are the destructive occupation of state levelers such as Robespierre, who even wished to force all the citizens of France to don the uniforms of the state. It is the recurring impulse of the Procrusteans—yardsticks always at hand—that drives the dystopias of *1984* and *Brave New World* discussed in Chapter Seven. Enforced equality smothers human talents; it extinguishes the spark of individual inspiration and thereby deprives us all of the gifts of genius.

If brotherhood is a spiritual or moral ideal, and equality is an ideal as we stand before the law, to what sphere does liberty belong? Clearly liberty is not suitable as the highest ideal before the law. Were liberty its ideal, the law would constantly aspire to the release of even the most heinous criminal. Instead, liberty is a political ideal. And while it is not the highest of all human ideals, it is the highest *political* ideal in that it allows us to live together productively in a polis—a city or a *civitas*—so that we can be *civilized* and not barbarians; this makes civilization possible. It is in the presence of freedom that people living together, unequal in other things, are able to pursue their unique gifts and preferences. Their very inequality in interests and abilities provides for the division of human labor. A thousand flowers bloom and civilization flourishes as free people seek ways to serve their fellows as a means in turn of providing for themselves and the satisfaction of their individual desires. The long sweep of human history and the contrast in conditions across national borders demonstrates that freedom is the political ideal that has enabled the march of human progress and makes prosperity possible.

The *liberté* of the French Revolution was the freedom of the Jacobins' Committee for Public Safety to order people to death, to dispense with courtroom formalities, and to pronounce sentence before trial. The French had their *liberté*, but it was not liberty for individuals. It was the unrestrained liberty of the state to do as it wished.

The artifice of equality of condition and outcome can only be implemented by the extinction of liberty. Or, as Goethe observed, freedom and equality can "only be enjoyed temporarily in the giddiness of madness." Madness was the prevailing condition of the terror regime in France that sought political means to address all human challenges. No such confusion contaminated the American Revolution. Thanks to the wisdom that prevailed among members of America's founding generation and the independent spirit of the colonists, their revolutionary objective was clear. Their aim was true: liberty. And thus Americans were spared the butchery that befell France.

The historical examples of the American and French revolutions illuminate the choices before us today.

- The French Revolution was the empowerment of the glorified collectivist state. Robespierre's ideal "Republic of Virtue" was set to be the dipenser of law. It sought to make the state the arbiter of all passions and virtues, the uplifter of all souls; all ambition would serve the state. The state was to be the fulfillment of the ages and encompass all philosophy; it would "accomplish the destiny of humanity."
- The American Revolution was a political event. It was not a revolution in the law; it did not seek to overthrow the common law, but instead incorporated it. It sought to provide for liberty by binding the state, checking its power, and dividing it against itself.
- The French Revolution vacillated between attempts to eliminate religion or, in the case of Robespierre, to create and direct his own religion of the state.
- The American Revolution sought to bar government from the business of religion.
- The French Revolution set out to be the guarantor of well-being for each individual. It sought to direct the economic life of the nation by directing labor, planning production, and controlling trade. It commandeered agriculture and created hunger. It set prices and applied the death penalty for their violation.
- The American Revolution was not the birth of a master plan. Instead it sought to allow people to direct their own economic affairs and to be self-reliant. It thereby set free the dynamo of millions of individual plans.
- The French Revolution represented the politicization of morals. Virtue consisted of love for "the fatherland," claimed Robespierre, while terror in the hands of the revolution was "an emanation of virtue."
- The American Revolution was not intended to be a substitute for the moral

obligations of individuals. It was not designed to regenerate the hearts of men and to make them love one another, but as a political event it did intend to create a political environment in which people could be free, live in peace, and prosper together.

While the American Revolution sought to create an environment in which each person could pursue his own ends, the French state would choose collective ends that all would serve. Out of its confusion and collectivism, the French Revolution culminated in horrors too grisly in its details to be recounted here except to say it included women and children buried alive, hacked up body parts fired from cannons, cannibalism, streets filled with bodies, and pyramids of corpses. And then there was Dr. Guillotin's invention. A thousand heads rolled in Paris in the first year and a half after the machine's introduction. While many thousands more were shot or drowned, as many as 17,000 persons met their end with "the national razor." Before the guillotine, errant members of the aristocracy would be beheaded by ax, while commoners were generally hanged. But now the French had their *egalité* in the application of the guillotine to the hapless of all kinds, as Wordsworth recorded:

Domestic carnage now filled the whole year
With feast-days; old men from the chimney-nook,
The maiden from the bosom of her love,
The mother from the cradle of her babe,
The warrior from the field—all perished, all—
Friends, enemies, of all parties, ages, ranks,
Head after head, and never heads enough
For those that bade them fall.

Perhaps a million people died in the madness of the French Revolution itself. But that is not the worst of it, because the revolution made foreign war a constant. When Washington delivered his farewell address in 1796 after two terms as president, he urged Americans, while extending commercial relations to all nations, to have as little to do politically with them as possible; to avoid the frequent controversies of foreign lands: "Why quit our own to stand upon foreign ground?" he asked. In the French Revolution, hundreds of thousands of French youth were drafted and sent off to foreign battlefields in wars with England, Austria, Spain, Prussia, the Dutch Republic, and elsewhere. But the worst of the carnage still lay ahead.

As the French Revolution collapsed, with many of the revolutionaries having long since devoured their own as they raced to send one another to the guillotine, France was so broken it became dependent on the plunder of war to pay its bills. So complete was the destruction of France from its ill-conceived revolution that the ensuing chaos gave rise to the military dictatorship of Napoleon and his sixteen years of war, empire, bankruptcy, and the deaths of many millions more.

The fruit of the American Revolution was different. The young country was growing in the environment of economic freedom and unleashed the ingenuity that would make it the wonder of the world. But in France, it would be forty years before capital, credit, and commerce returned to the levels that existed before its revolution.

Finally in France the futility of it all was apparent with the abdication of Napoleon in 1814. The revolution had come full circle, only to end up where it began. The Bourbon dynasty was restored to the throne and France became a monarchy once again. About the same time, the Americans, who, having no desire to be ruled, had sent George III packing once, repeated the feat.

Two revolutions: one a failure, one a success. Two models of man's relationship to the state. One releases the creative dynamic that makes prosperity possible. The other subordinates the race to autocrats. One allows individuals to do with their lives what they can as well as they can, making choices sometimes foolish and sometimes wise, but being chastened by the former and encouraged and improved by the latter. The other makes choice the perogative of a self-proclaimed elite. To be sure, wise choices are to be preferred to foolish ones, but what chain of thought arrives at the conclusion that a group of ambitious power seekers will choose wisely? It is simply too much to be hoped.

Behind the Curtain

The Republicans and Democrats of modern America—the red and blue faces of the state—have led us all down their yellow brick road of the welfare and warfare state. And now the curtain has been pulled back on the Great and Powerful Oz of Washington and its work of cheap flimflammery has been revealed for all to see. The roar of its might depended on the wealth it stripped from the people. Now it has no wealth left, only debt to burden the people with in their reduced circumstances. It promised to provide for the poor, but instead left the entire nation poorer. It promised to provide for the elderly in their retirement. But the only resources the Great and Powerful Oz had were the ones it took from them to begin with, and in so doing it altered the people's behavior so that they failed to provide for their own old age. It promised to provide for the general security. Instead it destroyed the people's financial security while it went abroad, propping up tyrants and meddling in affairs hither and yon. The security of the Great and Powerful Oz consists not of peace and tranquility, but in maintaining a perpetual state of alarm and making the people hated in far corners of the world. And in a foolhardy finale, it sought to solve the problem of insurmountable debt by piling on still more debt. Now the state must stop. Let the final curtain close on the humbuggery of the red party and the bunkum of the blue.

A change in the way people think about the state is inevitable, just as it was inevitable that tribal chieftains, the divine right of kings, the mandate of heaven, and the rule of churches should yield to the spread of freedom. It stands to reason that the hollowness of the state's promises should thrust this reconsideration on this generation at this time. But perhaps the generation is not equal to the demands of the age; perhaps we expect too much of a dependent, conditioned, and passive people. But if the people do miss the opportunity our economic distress provides to reassess the state, the opportunity of distress will be seized instead by those responsible for the calamity. They will use it to extend their authority and, yes, to increase the damage. As I described in *The Dollar Meltdown*, a command economy is an irresistible attraction to the power-seeking governing classes during economic distress. The hand of the state becomes a fist. Will Americans continue to succumb to the ways of statism as modeled by the French Revolution? Or will they recall the lessons of our own revolution and seek again to secure the blessings of liberty for ourselves and our posterity?

It should be clear that the decision before us is not the one presented by the major media outlets with their breathless coverage of the election horse races. It is not the one offered by the opinion makers with their constrained vision and tired habits of thought. It is not the choice between Republicans and Democrats that matters. It is the choice between statism and liberty. The sound-bite commentariat would have us choose whether the red team or the blue team should manage our lives. But America is not a sporting event, and we can manage our own lives. The future we are choosing is between want and abundance. The great achievements of mankind come not from slave labor, but from the self-motivated. Except for cigars from Cuba and vodka from the Soviet Union (if even that!), nobody anywhere with a choice is ever very interested in things made by unfree people living in command economies. Without the oxygen of freedom, creativity shuts down, inventiveness suffocates. When prodded like cattle, people move and act not as inspired, but as directed. All the spontaneity that organizes new forms of production, all the unexpected ways in which human life is improved, and the serendipity that delights us with enriching new experiences and opportunities—all flourish in an environment of freedom. Americans who know this face the task of persuading their fellows of both the self-evident moral preferability and the productive superiority of voluntary and contractual social relationships to coercive ones.

The things we have taken for granted in our material circumstances and the increase of ease in our lives—so many of the things we notice only in their absence—are the result of a free economy. So rich are its gifts, so abundant its bounty, so profuse its variety that we have come to think of prosperity as a given. And that is a good way to think of it—as a given. Like the cornucopia, the horn of plenty that is an icon of inexhaustible abundance that seemingly springs forth from nowhere, originating mysteriously only within itself, prosperity is a given, coming into being in the presence of free people in a free economy.

Liberty's gifts are many. This book has focused especially on prosperity because she appears to be slipping away from us. But prosperity is only one of liberty's daughters. Peace is another. And third among her daughters is opportunity. What a plague mankind suffers in the absence of liberty's gifts. What a cruel smothering of the human spirit to know only lack and insufficiency instead of the abundance of prosperity; to live in a time of constant strife and war, a time without the blessings of peace; and to experience a lifetime of frustrating limitation and futility, a world without opportunity.

A renewed appreciation of liberty will mean the growth of prosperity, peace, and opportunity. Her blessings await all who wish them.

APPENDIXES

APPENDIX I

I, Pencil

Ever since Adam Smith, author of the 1776 inquiry into the nature of prosperity, *The Wealth of Nations*, used the phrase "the invisible hand," it has been understood and misunderstood in countless ways.

Smith used the term to describe the way in which one seeking only his own economic objectives actually contributes to the well-being of others:

> He intends only his own gain, and he is in this, as in many other cases,
> led by an invisible hand to promote an end which was no part of his
> intention. Nor is it always the worse for the society that it was not part
> of it. By pursuing his own interest he frequently promotes that of the
> society more effectually than when he really intends to promote it.

Smith's metaphor has been ridiculed by opponents of the free economy to suggest that he somehow thought some metaphysical entity was going to do everything for you, from fetching the newspaper to brewing your morning coffee. Although that was not his meaning, it's hard to dispute that the free economy has even performed miracles on that front. You no longer have to put on your slippers each morning, go out, and try to find your paper in the bushes. You can have your news customized to your interests and delivered to your phone, tablet, or laptop, instantly and up-to-date before you even open your eyes in the morning. Meanwhile, thanks to companies like Starbucks and Keurig, you have personalized choices for morning coffee with a quality and convenience (and even temperature) unthinkable to Americans a generation ago, fresh and ready to go before you even get out of bed.

The meaning of Smith's "invisible hand" becomes clear elsewhere when he describes the way we are served by other people, each pursuing his own ends:

> It is not from the benevolence of the butcher, the brewer or the baker, that we expect our dinner, but from their regard to their own self-interest. We address ourselves, not to their humanity but to their self-love, and never talk to them of our own necessities but of their advantages.

In a delightful essay written from the point of view of a pencil, Leonard Read, the founder of the Foundation for Economic Education, describes the invisible hand at work in the production of a most commonplace item. It is a powerful essay about the way the creative forces of human beings work together in an environment of freedom to produce an item of such incredible complexity that no one alone could possibly make it.

> There is a fact still more astounding: the absence of a master mind, of anyone dictating or forcibly directing these countless actions which bring me into being. No trace of such a person can be found. Instead, we find the Invisible Hand at work.

Read's 1958 essay has become a classic. It should douse the fires of ambition of those who seek power to remake humans, orchestrate economies, and mastermind societies. First try performing a small miracle. Make a pencil.

I, Pencil: My Family Tree as Told to Leonard E. Read

I am a lead pencil—the ordinary wooden pencil familiar to all boys and girls and adults who can read and write.

Writing is both my vocation and my avocation; that's all I do.

You may wonder why I should write a genealogy. Well, to begin with, my story is interesting. And, next, I am a mystery—more so than a tree or a sunset or even a flash of lightning. But, sadly, I am taken for granted by those who use me, as if I were a mere incident and without background. This supercilious attitude relegates me to the level of the commonplace. This is a species of the grievous error in which mankind cannot too long persist without peril. For, the wise G. K. Chesterton observed, "We are perishing for want of wonder, not for want of wonders."

I, Pencil, simple though I appear to be, merit your wonder and awe, a claim I shall attempt to prove. In fact, if you can understand me—no, that's too much to ask of anyone—if you can become aware of the miraculousness which I symbolize, you can help save the freedom mankind is so unhappily losing. I have a profound lesson to teach. And I can teach this lesson better than can an automobile or an airplane or a mechanical dishwasher because—well, because I am seemingly so simple.

Simple? Yet, not a single person on the face of this earth knows how to make me. This sounds fantastic, doesn't it? Especially when it is realized that there are about one and one-half billion of my kind produced in the U.S.A. each year.

Pick me up and look me over. What do you see? Not much meets the eye—there's some wood, lacquer, the printed labeling, graphite lead, a bit of metal, and an eraser.

INNUMERABLE ANTECEDENTS

Just as you cannot trace your family tree back very far, so is it impossible for me to name and explain all my antecedents. But I would like to suggest enough of them to impress upon you the richness and complexity of my background.

My family tree begins with what in fact is a tree, a cedar of straight grain that grows in Northern California and Oregon. Now contemplate all the saws and trucks and rope and the countless other gear used in harvesting and carting the cedar logs to the railroad siding. Think of all the persons and the numberless skills that went into their fabrication: the mining of ore, the making of steel and its refinement into saws, axes, motors; the growing of hemp and bringing it through all the stages to heavy and strong rope; the logging camps with their beds and mess halls; the cookery and the raising of all the foods. Why, untold thousands of persons had a hand in every cup of coffee the loggers drink!

The logs are shipped to a mill in San Leandro, California. Can you imagine the individuals who make flat cars and rails and railroad engines and who construct and install the communication systems incidental thereto? These legions are among my antecedents.

Consider the millwork in San Leandro. The cedar logs are cut into small, pencil-length slats less than one-fourth of an inch in thickness. These are kiln dried and then tinted for the same reason women put rouge on their faces. People prefer that I look pretty, not a pallid white. The slats are waxed and kiln dried again. How many skills went into the making of the tint and the kilns, into supplying the heat, the light and power, the belts, motors, and all the other things a mill requires? Sweepers in the mill among my ancestors? Yes, and included are the men who poured the concrete for the dam of a Pacific Gas & Electric Company hydroplant which supplies the mill's power!

Don't overlook the ancestors present and distant who have a hand in transporting sixty carloads of slats across the nation.

Once in the pencil factory—$4,000,000 in machinery and building, all capital accumulated by thrifty and saving parents of mine—each slat is given eight grooves by a complex machine, after which another machine lays leads in every other slat, applies glue, and places another slat atop—a lead sandwich, so to speak. Seven brothers and I are mechanically carved from this "wood-clinched" sandwich.

My "lead" itself—it contains no lead at all—is complex. The graphite is mined in Ceylon [Sri Lanka]. Consider these miners and those who make their many tools and the makers of the paper sacks in which the graphite is shipped and those who make the string that ties the sacks and those who put them aboard ships and those who make the ships. Even the lighthouse keepers along the way assisted in my birth—and the harbor pilots.

The graphite is mixed with clay from Mississippi in which ammonium hydroxide is used in the refining process. Then wetting agents are added such as sulfonated tallow—animal fats chemically reacted with sulfuric acid. After passing through numerous machines, the mixture finally appears as endless extrusions—as from a sausage grinder—cut to size, dried, and baked for several hours at 1,850 degrees Fahrenheit. To increase their strength and smoothness the leads are then treated with a hot mixture which includes candelilla wax from Mexico, paraffin wax, and hydrogenated natural fats.

My cedar receives six coats of lacquer. Do you know all the ingredients of lacquer? Who would think that the growers of castor beans and the refiners of castor oil are a part of it? They are. Why, even the processes by which the lacquer is made a beautiful yellow involve the skills of more persons than one can enumerate!

Observe the labeling. That's a film formed by applying heat to carbon black mixed with resins. How do you make resins and what, pray, is carbon black?

My bit of metal—the ferrule—is brass. Think of all the persons who mine zinc and copper and those who have the skills to make shiny sheet brass from these products of nature. Those black rings on my ferrule are black nickel. What is black nickel and how is it applied? The complete story of why the center of my ferrule has no black nickel on it would take pages to explain.

Then there's my crowning glory, inelegantly referred to in the trade as "the plug," the part man uses to erase the errors he makes with me. An ingredient called "factice" is what does the erasing. It is a rubber-like product made by reacting rapeseed oil from the Dutch East Indies [Indonesia] with sulfur chloride. Rubber, contrary to the common notion, is only for binding purposes. Then, too, there are numerous vulcanizing and accelerating agents. The pumice comes from Italy; and the pigment which gives "the plug" its color is cadmium sulfide.

NO ONE KNOWS

Does anyone wish to challenge my earlier assertion that no single person on the face of this earth knows how to make me?

Actually, millions of human beings have had a hand in my creation, no one of whom even knows more than a very few of the others. Now, you may say that I go too far in relating the picker of a coffee berry in far-off Brazil and food growers elsewhere to my creation; that this is an extreme position. I shall stand by my claim. There isn't a single person in all these millions, including the president of the pencil company, who contributes more than a tiny, infinitesimal bit of know-how. From the standpoint of know-how the only difference between the miner of graphite in Ceylon and the logger in Oregon is in the type of know-how. Neither the miner nor the logger can be dispensed with, any more than can the chemist at the factory or the worker in the oil field—paraffin being a by-product of petroleum.

Here is an astounding fact: Neither the worker in the oil field nor the chemist nor the digger of graphite or clay nor any who mans or makes the ships or trains or trucks nor the one who runs the machine that does the knurling on my bit of metal nor the president of the company performs his singular task because he wants me. Each one wants me less, perhaps, than does a child in the first grade. Indeed, there are some among this vast multitude who never saw a pencil nor would they know how to use one. Their motivation is other than me. Perhaps it is something like this: Each of these millions sees that he can thus exchange his tiny know-how for the goods and services he needs or wants. I may or may not be among these items.

NO MASTER MIND

There is a fact still more astounding: The absence of a master mind, of anyone dictating or forcibly directing these countless actions which bring me into being. No trace of such a person can be found. Instead, we find the Invisible Hand at work. This is the mystery to which I earlier referred.

It has been said that "only God can make a tree." Why do we agree with this? Isn't it because we realize that we ourselves could not make one? Indeed, can we even describe a tree? We cannot, except in superficial terms. We can say, for instance, that a certain molecular configuration manifests itself as a tree. But what mind is there among men that could even record, let alone direct, the constant changes in molecules that transpire in the life span of a tree? Such a feat is utterly unthinkable!

I, Pencil, am a complex combination of miracles: a tree, zinc, copper, graphite, and so on. But to these miracles which manifest themselves in Nature an even more extraordinary miracle has been added: the configuration of creative human energies—millions of tiny know-hows configurating naturally and spontaneously in response to human necessity and desire and in the absence of any human masterminding! Since only God can make a tree, I insist that only God could make me. Man can no more direct these millions of know-hows to bring me into being than he can put molecules together to create a tree.

The above is what I meant when writing, "If you can become aware of the miraculousness which I symbolize, you can help save the freedom mankind is so unhappily losing." For, if one is aware that these know-hows will naturally, yes, automatically, arrange themselves into creative and productive patterns in response to human necessity and demand—that is, in the absence of governmental or any other coercive master-minding—then one will possess an absolutely essential ingredient for freedom: a faith in free people. Freedom is impossible without this faith.

Once government has had a monopoly of a creative activity such, for instance, as the delivery of the mails, most individuals will believe that the mails could not be efficiently delivered by men acting freely. And here is the reason: Each one acknowledges that he himself doesn't know how to do all the things incident to mail delivery. He also recognizes that no other individual could do it. These assumptions are correct. No individual possesses enough know-how to perform a nation's mail delivery any more than any individual possesses enough know-how to make a pencil. Now, in the absence of faith in free people—in the unawareness that millions of tiny know-hows would naturally and miraculously form and cooperate to satisfy this necessity—the individual cannot help but reach the erroneous conclusion that mail can be delivered only by governmental "masterminding."

TESTIMONY GALORE

If I, Pencil, were the only item that could offer testimony on what men and women can accomplish when free to try, then those with little faith would have a fair case. However, there is testimony galore; it's all about us and on every hand. Mail delivery is exceedingly simple when compared, for instance, to the making of an automobile or a calculating machine or a grain combine or a milling machine or to tens of thousands of other things. Delivery? Why, in this area where men have been left free to try, they deliver the human voice around the world in less than one second; they deliver an event visually and in motion to any person's home when it is happening; they deliver 150 passengers from Seattle to Baltimore in less than four hours; they deliver gas from Texas to one's range or furnace in New York at unbelievably low rates and without subsidy; they deliver each four pounds of oil from the Persian Gulf to our Eastern Seaboard—halfway around the world—for less money than the government charges for delivering a one-ounce letter across the street!

The lesson I have to teach is this: Leave all creative energies uninhibited. Merely organize society to act in harmony with this lesson. Let society's legal apparatus remove all obstacles the best it can. Permit these creative know-hows freely to flow. Have faith that free men and women will respond to the Invisible Hand. This faith will be confirmed. I, Pencil, seemingly simple though I am, offer the miracle of my creation as testimony that this is a practical faith, as practical as the sun, the rain, a cedar tree, the good earth.

Reprinted with permission from Foundation for Economic Education, Irvington-on-Hudson, NY. www.FEE.org.

The Broken Window Fallacy

Although I've cited Frederic Bastiat several times, I did not intend to include the short piece "The Broken Window" until a comment made by a prominent economist as I was writing reminded me how frequently the obvious point Bastiat makes in the essay is overlooked and how often it needs to be restated.

The comment represents a fault especially peculiar to economists of the Keynesian school, which means the great majority of economists in both government and academia. No one can illustrate this class more effectively than Larry Summers, himself a former World Bank chief economist, U.S. Treasury secretary, Harvard president, and current Kennedy School professor. In a television interview after the 2011 Japanese earthquake and tsunami, Summers said:

> This is clearly going to add complexity to Japan's challenge of economic recovery. It may lead to some temporary increments ironically to GDP as a process of rebuilding takes place. In the wake of the earlier Kobe earthquake Japan actually gained some economic strength.

One need only refer to Chapter Eight and Keynes's own flimflam prescription of hiding cash in bottles buried deep in a landfill as a creative and wealth-generating economic activity to recognize the common fault here: the belief that acts of destruction and make-work are great sources of new wealth.

Bush administration labor secretary Elaine Chao gave voice to the same view in the aftermath of Hurricane Katrina:

There is a bright spot in that new jobs do get created. And in the rebuilding. New Orleans, for example, is going to see one of the biggest construction booms that they have ever seen. So in the aftermath and the rebuilding of a devastated area, there will be a tremendous array of new jobs that are being created. And that is going to help the economic development.

Similarly, President George Bush expressed the belief that spending on his elective Iraq war was good for the economy, saying, "I think actually the spending in the war might help with jobs . . . because we're buying equipment, and people are working." The question to be asked of all such analysis is, where do the resources to level Iraq, rebuild New Orleans, and restore Japan come from?

The economic activity of bombing Iraq and then rebuilding schools has been seen on the evening news, as have the construction cranes in New Orleans and the crews removing rubble in coastal Japan. But the money to fund all those activities existed in the first place. If the destruction had not occurred, the schools and the buildings and towns would have continued to exist while the money spent on them would have been spent on other things—on new goods or investments. It is those additional goods and investments that are unseen in the pronouncements of Keynesians.

Chief among Bastiat's gifts was to pierce the fog that often accompanies economic discussions and to display the essential questions at issue in terms of parables and tales to which people can apply the common sense of everyday life.

"The Broken Window" is taken from an 1850 essay called "That Which Is Seen and That Which Is Unseen."

The Broken Window

BY FREDERIC BASTIAT

Have you ever witnessed the anger of the good shopkeeper, James B., when his careless son happened to break a square of glass? If you have been present at such a scene, you will most assuredly bear witness to the fact, that every one of the spectators, were there even thirty of them, by common consent apparently, offered the unfortunate owner this invariable consolation—"It is an ill wind that blows nobody good. Everybody must live, and what would become of the glaziers if panes of glass were never broken?"

Now, this form of condolence contains an entire theory, which it will be well to show up in this simple case, seeing that it is precisely the same as that which, unhappily, regulates the greater part of our economical institutions.

Suppose it cost six francs to repair the damage, and you say that the accident brings six francs to the glazier's trade—that it encourages that trade to the amount of six francs—I grant it; I have not a word to say against it; you reason justly. The glazier comes, performs his task, receives his six francs, rubs his hands, and, in his heart, blesses the careless child.

All this is that which is seen.

But if, on the other hand, you come to the conclusion, as is too often the case, that it is a good thing to break windows, that it causes money to circulate, and that the encouragement of industry in general will be the result of it, you will oblige me to call out, "Stop there! Your theory is confined to that which is seen; it takes no account of that which is not seen."

It is not seen that as our shopkeeper has spent six francs upon one thing, he cannot spend them upon another. It is not seen that if he had not had a window to replace, he would, perhaps, have replaced his old shoes, or added another book to his library. In short, he would have employed his six francs in some way, which this accident has prevented.

Let us take a view of industry in general, as affected by this circumstance. The window being broken, the glazier's trade is encouraged to the amount of six francs; this is that which is seen. If the window had not been broken, the shoemaker's trade (or some other) would have been encouraged to the amount of six francs; this is that which is not seen.

And if that which is not seen is taken into consideration, because it is a negative fact, as well as that which is seen, because it is a positive fact, it will be understood that neither industry in general, nor the sum total of national labour, is affected, whether windows are broken or not.

Now let us consider James B. himself. In the former supposition, that of the window being broken, he spends six francs, and has neither more nor less than he had before, the enjoyment of a window.

In the second, where we suppose the window not to have been broken, he would have spent six francs on shoes, and would have had at the same time the enjoyment of a pair of shoes and of a window.

Now, as James B. forms a part of society, we must come to the conclusion, that, taking it altogether, and making an estimate of its enjoyments and its labours, it has lost the value of the broken window.

When we arrive at this unexpected conclusion: "Society loses the value of things which are uselessly destroyed"; and we must assent to a maxim which will make the hair of protectionists stand on end—To break, to spoil, to waste, is not to encourage national labour; or, more briefly, "destruction is not profit."

What will you say, Monsieur Industriel—what will you say, disciples of good M. F. Chamans, who has calculated with so much precision how much trade would gain by the burning of Paris, from the number of houses it would be necessary to rebuild?

I am sorry to disturb these ingenious calculations, as far as their spirit has been introduced into our legislation; but I beg him to begin them again, by taking into the account that which is not seen, and placing it alongside of that which is seen.

The reader must take care to remember that there are not two persons only, but three concerned in the little scene which I have submitted to his attention. One of them, James B., represents the consumer, reduced, by an act of destruction, to one enjoyment instead of two. Another under the title of the glazier, shows us the producer, whose trade is encouraged by the accident. The third is the shoemaker (or some other tradesman), whose labour suffers proportionably by the same cause. It is this third person who is always kept in the shade, and who, personating that which is not seen, is a necessary element of the problem. It is he who shows us how absurd it is to think we see a profit in an act of destruction. It is he who will soon teach us that it is not less absurd to see a profit in a restriction, which is, after all, nothing else than a partial destruction. Therefore, if you will only go to the root of all the arguments which are adduced in its favour, all you will find will be the paraphrase of this vulgar saying—What would become of the glaziers, if nobody ever broke windows?

Reprinted with permission from Foundation for Economic Education, Irvington-on-Hudson, NY. www.FEE.org. Translated by Patrick James Stirling in *Essays on Political Economy,* Provost & Co., London, 1873.

BIBLIOGRAPHY

Allman, T. D. "Blow Back." In Mike Gray, ed., *Busted: Stone Cowboys, Narco-Lords, and Washington's War on Drugs*. New York: Thunder's Mouth Press/Nation Books, pp. 3–16.

Appel, Jacob M. "Beyond Fluoride: Pharmaceuticals, Drinking Water and the Public Health." The Huffington Post, December 21, 2009. http://www.huffingtonpost.com/jacob-m-appel/beyond-fluoride-pharmaceu_b_398874.html.

Barlett, Donald L., and James B. Steele. "Billions over Baghdad." *Vanity Fair*, October 2007.

———. "Deadly Medicine." *Vanity Fair*, January 2011.

Bastiat, Frederic. *Economic Sophisms*. Irvington-on-Hudson, NY: Foundation for Economic Education, 1964.

———. *The Law*. Irvington-on-Hudson, NY: Foundation for Economic Education, 1979.

Beinhocker, Eric. *The Origin of Wealth: Evolution, Complexity, and the Radical Remaking of Economics*. Boston: Harvard Business School Press, 2006.

Bernstein, William J. *A Splendid Exchange: How Trade Shaped the World*. New York: Atlantic Monthly Press, 2008.

Bradlee, Ben. "Deceit and Dishonesty" (the first James Cameron Memorial Lecture). London: *The Guardian*, April 29, 1987.

Breggin, Peter R. *Medication Madness: The Role of Psychiatric Drugs in Cases of Violence, Suicide, and Crime*. New York: St. Martin's Griffin, 2009.

Center for Public Integrity. *The Helicopter War*. Washington, DC, 2008. http://projects.publicintegrity.org/report.aspx?aid=260&sid=100#.

Crews, Clyde Wayne. *Ten Thousand Commandments 2010: An Annual Snapshot of the Federal Regulatory State*. Washington, DC: Competitive Enterprise Institute, 2010. http://cei.org/studies-issue-analysis/ten-thousand-commandments-2010.

Dostoyevsky, Fyodor. *The Brothers Karamazov*, trans. Constance Garnett. New York: Vintage Books, 1950.

Flynn, John T. *As We Go Marching*. New York: Free Life Editions, 1973.

Fry, Eric. *Outing Ben Bernanke*. *The Daily Reckoning*, December 15, 2010. http://daily reckoning.com/outing-ben-bernanke/#ixzz1Hadw1Eeb.

Galbraith, James K. *The Predator State: How Conservatives Abandoned the Free Market and Why Liberals Should Too*. New York: Free Press, 2008.

Goldberg, Jonah. *Liberal Fascism*. New York: Doubleday, 2007.

Greenspan, Alan. *The Age of Turbulence: Adventures in a New World*. New York: Penguin Press, 2007.

Hayek, Friedrich A. *Denationalisation of Money: The Argument Refined*. London: Institute of Economic Affairs, 1990.

———. *Individualism and Economic Order*. Chicago: University of Chicago Press, 1948.

———. *Law, Legislation and Liberty*, vol. 1, *Rules and Order*. Chicago: University of Chicago Press, 1973.

———. *Law, Legislation and Liberty*, vol. 3, *The Political Order of a Free People*. Chicago: University of Chicago Press, 1979.

———. *The Road to Serfdom*. Chicago: University of Chicago Press, 1944.

———. *The Use of Knowledge in Society*. Library of Economics and Liberty, 1945. http://www.econlib.org/library/Essays/hykKnw1.html

Hazlitt, Henry. *Economics in One Lesson*. New York: Three Rivers Press, 1979.

Hedges, Chris. *American Fascists: The Christian Right and the War on America*. New York: Free Press, 2006.

———. *War Is a Force That Gives Us Meaning*. New York: Public Affairs, 2002.

Hellman, Christopher. "The Real US National Securities Budget: The Figure No One Wants You to See." National Priorities Project, March 1, 2011. http://nationalpriorities.org/en/pressroom/articles/2011/03/01/tomgram-chris-hellman-12-trillion-for-national-sec/.

Huxley, Aldous. *Brave New World*. New York: Harper and Row, 1946.

Johnson, Chalmers. *Dismantling the Empire: America's Last Best Hope*. New York: Metropolitan Books, 2010.

———. *Nemesis: The Last Days of the American Republic*. New York: Metropolitan Books, 2004.

Johnson, Paul. *A History of the American People*. New York: HarperCollins, 1997.

———. *Modern Times: The World from the Twenties to the Eighties*. New York: Harper and Row, 1983.

Jung, Carl G. *The Undiscovered Self*. New York: Mentor Books, 1957.

Karmin, Craig. *Biography of the Dollar: How the Mighty Buck Conquered the World and Why It's Under Siege*. New York: Crown Business, 2008.

Kuehnelt-Leddihn, Erik von. "Operation Parricide: Sade, Robespierre and the French Revolution." *Fidelity Magazine*, October 1989. http://www.culturewars.com/Culture Wars/Archives/Fidelity_archives/parricide.html.

LeShan, Lawrence. *The Psychology of War: Comprehending Its Mystique and Its Madness*. Chicago: Noble Press, 1992.

Mises, Ludwig von. *Economic Policy: Thoughts for Today and Tomorrow*. South Bend, IN: Regnery/Gateway, 1979.

———. *Human Action*. Chicago: Contemporary Books, 1963.

Orwell, George. *1984*. New York: Alfred A. Knopf, 1992.

Pew Research Center for the People and the Press. "America's Place in the World 2009." Washington, DC, 2009. http://people-press.org/files/legacy-pdf/569.pdf.

Powell, Jim. *FDR's Folly: How Roosevelt and His New Deal Prolonged the Great Depression*. New York: Crown Forum, 2003.

———. *The Triumph of Liberty: A 2,000 Year History Told Through the Lives of Freedom's Greatest Champions*. New York: Free Press, 2000.

Rand, Ayn. *Atlas Shrugged*. New York: Random House, 1957.

Reed, Lawrence W. *Great Myths of the Great Depression*. Irvington-on-Hudson, NY: Foundation for Economic Education, 2009. http://fee.org/articles/great-myths-of-the-great-depression.

Rogers, Jim. *Adventure Capitalist*. New York: Random House, 2003.

Rothbard, Murray N. *America's Great Depression*. Los Angeles: Nash Publications, 1972.

———. *Egalitarianism as a Revolt Against Nature and Other Essays*. Auburn, AL: Mises Institute, 2000.

———. *The Ethics of Liberty*. New York: New York University Press, 1998.

———. *Man, Economy, and State with Power and Market*. Scholar's ed. Auburn, AL: Mises Institute, 2009.

Schoolland, Ken. *The Adventures of Jonathan Gullible: A Free Market Odyssey*. Honolulu: Small Business Hawaii, 1995.

Solomon, Norman. *War Made Easy: How Presidents and Pundits Keep Spinning Us to Death*. Hoboken, NJ: John Wiley and Sons, 2005.

Sorokin, Pitirim A. *The Reconstruction of Humanity*. Boston: Beacon Press, 1948.

Soto, Hernando de. *The Mystery of Capital: Why Capitalism Triumphs in the West and Fails Everywhere Else*. New York: Basic Books, 2000.

Sowell, Thomas. *Basic Economics: A Citizen's Guide to the Economy*. New York: Basic Books, 2000.

Taibbi, Matt. "The Great American Bubble Machine." *Rolling Stone*, April 5, 2010.

———. "The Real Housewives of Wall Street." *Rolling Stone*, April 12, 2011.

Weaver, Henry Grady. *The Mainspring of Human Progress*. Irvington-on-Hudson, NY: Foundation for Economic Education, 1953.

White, Andrew Dickson. *Fiat Money Inflation in France*. Caldwell, ID: Caxton Printers, 1958.

Whitt, Joseph A. "The Mexican Peso Crisis." *Economic Review* (Federal Reserve Bank of Atlanta), January/February 1996. http://www.frbatlanta.org/filelegacydocs/J_whi811.pdf.

Wolf, Naomi. *The End of America: Letter of Warning to a Young Patriot.* White River Junction, VT: Chelsea Green Publishing, 2007.

Woods, Thomas E. *Meltdown: A Free-Market Look at Why the Stock Market Collapsed, the Economy Tanked, and Government Bailouts Will Make Things Worse.* Washington, DC: Regnery Publishing, 2009.

INDEX